I WILL

YOUR

GOD

I WILL BE
YOUR
GOD

HOW GOD'S COVENANT
ENRICHES OUR LIVES

T. M. MOORE

PUBLISHING
P.O. BOX 817 • PHILLIPSBURG • NEW JERSEY 08865-0817

Page design and typesetting by Lakeside Design Plus

Printed in the United States of America

Library of Congress Cataloging-in-Publication Data

Moore, T. M. (Terry Michael), 1949-
    I will be your God : how God's covenant enriches our lives / T.M. Moore.
       p. cm.
    Includes bibliographical references and index.
    ISBN 0-87552-558-X (pbk.)
    1. Covenant theology. 1. Title.

BT155.M58 2002
231.7'6—dc21

2002074917

FOR DR. O. PALMER ROBERTSON

CONTENTS

INTRODUCTION

I remember vividly when I began to experience the power of a covenantal understanding of Scripture and the life of faith for the first time.

In the summer of 1973, I went off to seminary a young believer whose early nurturing in the faith had been in an unconsciously (for me) dispensational environment.[1] I would describe my approach to Scripture and the life of faith in those days as purely pietistic and practical. That is, my primary concerns were with maintaining a sense of spiritual well-being and applying the teaching of Scripture to the task of making the gospel known to others. I approached the New Testament as a handbook for Christian relationships and mission, while I regarded the Old Testament as little more than a sourcebook of spiritual exemplars and moral guidance.

My devotional journals from those early years are filled with reflections on the application of the faith to my personal struggles. My view of salvation was strictly individualistic and pragmatic. Faith for me was a constant struggle to find peace in the midst of the storms of life, where Christ was my personal Rescuer and His Word was my Guide. The world was going to hell in a handbasket, and my job was to invite and urge others to receive Jesus as their Savior and be drawn aboard the lifeboat of grace. Together we would ride out the tempests of this life, offering life preservers to as many as possible, until we reached the shores of eternity by the grace of God.

As for the affairs of the world, they were of no concern to me. Apart from a few "end-times" fantasies, I had not read a book in years, did not get a daily paper, and paid almost no attention to the news. I regarded the breaking Watergate scandal and the last days of the tragedy of Viet Nam as worldly matters for which I had little time. I was not even aware of the *Roe v. Wade* ruling in January 1973. I would describe my overall outlook on life at that time as self-centered and solemn, even a little cynical, and generally lacking in contentment. Although I was committed to Christ and devoted to making Him known, my world-view—although I would not have used that term—was not far removed from the proverb that says concerning those of my heritage, "An Irish-man has an abiding sense of tragedy that sustains him during inter-mittent periods of joy."

I came to seminary to prepare for what I hoped would be a larger arena of service than the campus ministry I had known for four years. During the fall semester I began to be exposed to ideas and terms that, while I'm certain I had encountered them in my reading of the Scrip-tures, somehow never managed to hold my attention—ideas such as the sovereignty of God and the lordship of Jesus Christ, and terms like "providence," "grace," and "covenant." I heard the term "world-view" for the first time that fall, but had no idea what it meant. Yet I was listening very carefully.

Listening, but not understanding. If anything, I was becoming con-fused. If what these ideas and terms suggested was true, then my view of the life of faith was sorely deficient. But if that was true, if my "lifeboat" view of the faith was not the whole story, then what were the implications of *that* for Christian living in the world, and for my own life in particular? And where did the commitments I had always em-braced—to personal piety and aggressive evangelism—fit in this con-fused and expanding picture?

In the spring of the following year I participated in a series of semi-nars on God's covenant led by Dr. O. Palmer Robertson. Dr. Robertson explained the comprehensive and unbreakable nature of God's covenant, demonstrating how all the promises of Scripture have realized their fulfillment in Jesus Christ. Because of what Christ has accomplished, those promises are ours to claim. And in the new context of the unfolding kingdom of God and the power of the indwelling Spirit of Christ, all that stands in the way of our realizing full, abundant, and victorious life is our own faulty vision—that and simple unbelief. I began to see that all of life is there for taking and remaking—a richer devotional life, sustained growth in the Lord, renewed and more loving relationships, meaningful work and leisure, and the calling to transform every institution, all of culture and society, according to the wisdom and grace of God. God has entered into a relationship of everlasting, irresistible power with His people, and for two thousand years the faithful have been realizing the fullness of His grace in ways that have turned the world upside down for Jesus Christ.

I had never heard the Christian faith explained in such cosmic and powerful terms. I was stunned. Where had I been? Why was my own experience of Christ so shallow and self-centered? What was I thinking as I glibly mouthed my faith in Christ as Lord, then lived as though that great reality had merely personal and, frankly, fleeting implications? How could I have so blithely treated as mere rhetoric those incredible, unfathomable biblical truths? All at once, as if in a moment, I experienced a stretching of my mind, a reenergizing of my soul, and a kindling of fervor in my heart such as I had never known before. Now I began to see that the world and everything in it belong to the Lord. Everything is ours to be taken up, restored, enjoyed, and deployed in the service of the King of kings and Lord of lords. We have His mandate for it and His Word on it! We dwell within the living framework of His unfathomable power! We are a royal priesthood, a chosen generation, a people of God's possession, and we have been sent to declare His excellencies to a desperate world in all our relationships, roles, and responsibilities!

From that moment I began to explore with greater earnestness, attention, passion, and resolve an understanding of who I am in Jesus Christ. I wanted to take *seriously* the promises of His Word for every aspect of my life, as well as for all of human life and interest. The things that had always concerned me—finding peace in the midst of trials, helping others to know the Savior, and getting through each day without falling backward in my faith—took on a whole new prospect in the light of my new understanding. The seeds of hope, confidence, vision, and enthusiasm burst to life in my soul and began to bud and blossom in new and exciting ways. My outlook on life, now increasingly grounded in a covenantal understanding of the Word of God and the deeper, richer experience of salvation that understanding provides, was dramatically transformed, and I came to believe, as Jesus had taught, that "with God all things are possible" (Matt. 19:26). From that moment on, nothing in my life has been the same.

This book is an attempt to spread the happy virus of a covenantal outlook on life, to share with great urgency and delight the secret of learning to see our lives within the framework of the promises of God, whose faithfulness reaches to the skies (Ps. 36:5). Many Christians, particularly those in the Reformed tradition, acknowledge the role of God's covenant in His redemptive plan, that He is, through our Lord Jesus Christ, calling a people unto Himself for His own glory. But how many of us actually understand and are daily experiencing the powerful, life-changing implications of that glorious calling for every aspect of our lives?

For how many of us are our devotional lives and our worship life-transforming encounters with the glory of God? How many of us carry out our daily activities with a mind-set of taking every area of our lives—our families, work, recreation, and all the rest—captive for the cause of Christ and His glory? How many are committed to building communities characterized by heartfelt worship, mutual service and love, and determined mission to the lost, both in our neighborhoods and around the world? How many are devoted to the task of restoring our cherished traditions and institutions, working to bring the truth and glory of God to light in every arena of life? And how many experience the Christian life as a thrilling ride on the crest of a growing sense of victory, promise, hope, faith, and joy in the power of God's Spirit and the light of His truth?

This book is dedicated to promoting such an outlook on life, which comes through a better understanding of the nature, meaning, and implications of living in God's covenant. The chapters that follow explore the meaning of God's covenant for Christian living in our modern/postmodern society. Each chapter includes a series of questions that individuals or groups can use to discover personal applications of God's covenant. Much has been written of late about God's covenant, as more and more scholars are coming to understand the central place of the covenant, in both the organic development of the Word of God and the progress of His redemptive plan.[2] This is a most welcome and encouraging development.

At the same time, however, little has been done to help rank-and-file believers understand the glorious implications of our covenant relationship with God. As powerful, all-comprehending, and totally integrating a concept as the covenant is for understanding the Bible, it is, if anything, even more so for the life of faith. By understanding, embracing, and beginning to live self-consciously with a covenantal outlook, we can discover new vitality, direction, and power for the life of faith, that, if my own experience is any kind of guide, can set our hearts aflame with love for Christ and channel the heat of our renewed passion for Him into life-changing service in His Name. May God be pleased to use these words to nurture such an experience of the life of faith among all who read them.

1

GOD'S COVENANT

But I will establish My covenant with you. . . .—Genesis 6:18

The sovereign Lord of heaven and earth dictates the terms of his covenant.—O. Palmer Robertson[1]

I could tell as he walked into my office that Roger was a man in trouble. He was downcast and somewhat disheveled; he walked with the slow gait and stooped shoulders of a man whose burden was about to crush him.

Roger had just begun coming around the church, although, as I observed him week after week, I noted that he seemed to be acquainted with several members of the congregation and was familiar with the liturgy. Perhaps, I reasoned, he was something of a prodigal returning to his Father's estate after a season of wandering and disappointment. That preliminary assessment would prove to be on the mark.

"My life is out of control." Thus Roger began the lengthy account of his life. Brought up in the congregation where I had recently begun to serve as pastor, he had departed from the church and the things of the Lord, married, and started a family, only to see his marriage go sour at the same time his job was becoming increasingly pressure-filled and dissatisfying. He had come back to church after many years in order to find some peace and guidance, but his situation only continued to deteriorate.

His relationship with his wife involved constant quarreling and bitterness; she had begun proceedings to divorce him. His children were angry and distant, and one had ventured into the drug scene. Neither would have anything to do with him. He was routinely "shafted"—to use his term—at work, never given full credit for the sales he made and always passed over for someone else when a new and potentially lucrative account was assigned. He hated himself and felt like his life was unraveling faster than he could keep all the loose ends together. He was fighting against his own self-centered past; the pressures of work, culture, and society; his family's desire for independence from his oppressive ways; and a rapidly approaching future that held little in the way of hope. And, as he told me through a torrent of tears, he was losing the battle.

"I don't know what to do, where to turn. Everything in my life has gone out of sync, and I can't keep it or myself together any longer. I thought that coming back to God might help, but I haven't found any peace or direction, and things just keep getting worse at home, at work, and in every area of my life. My life is out of control, and I'm getting near the end of my rope."

"My life is out of control."

How many people feel this way at one time or another? As they see it, their lives have become like a line out of Yeats: "Things fall apart, the centre cannot hold." All the things they have depended on for stability and satisfaction are fractured and failing, and they cannot seem to find any larger framework within which to make a stand, halt the erosion of their well-being, or make sense out of their lives. They become depressed, angry, and fearful, all at the same time, and they seek relief from the pressures that are threatening to undo them. Just like Roger. Indeed, just like I did for so many years, including those early years of my walk with the Lord.

Many Christians have felt this way at times as well, Bible-believing, Christ-loving disciples of the Lord whose lives seem to be coming apart at the seams and who feel powerless to do anything about it. Frustrated and fearful, they fall into fits of anger or depression, hating themselves and taking their self-hate out on the ones closest to them, making their situation even worse than it was before. They feel their lives have begun to spin out of control, that they're in for a rough ride of indeterminate duration, and that the best they can do is hold on, seek help, and hope for the best.

They are a little like Elisha's servant who, upon seeing the approaching armies of the Syrians, went into a panic and began to fear the worst (2 Kings 6:15–17). Their problems are so many and are pressing in on them so closely, that they feel they can't breathe, can't do anything right, and can't go on like this. They come to the church or to the pastor's study seeking advice, affirmation, and some alleviation of their distress, yet they often go away unhelped and unchanged. Circumstances are in the driver's seat of their lives, and they seem determined on a course of unmitigated disappointment and dismay.

What such people need is for someone to draw back the veil of eternity, allowing them a clear and compelling glimpse into heavenly truths and divine realities. For their problem is not one of *control*, but one of *perspective*. It is all too easy in the crush of things to lose sight of the eternal, covenant framework within which we live and move and have our being. Once our focus on heavenly verities begins to waver, the result of any number and variety of temporal pressures and distractions, our confidence falters, our priorities become confused, and we set ourselves up for an experience like Roger's. All our happiness, hope, and security in life become locked up in the frail and unreliable realities of our day-to-day existence. As they go, so do we: when they're up, we're up; when they're down and crashing, we are too.

But the changing circumstances and fickle vicissitudes of our everyday lives do not for a moment alter the covenant relationship that we who believe in Jesus Christ have entered into by the grace of God. Our lives may be storm-tossed from time to time, the deck chairs all askew, normal routines postponed or canceled, and we unable to get our sealegs. But the ship in which we are journeying is intact, unsinkable, and in the hands of an experienced and reliable Captain who not only built

3

and commands our vessel and specially chose us for this journey, but rules the winds and waves and everyday circumstances of life as well.

A COVENANT PERSPECTIVE

Understanding and learning to live within the covenant God has entered into with us can enable us to sail above our circumstances. The sextant of our lives constantly fixed on the North Star of God's grace and truth, our confidence and hope will rest in Him, and not in our circumstances or ourselves. Similarly, maintaining a covenant mind-set can help us in setting the kind of priorities in life that will enable us to serve and honor God each day. Living self-consciously in the light of God's covenant can guide our decisions and choices in the path of righteousness, and move us to undertakings of faith that we might not otherwise consider or think ourselves capable of. The covenant can embolden us in the face of adversity and trial, fill us continuously with the joy of our salvation, give us the wisdom and strength to serve others in love, and make our lives an ongoing service of worship to the living God.

Ironically, however, such an experience of life does not, in the end, depend on our ability to keep our minds and hearts properly focused on those heavenly realities that orbit around Christ, seated at the right hand of the Father (Col. 3:1–3). True, we must strive to gain and maintain God's covenant perspective on our lives. But, as we shall see, even our ability to appropriate the blessings of the covenant depends upon the *nature* of the covenant and the God who stands back of it.

The power that makes all things new in our lives and sustains us over the rough waves and storm-tossed seas of everyday living inheres in God Himself and flows to us within the framework of His covenant. That power is always and in all places available to us, so that we might know the peace that passes understanding and the grace that makes all things new continuously, and in dramatically life-changing ways. As we become more and more mindful of that covenant relationship and grow in our ability to tap into God's power and grace, we will be better able to avoid the sand bars and the icebergs of life and to experience more of the smooth sailing that life in Christ can be.

The Scriptures speak frequently of the mind-set that we allow to chart the course of our lives. We are exhorted to be renewed in our minds and to set them squarely and unswervingly on the heavenly realities that surround and devolve from the throne of Jesus Christ (Eph. 4:23; Col. 3:1–2). Yet this will be difficult to do and to sustain without a good understanding of these realities, especially of the covenant framework within which we who know and love the Lord live and move and have our being. For that covenant itself, God's covenant, holds the key to the full and abundant life we earnestly desire. In the paragraphs that follow we will examine some of the foundational elements of God's covenant, the building-blocks upon which the subjects of succeeding chapters are erected and stand.

GOD'S COVENANT IS *HIS*

In the most generic terms, a covenant is an arrangement entered into by various parties for the purpose of establishing a mutually beneficial relationship involving privileges and obligations. Business contracts, neighborhood covenants, and financial notes are all examples of covenants as they are employed today. Covenant making was a common activity in the ancient Near East. In its most public form, great leaders who were seeking to live together in peace would agree on terms of an arrangement between them, declare those terms publicly before their families and subjects, seal their covenant with a special ceremony, and enjoy a meal together as a token of their mutual good will.[2] We can discern the outlines of this covenant-making activity in Genesis 21:21–23, the covenant between Abraham and Abimelech, and Genesis 26:26–31, the covenant between Isaac and the same man. There are many other examples in the historical and archaeological record of the ancient world to show that this kind of covenant making was not uncommon.

Entering into covenants, therefore, was a practice with which ancient Near Eastern folk—including biblical peoples—would have been quite familiar. They would have understood well what was implied in such a relationship. When, therefore, God established His relationship with His people in the form of a covenant, they would have understood very well what His intentions were, as well as their privileges, duties, and obligations.

God's covenant, however, is unique as an expression of this covenant idea. His covenant, while it partakes of various attributes of human covenants, is *sui generis*. It exists in a category all its own, and that for a variety of reasons.

In the first place, God's covenant is precisely that—*His*. He consistently refers to it in that way—not as *our* covenant or merely *a* covenant, but *My* covenant, as we see from the very first mention of His covenant in Genesis 6:18, as well as in numerous other passages of Scripture (cf. Gen. 17:2, 4, 13; Ps. 50:16; Hos. 8:1; etc.).

This distinctive aspect of God's covenant implies several features. (1) *God conceived the covenant.* He did not devise it in consultation with men or angels. It is not the result of negotiation, give-and-take, or compromise. Rather, God's covenant is His idea, first to last. Robertson observes, "No such thing as bargaining, bartering, or contracting characterizes the divine covenants of Scripture."[3] Its design and purpose are entirely of God's making. All the elements and promises of the covenant are the fruit of His eternal, holy, perfect, and good will. Because of this, we do not have to worry about whether the covenant is adequate, or if it might be flawed. Since men had no hand in its design, but only the good and perfect counsel of the all-wise God, we can rest assured that God's covenant is exactly fitted to His interests, as well as our needs. The covenant is God's covenant, in the first place, because He alone had input into its nature, purpose, elements, focus, and design.

(2) Further, *He initiated the covenant.* Throughout Scripture it is God who takes the initiative with people, seeking them out in their sinfulness or suffering and reaching out to them with the promise of grace. God's covenant in *all* its expressions[4] is a covenant of grace. God is sovereign in the timing, disposition, and implementation of His covenant, even as He is in its continuing administration. People are but the re-

cipients of His gracious initiative. And, while entering into covenant with God does involve them in certain privileges, duties, and obligations, even these cannot be fulfilled apart from the operative grace and power of God in their lives.[5]

(3) God shows further that the covenant is His in that *He extends it to whomever He will.* Nothing about the people with whom God initiates His gracious relationship can commend them to Him. Abraham was the son of an idolater. The Israelites were a slave people, despised by all and condemned to extermination. David was a rising political star with feet of clay and an uncertain future. We who have come into covenant relationship with the living God were His enemies and fleeing from Him when He gave His Son for our salvation and mercifully brought us to Himself (Rom. 5:10). Yet, in His sovereign wisdom, and for His delight and glory, God was pleased to extend His covenant, not to the wealthy and powerful or the potentially rich and famous—to those, that is, who may seem to have earned or deserved it, or otherwise to be worthy of it—but to aliens and strangers, those who were spiritually bankrupt and without hope, so that we might become members of His household and heirs of His promise (Eph. 2:11–22).

Let us not despise the sense of unworthiness that comes over us from time to time as we think about the goodness God has shown us in His covenant. Rather, let us accept that we are unworthy, and let us praise Him who freely and lovingly extended His grace to us in the mystery of His covenant love.

(4) Finally, the covenant is God's because *He alone exercises accountability over it.* Having defined its terms and conditions and extended it to whomever He will, God stands over His covenant, enforcing its terms with blessings and curses designed to shape a people of His own choosing into the salt of the earth and the light of the world, and to bless and prosper them and glorify Himself. God takes His covenant seriously. It has ramifications and implications for all people, not only those who have come to know Him through Jesus Christ. God faithfully and continually exercises accountability over all people, striving with some to bring them to a knowledge of Himself, giving others up to the sinful consequences of their ingratitude and disobedience,

blessing the obedient and those who favor them, and cursing those who are obstinate and rebellious toward Him. God is ever active in holding Himself and His creatures accountable for the terms of the covenant He has declared. He alone is able to distribute its blessings and enforce its prohibitions, and He does so through His lovingkindness and faithfulness at all times.

Thus God's covenant is altogether unique in the first instance because He alone has authority to define, distribute, administer, and enforce it. It is *His* covenant. And just as the design and implementation of God's covenant rest in His hands alone, so also does its success, its power to bring blessing to His people and glory and honor to Himself.

GOD'S COVENANT IS *ETERNAL*

Second, God's covenant is unique in that it is *eternal*. We shall have more to say about this in a later chapter. For now a few remarks will suffice.

(1) *An eternal covenant is unchangeable*. What God planned and promised from the beginning remains unalterably in effect throughout the life of the covenant, that is, forever. What He has declared will never be retracted. What He has determined cannot be opposed. What He wills most definitely comes to pass. His Word is faithful and reliable in all generations. What the earliest beneficiaries of His covenant hoped for continues unchanged within the framework of God's everlasting covenant, and remains as the aspiration and longing of covenant people today (Heb. 13:20–21). What McComiskey says of the promise to Abraham is equally true of all the various temporal expressions of God's covenant: "Since the promise covenant given to Abraham continues in force, the authority of the oath that backs it has never been vitiated. *It remains the sworn intent of God to carry out his purposes for the people of God in all ages.*"[6]

(2) In the same way, *God's eternal covenant cannot be interrupted*. It cannot be diverted, obstructed, or set aside. Once initiated, the terms of God's covenant are perpetually in force, and the objects of His covenant attention can expect to realize either its blessings or its curses

according to their response to His grace. Like a stream of divine power that flows ineluctably down the course of history, God's covenant continues unabated, undiverted, and undammed, ever flowing to its final destination in the new heavens and the new earth (Ps. 46:4–5).

(3) While God's covenant is eternal, *it is not timeless*. That is, the manner of God's administering His eternal covenant can be expected to change according to the circumstances of time and place of the people to whom God extends it. This is the reason why we find in Scripture different events of covenant making between God and representatives of His people, and different periods in which one or another temporal expression of the divine covenant is in force. The basic elements of the one divine covenant remain the same, but the ways that God implements and fulfills His covenant are adjusted from time to time in order to ensure maximum enjoyment of its privileges and maximum adherence to its obligations. God's eternal covenant has a built-in cultural and historical flexibility that makes it relevant to every generation of those to whom God extends it. For us, this means that the promises of God's covenant have unique applications for our own day, as we shall see.

GOD'S COVENANT IS *COMPREHENSIVE*

Nothing is outside the scope of God's covenant. Another way of saying this is that God's gracious and powerful attention is addressed, in at least some way and at all times, to everything He has made.[7] While certain aspects of His covenant will be more sharply focused than others, still all that exists falls within the scope of God's declared intentions, promises, and will.

(1) God's covenant *encompasses all the patterns, processes, laws, and aspects of the created order* (Jer. 33:25). Scientists speak of the *laws* of nature, those material processes that determine the shape and direction of every created thing. Yet, in actuality, no such laws exist. Rather, the patterns and processes we observe in the natural world are nothing less than descriptions of the ways and means by which the faithful God upholds, directs, and governs the cosmos by the Word of His power

(Ps. 47:15–20; Heb. 1:3).[8] God is a God of order; He is infinitely faithful, wise, and strong; and His creation manifests in all its operations these aspects of His character and His covenant. All creation benefits from God's covenant, enabling it to flourish and produce many good and wonderful things.

(2) In the same way, God's covenant *extends to every living creature* (Gen. 9:8–15). God gives them life and breath, provides them with food and shelter, brings good things into their lives, and sets the bounds and limits of their existence (Ps. 104:1–30). Without God's covenant ordaining and sustaining them, no living creature would have life or health, and we would enjoy none of the mystery, beauty, wonder, and blessings that the living creatures afford.

(3) God's covenant also *reaches to all people* (Gen. 12:1–3). He provides them with blessings in abundance and disciplines them when they wander from His path (Matt. 5:45; Acts 14:17; Rom. 1:21–32). He divides them into nations and peoples and determines the arrangements by which they live together in mutual benefit upon the earth (Acts 17:24–27). He makes Himself undeniably known to all men so that they might seek Him, give thanks and praise to Him, and enter more fully into His covenant blessings (Rom. 1:18–21; Acts 17:27). He gives them many good and wondrous gifts with which to bless themselves and others, and to give Him thanks and praise (Ps. 68:18). That most men do not honor God is no failing of His covenant, since those who turn from Him to idols bring down on themselves the curses He has built into the warp and woof of this relationship that reaches to all creation and all men (Rom. 1:18–32).

All creation exists and thrives because God has been pleased to extend His blessings to it in the covenant that He has declared. His covenant is comprehensive of all that He has made. Nothing that exists is outside the scope of His covenant rule. We who participate in a special way in that covenant by virtue of God's special love for us thus have the assurance, as Paul reminds us, that God is causing all things—every created reality, daily circumstance, and event—to work together for our good (Rom. 8:28). The whole creation is at His disposal to do with, for, and through it as He will, according to the design and purposes of His eternal covenant (Ps. 119:90–91).

GOD'S COVENANT IS *ALL OF GRACE*

We shall have more to say later about other aspects of God's covenant—its unity and diversity as well as its promises and purpose. Here we wish to clarify what was mentioned earlier, namely, that God's covenant is *all of grace*. It springs from, is sustained by, and brings us into the experience of His sovereign, mysterious love. Grace—unmerited, undeserved love—is the foundation and operative principle of God's covenant. God is in no way, and at no time, obligated to relate Himself to any of His creatures—or, for that matter, even to have created them in the first place.[9] All that He has planned and all that He does in His covenant are expressions of His love, for Himself and His glory as well as for His creation and His people. All the blessings we enjoy, as well as all the adversity to which we are subjected, come from the hand of God and are motivated by His love.

As we learn more and more how to live within the framework of God's love and to recognize and wait upon His love in all the situations of our lives, we will be able to live a life of thanksgiving, rejoicing, purpose, power, and peace without complaining or fear. His grace sustains and guides us, as He has shown us supremely in the giving of His Son for our salvation. What have we to fear from anything that might come our way, knowing that the grace of God in Jesus Christ envelops and sustains us at all times (Ps. 27; Rom. 8:32, 35–39)?

Indeed, we might go so far as to say that the *power* of God's covenant, that power which makes all things new in our lives, is a function of the *grace* of God. As God reaches out to us in love within the framework of His covenant, we come to experience the power that reminds us that our lives are not out of control. By His grace God enables us to know that the Captain is still at the helm, the ship is sound and secure, and we shall reach our destination. With this in mind, therefore, we begin to know more and more His power, which enables us to carry out our assigned duties in confidence, hope, and joy. Our duty and privilege as His covenant creatures, therefore, is to *seek His grace* and to *appropriate His power*, a duty and a privilege uniquely available to us through the finished work of our Lord Jesus Christ.

A Covenant for Today

Over a period of many weeks and months, as Roger and I searched the Scriptures together, he began to seek the grace of God more consistently, trusting through meditation, prayer, and waiting on the Lord that the renewing power of His covenant would become a reality in his life. Slowly Roger began to recover a perspective on his life that focused on God's covenant and his own place in that wonderful arrangement of grace. His hope revived and his joy began to return. He started to grow in confidence that God could make something worthwhile out of his life.

Roger explained what he was beginning to understand about the grace of God to his family, and he sought forgiveness from his wife and children. He started working hard at showing the love of God to them, trusting the Lord to help him deal with his negative and self-centered attitudes and to enable him to show the love of Christ to his wife and daughters. He changed jobs so that he could work in a setting where he was better able to see God at work in and through his labors, and where he could be closer to home and family. He became an earnest student of God's Word, a man of increasing prayer and faithfulness, a willing servant of the church, and a bold witness for Christ.

Increasingly Roger saw himself as safe within the framework of God's love and power, and he began to learn how to draw on the promises of God's covenant more and more. Gradually, he became a changed man, the old Roger slowly dying away while the new Roger in Christ Jesus became increasingly evident to all. Roger's growth brought laughter and enthusiasm back to his life, as even his wife and children testified.

Roger's changed life was the result of a renewed perspective. No longer did he view his life as out of control and himself as the victim of fickle circumstances and unfortunate, unhappy choices. More and more he came to see himself as a child of God, an heir of His covenant, and a servant of His grace. He learned to believe and claim God's promises, to bank on His mercy and grace, to identify with His purpose, and to draw on His power. As his understanding grew, his personal life vision was transformed, and his daily activities and responsibilities took on an air of mission and purpose. The revival that Roger experienced was the result of the grace of God bringing a renewed perspective—a recovered understanding of and focus on God's covenant and of himself as a child of that blessed relationship.

Today, when so many Christians are captive to the schedules, demands, and priorities of an increasingly secular and postmodern age, many need a renewed touch of the grace of God, enabling them to recover an understanding of and to learn to live within God's covenant as the framework, purpose, and sustaining power of our lives. The power this generation of Christians needs in order to break free of the ever-tightening shackles of worldliness lies not in new programs, new preachers or teachers, or even new resolve. Rather, it lies in a grace-renewed perspective concerning who we are in Jesus Christ, what God has designed for us, what He purposes and promises, and what He will do in, for, and through us as we trust wholeheartedly in Him.

The people of God today need to discover once again the power of God's covenant for the renewing of their minds and transformation of their lives, and for full and abundant life in Jesus Christ.

QUESTIONS FOR STUDY AND DISCUSSION

1. In what ways do you find that your own sense of well-being—your happiness, enthusiasm, and zeal—is determined by the things of this world? How does this affect you day-in and day-out?

2. Does this focus on worldly matters in any way hinder your service to Christ? Do you find that you are too exhausted, distracted, or discouraged to devote yourself to growing in Him, serving Him in the church, or living as His witness to the people around you? Does serving in the church sometimes seem not all that important, compared with all you have to do each day?

13

3. What does God's covenant mean to you at this time? How well do you understand His covenant—what it is for, how it operates, what hope it holds out, what its promises are, how it obligates and enables us?

4. To what extent, and in what specific ways, does your understanding of God's covenant—and your place in that covenant—influence and affect your daily decisions, choices, and activities? How would you like to see this change?

5. As you begin this study of God's covenant, in what ways would you like to change? How do you hope that this study will help you to grow in love for the Lord? For your neighbor? Which aspects of your spiritual life—disciplines, obedience, vision, hope—would you like to see affected, and in what ways? What will convince you, at the end of this study, that your study of God's covenant has been worthwhile?

2

THE COVENANT
OF PROMISE

His divine power has given to us all things that pertain to life and godliness, through the knowledge of Him who called us by glory and virtue, by which have been given to us exceedingly great and precious promises. . . .—2 Peter 1:3–4

Because the promise is eternal, it is in force today, defining God's work in the world relative to the formation of a people for his name.
—Thomas Edward McComiskey[1]

Every four years Americans enter a season of exceedingly great and *specious* promises. The political campaigns that erupt throughout the land are, among other things, a tour de force of promise making, each candidate trying to outdo the other in the number and kinds of things he or she will promise voters in an effort to gain their support.

Americans are ambivalent about such political promises. On the one hand, we would like to believe that politicians mean what they say and will do what they have promised if they manage to be elected. What candidates promise is part of the reason we vote the way we do. On the other hand, we know in our hearts that many political promises are not worth the words by which they are spoken. We bear in mind such images as George Bush saying, in the secular equivalent of swearing on a stack of Bibles, "Read my lips: No new taxes!" only to go on and raise taxes shortly after he came into office.

We want to believe our politicians, but we suspect that they don't really mean what they're saying and have already decided on a course of "spin" to justify breaking their promises once in office. Or they may be sincere and really mean to keep the promises they make; yet, once in office, they will not have the power they need to be able to implement those promises. Other political forces and priorities conspire to keep them from being able to do what they have sworn and may sincerely want to do.

But political campaigns do have this virtue at least: they remind us of how thoroughly our lives are determined by the promises we hope to realize. Hardly an aspect of our everyday lives is not governed by our sense of the promise this or that activity, relationship, or commitment holds for our well-being. We choose a life partner because we believe this relationship holds the promise for our maximum happiness in marriage. We pursue careers and change jobs in the hope that we will realize the promise of greater satisfaction and reward. All our purchases, the ways we use our time, the relationships into which we enter, the avocations we pursue, and the priorities we choose are governed by our sense of the promise such things hold to bring happiness and fulfillment into our lives. We are creatures of promise: our lives are ruled by promise and our happiness and well-being are determined, in no small part, by the extent to which the realities of our lives match up to the promises we believed we would realize.

Sadly, for many of those who identify themselves as followers of Jesus Christ, the promises held out to them by the opportunities and relationships of their lives in the world provide their primary motivation for daily living, and are the principal source of their happiness. They get up in the morning to go to work, hoping to find some satisfaction there and to earn enough income to provide for their wants and needs and those of their families. They come home at night after an exhausting day seeking the promise of rest, relaxation, and relief that family, television, or any of a hundred other diversions hold out. They go on vacation, hoping to find the promise of rest and renewal; purchase new cars for the promise they offer of self-esteem (and maybe a little better gas mileage); and send their kids to this or that school for the promise it offers of a better job or a more moral and satisfying life.

When what they hoped for in these choices is realized, then happiness and a sense of well-being ensue; when the hoped-for boon does not pan out, they are disappointed and fall into moods of meanness, anxiety, and despair. Having hitched their wagons to uncertain stars, the only happiness they can know is fleeting, and the only fulfillment they can realize is tentative and rarely, if ever, as satisfying as hoped.

The problem is not with living according to the hope of promises; the problem is that, for many of the followers of Christ, their promises are just too puny. And there is no certainty in this uncertain world that even their relatively puny promises will enable them to realize the hoped-for boon. So the level of joy, enthusiasm for life, and earnest purpose that characterizes many Christians is not that much different from that of their secular friends and acquaintances. With all the same promises as the guiding force in their lives, how could it be otherwise?

The great privilege that is ours as followers of Christ is that we are the recipients of better promises than the fleeting, materialistic, and temporal hopes that come from jobs, families, and diversions. As important as these are, they are not sufficient to fill our lives with enduring purpose or to summon us to the courage of our convictions when our faith is on the line. We need better promises than these, and some kind of guarantee that those promises are not mere empty gestures. This is precisely what we have in God's covenant, "exceedingly great and precious promises" and a sovereign, faithful God who keeps His promises in exhaustive detail.

THE PROMISE OF GOD'S COVENANT

The first and fullest statement of what God promises His people in His covenant is in the meeting between God and Abram recorded in Genesis 12:1–3. Here we see God making a sixfold promise of blessing, purpose, and power to the wealthy son of idolaters in the pagan land of Ur of the Chaldees.[2] Immediately we note the divine character of the proffered covenant: God defines the terms, bestows it on a most un-likely man, and underwrites His promises by His own authoritative and faithful Word. All the world will be affected by this divine initiative. Abram is not asked his opinion, he is not given the option of choosing among the promised blessings, and he is not allowed to dicker over the terms whereby those promises will be fulfilled. The covenant with Abram is God's covenant, first to last, and the six promises it includes issue from the conception and initiative of the God of grace, to be su-perintended by His lovingkindness, faithfulness, and power.

(1) Abram is first promised that *God will make of Him a great people* (v. 2). Here we must think in strictly numerical terms. As God would later reaffirm, the nation that would be created out of Abram's loins would be as numerous as the dust of the air and the stars of the heav-ens (Gen. 13:16; 15:5). Although he was being called to leave home, family, and country, Abram believed that God would greatly increase his offspring, more than he might reasonably expect were he to con-tinue in his fatherland and familiar occupation. Abram was motivated by the promise of becoming a great nation to follow God to an un-known, distant land in the belief that there, in His way and time, God would raise up a mighty people who would trace their origins to him.

(2) Next, *God promised to bless Abram in ways far beyond any tempo-ral prospect held out by his continuing in Ur* (v. 2). We recognize in the word "bless" the suggestion of good things to come. Specifically what those things might be was left to Abram's eager and fertile imagination. But something far beyond temporal enjoyments was in view here.

The root of the word, "bless," in both its substantive and *hiphil* verb forms, refers to the knees. Although it is unlikely that Abram could have understood all the ramifications of this, it seems clear that God was saying He would establish the patriarch in a special relationship with Himself, one characterized by his "being on his knees" before the sovereign God. In such a posture he would be ready to hear and able to receive good things from his covenant God. Like Adam and Eve in the day that God blessed them (Gen. 1:26–28), Abram would have access to the presence of God, would live before Him in a posture of worship and service, and would receive from Him unknown but wonderful blessings as a result. That Abram understood this to be something of the meaning of his being blessed of God is indicated by his erecting altars to the living God as a means of coming into His presence, attending to His Word, and preparing for a life of service and blessing before Him (cf. Gen. 12:7–8).

Abram believed that God would receive him into His presence, would guide him in his daily life, and would fill his life with many good things appropriate to one who was an obedient servant of God and of His covenant. Abram was motivated to worship and serve God by the promise of blessing.

(3) *God also promised to make Abram's name great* (Gen. 12:2). He would be a man of influence, a man to be reckoned with by neighbors and remembered by posterity. His words would matter, and his testimony would carry great weight. Doubtless in Abram's mind this third promise only made sense, given the preceding promises of a great nation and access to the divine presence and blessings. Abram could see himself as a man to whom others would look for guidance, one to whom they would defer in important issues and whom, because of their respect for him, they would treat with fairness in all matters. How this must have been confirmed for him in the affair with Pharaoh and Sarai (Gen. 12:10–20)! We see it also, much later, when Abram (now Abraham) went to purchase a burial plot for his deceased wife. The sons of Heth, greatly flattered by Abraham's interest in their real estate, wanted to give the burial cave to him. What a feather in their caps that would have been! But Abraham insisted on paying fair market price, and his wishes in the matter were respected (Gen. 23). Even in his lifetime Abraham's name became great among his neighbors; how much more so was his greatness increased with each successive generation of the sons of Israel. Filled with the hope of this promise, Abram would begin to live as one who expected to be a noteworthy person among his contemporaries, and whose name would exert influence for generations to come.

(4) *God promised to make Abram a blessing to others* (Gen. 12:2). In his mind this must have registered that Abram would be a source of good to his neighbors, a means to their help, guidance, and prosperity.

But more than this, God seems to have been suggesting that, through Abram, others would be able to come into that special relationship with God that he himself enjoyed. The race of those who knew the Lord—worshiped, served, and enjoyed Him—would be greatly enlarged by Abram's living and spoken witness to the God of the covenant. He would be a channel of blessing, a conduit of grace to the nations, God's chosen vessel for spreading the knowledge of God abroad among the peoples of the earth.

(5) *God promised to protect and provide for Abram in sovereign and efficient ways* (v. 3). He would bless the peoples who blessed Abram, who allowed themselves to be God's means of enriching and providing for him; and He would curse with trouble and calamity those who looked askance at the patriarch and sought his downfall. What confidence this must have instilled in Abram as he wondered just how God would fulfill all that He was promising to him! He believed that God would take care of him, would fill his life with good things and keep him out of—or preserve him in the midst of—harm's way. The episode of Abraham's dramatic and remarkable rescue of Lot from the ravaging kings of the east must have confirmed this promise for the patriarch in a powerful and convincing way (Gen. 14). That Abram even believed he might prevail against so overwhelming a force suggests the strength with which he clung to the promise of God to protect and provide for him and his family.

(6) *Through Abram God promised to extend His blessing to "all the families of the earth."* This must have registered in both geographical and historical terms to Abram. God, who was making such exceedingly great and precious promises to an unworthy man such as he, would do the same for all people, both those living and those yet to come. That Abraham was careful to pass these promises on to his own son indicates that he expected God to fulfill His promises to the generations to come. His own reach to "all the families of the earth" was strictly minimal; through his offspring it would continue until the blessings of God covered the earth.

How Abram's brain must have buzzed with the thought of these promises being granted to him! What visions of wealth, ease, respect, goodness to others, and progeny must have filled his mind! What immense spiritual satisfaction he must have felt as his mind dwelled on all that God had promised! He could not, of course, have envisioned all the details, but he knew enough about the good things of life to understand that God's purposes for him were for good, and not for evil, and that what he was being offered was vastly much more than awaited him in Ur of the Chaldees. He certainly could not have seen all the way through to the ultimate fulfillment of these promises in Jesus Christ (2 Cor. 1:19–20), but his imagination undoubtedly took in questions of eternity and blessedness beyond the grave. He knew that God, being who He is, would somehow extend His exceedingly great and precious promises to him and all those blessed in him to an eternal existence of peace, joy, and abundance.

And Abram believed God, demonstrating his belief by uprooting himself and his family and moving hundreds of miles away to an unfamiliar land, there to wait on the Lord to fulfill all that He had promised. In the land of Canaan Abram would grow in his faith in the Lord, learning through trial and error to prefer the promises of God to the material prospects of neighboring peoples. He would learn how to rely on God's Word, to trust in Him as faithful and unerring, and to keep *His* promises in view rather than be content with mere temporal satisfactions. At times this would require him to endure hardship and sacrifice in order to show good faith in the Lord. He would learn obedience through disobedience, trial, and hardship, but he would never waver in his ultimate commitment to keep the promises of God in view and to do whatever the Lord commanded in order to realize them. We can imagine that all manner of temptation accosted him from time to time, suggesting that his move had been a mistake and that he ought to return to his familiar country and take up the work that he knew well and had prospered in before. But he resisted all such temptations and persevered in the Lord, even to the point of offering his only, long-awaited son, as a sacrifice to the Lord in obedience to His command (Gen. 22).

The sacrifice of Isaac was the ultimate test of Abraham's faith, giving him the opportunity to show just how much he believed the Lord, how certain he considered His promises, and how devoutly obedient he would be. The reward of his life of faith—a faith deriving from God's gracious initiative with him—was both a "down payment" on those exceedingly great and precious promises—wealth, protection, progeny, respect, and blessing—and the confident assurance, which he passed on to his son, of greater and more wondrous blessings to come.

What peace Abraham came to know, and what purpose and power for living in God's covenant were increasingly evident throughout his life! Abraham understood the importance of living with a view to eternal verities and divine promises, and his life took on the piety, prospect, and prosperity that such living in God's covenant provides. He might have done better for himself materially had he stayed in Ur of the Chaldees. But that promise of material prosperity paled against the fuller promises of the blessings of God Abraham came to know. Had he stayed in Ur, he would have known nothing like the confidence, hope, and spiritual rest that he enjoyed living in God's covenant in the land of Canaan.

THE GOD WHO PROMISES

Somehow (we do not know exactly how) Abraham came to understand that God is not like the false gods of materialistic men. Nor is He like the contemporary politicians who litter the campaign trail with exceedingly great and specious promises every few years. He knew God to be powerful and faithful, able to thwart the intentions of the greatest kings in order to protect His own people and keep His Word to them. He knew His promises to be sure, and that He would provide a son for Abraham, even against all hope of such an event. He learned that God's Word was reliable, if incredibly mysterious, and he came to understand that the promises of God's covenant held out the hope of blessing not only for him but for his children and all people as well.

The God who offers such exceedingly great and precious promises to the spiritual descendants of Abraham today is *a God who cannot lie* (Titus 1:1–2). It is contrary to His character to declare something that is not true or that He does not intend to fulfill. As unlikely or unfeasible as His promises may seem to puny-minded people such as we, they are as sure as He Himself is. Nothing can keep them from coming to fruition, for back of them stands the God who conceived and made them and who cannot lie. The only question is whether we will enter fully and with complete faith into His covenant of promise, or if those promises will await fulfillment for other, more faithful, men and women.

He is also *a God who cannot fail*. We may not be able—as Abraham undoubtedly was not—to see how God can fulfill all that He has promised. Indeed, we may consider that our lives are so hopeless and God's promises so far-fetched that we may despair of ever knowing the blessedness of His covenant. But He is able to do exceedingly abundantly above all that we could ever ask or think (Eph. 3:20). No counsel or scheme of men or demons can thwart Him as He moves to carry out His promises. He looks only for the heart of faith and the life of obedience as the arena in which to make His exceedingly great and precious promises known.

Abraham dared even to think the unthinkable about this faithful and powerful God. So certain was he that God's promise would not fail, that He would do all that He had declared, regardless of what had to be overcome at the human level, that Abraham allowed himself to believe that, were it necessary, God could even raise Isaac from the dead in order to keep His covenant operative and in force (Gen. 22:5: note the "we"; Heb. 11:17–19). Such a thing had never been seen before. Humanly, it was impossible. *But Abraham was not thinking humanly as he set out to obey the Lord's command. He was thinking God's thoughts after Him, focusing on His Word of promise, and learning to believe beyond what was humanly possible, given the faithfulness and almighty power of the God of the covenant.*

This is what living in God's covenant enables us to do—to begin to think like God so that we may act in accordance with His purposes and promises, in the full hope and expectation that He will never fail us nor forsake us (Heb. 13:5).

How many believers today are stifled in their witness for Christ because they have never shared their faith before and cannot imagine being able to do so? How many give stingily to the work of the Lord because they believe that, if they gave more, gave in obedience to the Lord's requirements, they would somehow not have enough for themselves? How many have hardly given a thought to what is required of them in loving their neighbors as themselves, just because they do not know their neighbors or cannot imagine how they might begin to fulfill this second great commandment? How many mumble and stumble their way through a worship service because their vision of God is no bigger than the printed liturgy in their bulletins?

How many balk at some new opportunity to serve the Lord because they are focused more on their abilities than on His unlimited resources? How many live lives of disappointment, defeat, distraction, and despair because they have allowed the puny promises of mundane living to obscure the exceedingly great and precious promises of God's covenant? How many have never known the excitement of living by faith, the power of God's Spirit bearing witness in and through them, the joy inexpressible of worshiping God in spirit and in truth, and the resolute kingdom purpose from which nothing can cause them to swerve, *all because they are holding fast to the promises of this brief life and have never learned how to live within the exceedingly great and precious promises of the faithful and all-powerful covenant God?*

The Recipients of God's Promises

But is it not presumptuous, if not simply wrong, for us to think that the promises made to Abraham are still available to us today? Has not that covenantal dispensation passed into the circular file of revelation and history, so that it is no longer a source of hope and guidance for us today? Although we shall have more to say about this in the excursus that follows this chapter, the following comments will suffice for now.

(1) We must note, in the first place, that *all the promises made to Abraham have come to their fulfillment in the Person and work of our Lord Jesus Christ* (2 Cor. 1:19–20). In Him, all the promises are Yes! and Amen! A simple review of the promises of the Abrahamic covenant

will show this to be true. Those who claim the Name of Jesus Christ are an uncountable host, millions if not billions of people alive today, and at least as many from previous generations, a great nation and a holy people (as we shall examine more fully in chapter 6). Through His blood and intercession they are blessed of God and have access to His throne of grace, coming before Him on their knees with their praises and requests, and finding help and satisfaction in His loving gaze. Their name, while the object of scorn by many, has been one of great influence in moral, social, and cultural affairs over the years. Kings and tyrants have yielded to the advice and admonitions of the followers of Christ, nations have been revived, the oppressed have been delivered, great undertakings in the arts and sciences have issued forth, and the downcast and despairing have been lifted up by words of truth and hope from those who bear His Name on them.

Further, many have come into that arena of blessing which is found before the throne of grace as a result of the witness of the spiritual offspring of Abraham, and have found there blessings abundant to meet their every need. Those who live in the covenant that God entered into with Abraham and consummated in Jesus Christ have known His protection and provision in ordinary and extraordinary ways. And their tribe has reached across time, cultures, classes, and tongues to constitute the single most remarkable race of all human history. Clearly Paul's straightforward summation of the full realization of God's promises in Christ is absolutely on the mark. And yet, this is just the down payment on richer, fuller, more glorious and blissful blessings to come.

(2) That those exceedingly great and precious promises are for us who have come to Christ is clear from the words of the apostle Paul in Ephesians 2:12–13. Here Paul, speaking to the Gentile believers in the church in Ephesus, reminds them that there was a time when they had no part with their Jewish brethren in the things of the Lord. They did not know Christ, had no faith in God and no hope, and were "strangers to the covenants of the promise" (according to the original Greek, v. 12).[3] This is a most interesting phrase, since it clearly intends to embrace the whole of Old Testament covenant making under the umbrella of the promise God made to Abraham (we shall have more

to say about this in chapter 6).[4] *All the covenants of Scripture are to be seen within the overarching framework of the promises of God.*

But now, Paul tells them, "you who formerly were far off have been brought near," that is, made to participate in the promises of God's covenant along with the Jews who trusted in God in Ephesus. How was that possible? For both Jews and Gentiles alike it was "the blood of Christ" that brought them near (v. 13). He in whom the covenant finds its consummation is also the One who is able to bring men and women under the umbrella of its divine protections and extend to them the full measure of His grace.

Thus, all who have come in faith to Jesus Christ, who have understood that His righteous blood spilled on the cross for them was for their redemption, and who have been washed in that blood unto newness of life in Him, are no longer strangers to the promises of God's covenant. They are now "fellow-citizens with the saints, and are of God's household," heirs of eternal life and possessors of the promises of God's covenant (v. 19).

Living in God's Promises

Having this rich treasure as our possession, therefore, how shall we live in it so that we might know the fullness of life in the arena of God's grace?

In a day when so many followers of Christ are leading drab, defeated lives, we must wonder to what promises they are clinging for purpose and joy in life. *For the prospect of living each day in the bright glow of peace that passes understanding, joy unspeakable, a heightened sense of purpose and expectation, and the presence and power of the Lord of glory has not diminished one whit from what previous generations of the followers of Christ have known.* Yet this is only available within the framework of God's covenant and His promises. As the followers of Christ in all ages have lived overcoming, victorious lives, turning their world upside down for Christ and living in the full confidence of His blessings and power, so we today may live as well. That so few contemporary Christians experience the life of faith like this is testimony to the fact that we are con-centrating on the wrong promises.

The promises held out by our mundane experience, as valid as they may be, can easily become idols, created objects in which we place all our hope and to which we give the greatest measure of our devotion, expressed as time, energy, and mind-set. As long as our primary focus in life is on the promises of work, home, wealth, relationships, or di-version, we consign ourselves to a life of defeat and disillusionment as Christians. We hope to know the full and abundant life in Christ while we trust in the promises of our own hands. We must learn instead to put the activities of our daily lives, and all the promise they hold, into the perspective of God's covenant and the exceedingly great and pre-cious promises He holds out for us there. Only then will our joy and peace be informed by God's Word and not the works of our own hands. And only then will we know the kind of purpose and power for living that is able to take us beyond ourselves into new realms of spiritual experience as the servants of the living God.

How do we begin to do this?

(1) *See the promises of Scripture.* We must learn to see the promises of God throughout His Word, earnestly seeking the grace of God and claiming those promises as our own. When I was a new believer I would often use a colored pen to mark my Bible, underlining commands in red, doctrinal passages in blue, and promises in green. Over the years of doing this I was amazed to see how much green ink appeared on the pages of my Bible! The promises of God are so many and varied, yet they all fall nicely under one of the six promises made to Abraham, all of which are fulfilled in our relationship with the Lord Jesus Christ.

We tend to read the Bible only for new insights into deep doctrinal truths, or for crisp commands or pithy platitudes to guide our daily paths. But until we begin to notice, meditate on, claim for ourselves, and act in our daily experience on those exceedingly great and precious promises of God's covenant, we shall never know more than the most meager morsel of the full and abundant life we have in Christ. Until we see those promises as *our* promises and begin to lay hold of them for our daily experience in Christ, our Christian life will continue to be clouded by the idols of our mundane experience and, therefore, will lack the fullness He Himself wants us to have.

(2) *Let the promises form our vision.* Like Abraham, we need to allow the promises of God to inform and shape our vision of the kind of life we want for ourselves. What faith Abraham showed to offer his son Isaac to the Lord! How could he do that? Only because, in his mind, he had become convinced, based on his experience with the Lord and the promises of His Word, that Isaac was the chosen seed through whom the promises of God's covenant would begin their descent to the generations to follow. God would rescue him, would do something only He could do to keep this boy from perishing, even if He had to raise him from the dead. Abraham's was a vision fixed on eternal truths and sustained by the power of God, and not merely his own understanding.

How small the vision of most Christians appears by contrast! How do we as the followers of Christ see ourselves in this postmodern world? Obviously, for the millions of believers who immerse themselves in eschatological fantasies of an imminent rapture, their vision is one of merely holding on and waiting. No need here to claim promises about being a blessing to the nations or of raising up succeeding generations in the knowledge of the Lord. We're not going to be around long enough for any of that. Millions of other believers are so caught up in the mundane world of getting and spending that they have little time to devote "on their knees" to knowing and enjoying the Lord and living as His servants in the world. And millions more are content with a merely cultural Christianity that finds them going to church, perhaps reading their Bibles and praying at meals, and trying to keep their noses clean before their neighbors.

Here are no visions of mighty divine interventions enabling us to do exceedingly abundantly above all that we could ever ask or think. No commitment to overcoming our fears and reticence in order to become powerful witnesses to the resurrection of Jesus Christ. No determination to invest our time, talents, and resources in bringing the blessings of God to bear through our lives on the culture and society of our day, so that others may know the blessings of God as well. No sense of the thrill of sacrificial living; little knowledge of the life-changing power of God; no strength to stand firm in the face of temptation; no adamant determination to seek the kingdom of God above all else.

How do we see ourselves as heirs of the covenant and children of the King? Unless we nurture a vision more firmly rooted in the promises of God's covenant and the almighty power of God to do in, for, and through us more than we might otherwise expect, we shall never know the power of those exceedingly great and precious promises in anything more than a perfunctory manner. But by understanding those promises, meditating on them deeply and long, imagining their impact on our own lives and the lives of our fellow Christians; by arranging them into components of a personal vision and calling upon God for grace to live according to that vision; and by going forth to follow that vision in our daily lives, we can begin to know more of what Abraham must have experienced on that mountain when the Angel of the Lord stayed his hand, commended his faith, and pointed him to another sacrifice.

(3) *Live out our vision.* We need to live according to our promise-informed vision, and not according to the limits of our circumstances or our abilities—the puny promises of our mundane life. I was once asked by a student whether I thought that most pastors were working to the level of their ability. He had expressed disappointment in the work ethic and general productivity of pastors he had known and was seeking some explanation. I told him I did not think so. I'm certain that most pastors are highly gifted and capable individuals, who could be much more productive in their service for the equipping of the saints for the work of ministry. However, as I told my student, I do believe that most pastors are working up to the level of their *vision*. They are doing in their callings what they understand to be expected of them. The problem is that many of their expectations are ill-informed, misguided, or simply wrong. And the vision they have constructed for themselves fits well with their personalities, interests, and natural abilities; so this has become the "com-

fort zone" for their ministries. Fettered by such puny vision, it is no wonder they are not more productive.

What is true of many ministers is true of many other Christians as well.

As we begin to develop personal visions richly infused with the great and precious promises of God's Word, we will begin to "dream dreams and see visions" of how our lives might be different, according to what *God* has promised and not what we have always known to be true about ourselves. We will see ourselves doing things—undertaking ministry activities, giving more liberally and joyously, sacrificing our time and personal interests, standing firm for the gospel before our postmodern friends and associates, serving in our local church—that we have neither experienced before nor imagined being able to do. But, believing God's promises, we will begin to prepare for such activities, setting aside the time, getting the training, and beginning to pray for the open doors of opportunity that will allow us to claim those promises in the day-to-day realities of our lives.

And then we will see our lives begin to change. We will experience new surges of divine power within us, find new boldness in bearing witness for Christ and new joy in sacrificing for Him. We will know the reality in us of the faithful and powerful God who made us, who gave us His promises, and who is pleased to enable us by His Spirit to know those promises in greater and greater fullness each and every day. And as this begins to happen, we will discover the unshakable peace and joy of a life committed to God and lived within the framework of His covenant of promise. We will understand what it means to walk by faith and not by sight (2 Cor. 5:7); will find ourselves swept up in a new sense of purpose in life and a new vision of ourselves as servants of the living God; and will begin more and more to realize those exceedingly great and precious promises as the wellspring of our own happiness and strength.

QUESTIONS FOR STUDY OR DISCUSSION

1. To what extent would you say that the promises God made to Abraham provide a focus for your own life? In what ways is this

so? To what extent is your life governed more by the promises of your daily life in the world than the promises of God's covenant?

2. Why do you suppose so many Christians have a hard time keeping these exceedingly great and precious promises in mind? What do they seem to be focusing on instead?

3. Would it make a difference in your church if more of your members understood God's promises and were making a conscious attempt to live within them? What kind of difference?

4. What steps might you begin to take in order to allow the promises of God to be more of a molding and shaping influence in your own life? How would you expect this to begin to change your life?

5. Review the goals you set for this study. What is the most important lesson you have learned from this chapter? How do you think this might help you to realize your goals?

3

EXCURSUS: THE COVENANT OF PROMISE IN THE NEW TESTAMENT[1]

And he received the sign of circumcision, a seal of the righteousness of the faith which he had while still uncircumcised, that he might be the father of all those who believe . . . who not only are of the circumcision, but who also walk in the steps of the faith which our father Abraham had. . . .—Romans 4:11–12

The patriarchal hope in God's promises continues to be the hope of the church.—Willem VanGemeren[2]

We need to linger a bit, at the risk of becoming momentarily sidetracked, on this matter of the promise of God's covenant—the Abrahamic covenant—for two reasons.

The Abrahamic covenant is one of the most recurrent themes in the Bible. Hardly a section of Scripture is devoid of some reference to it. The Mosaic covenant is based upon it (Exod. 2:24–25), and David, with whom a remarkable manifestation of God's covenant was initiated, never loses sight of its ongoing relevance (cf. the many references to the patriarchs, covenant, promise, the land, God's blessing to the nations, etc. in such psalms as 20, 22, 25, 37, and so forth). The significance of God's dealings with Abraham appears over and over in Scripture as foundational to everything else that God would do with and for His people.

At the same time, *many contemporary Bible scholars and teachers regard the covenant with Abraham as merely a temporary arrangement* that was eclipsed in successive eras of covenant making between God and men. The effect of such a view of God's covenant making activity is to cut off the generations of those who came after Abraham—including the present generation—from the exceedingly great and precious promises God held out for him. According to this view, the generations who succeeded Abraham came under a new way of relating to God, so that they could hope to know and enjoy God through obedience to His Law or His appointed king, rather than by a faithful longing for His promises and an eager expectation of His promised Seed (Gal. 3:16). According to such teachers, the promises made to Abraham were of strictly temporary import, and have no abiding relevance beyond his day, or in our own.

However, as we have suggested and as we shall see, the New Testament regards the covenant of promise as foundational to the New Covenant and contends that the promises of that covenant realized their fulfillment in the person and work of Jesus Christ. The New Testament treats the covenant between God and Abraham as a *revelational key* in helping us to understand more clearly the general intent of God's revelation, and as an *overall framework* of life, for both grasping the scope of Christ's achievement and understanding the life of faith and ministry that has come down to us in the church today.

Our purpose in this excursus, therefore, will be to examine the place of the covenant of promise—God's covenant—in the New Testament. We will consider the uses of the Abrahamic covenant in the New Testament and offer some conclusions and a caveat that would seem to follow from our investigation. We will see the continuing validity of the Abrahamic covenant, as well as its supreme relevance for the life of faith today.

THE ABRAHAMIC COVENANT IN THE NEW TESTAMENT

There are two ways in which the Abrahamic covenant—the covenant promise of God—is referenced in the New Testament. The first we might call the *incidental* uses, and the second, *integral* uses.

34

(1) *Incidental uses*. Incidental references occur in various places in the New Testament in the context of some larger point the writer or speaker is making. In that context references to the covenant with Abraham serve to illustrate, supplement, or otherwise focus the particular point or claim the writer is making in the passage as a whole.

We can also see that these incidental uses of the Abrahamic covenant are made by two different groups of people. First, there are those made by *the unbelieving Jews*. In John 8:33, for example, we see the Jews trying to subvert the exclusivistic teaching of Jesus by claiming to be the children of Abraham not in need of any deliverance that He might offer. The implicit claim in this is that mere physical descent from the patriarch was sufficient for having a place in God's covenant. In the view of the religious leaders of Jesus' day, no one could be greater than Abraham, and to be tied to him by blood descent was as much spiritual insurance as anyone needed.

It was this same spiritual pride that John the Baptist discerned in those unbelieving Jews who came out to him (Matt. 3:7–9). In this, as in the previous case, their inclination to appeal to physical descent from Abraham in order to justify their opposition to the gospel was incidental to their real concern, which was to resist, discredit, and destroy all threats to their place of power and privilege (John 11:48). They appealed to the covenant with Abraham as the sole means of finding favor with God.

Not only the Jews but *the faithful as well* make incidental reference to Abraham and the covenant into which God entered with him. Matthew, for example, notes that Jesus is the Son of Abraham as part of his presentation of the kingly descent of the Messiah (Matt. 1:1). In Matthew 8:5–13 Jesus Himself makes reference to Abraham in order to make the point that the kingdom of God is for those who believe, not merely those who can trace a physical descent from the patriarch. He makes the same point in a similar way in Luke 13:28–29. In that same chapter Jesus uses the phrase "daughter of Abraham" to refer to a woman whose faith had brought her healing. He thus commends her understanding of and submission to the requirement of faith in order for one to receive the blessings of God's grace (Luke 13:16).

The apostles Peter and Paul make use of the Abrahamic covenant as a means of establishing common ground and credibility for their preaching, Peter in Acts 3:13 and Paul in Acts 13:36. In each case their main point is the sufficiency and supremacy of Christ as the way of salvation. The references to Abraham aided them in keeping the audience's attention and provided a frame of reference for their preaching. The suggestion in each case is that the great redemptive work God began with Abraham realized its fulfillment in Jesus Christ.

There are many other such incidental uses of the Abrahamic covenant in the New Testament. The few cited here should be sufficient to help us see that *the importance of this idea—of a covenant between God and Abraham—was firmly established and of enormous significance in the days of the gospel's beginnings.* The idea of Abraham and the special relationship he enjoyed with God was part of the "cultural literacy" of the time. Moreover, it seems to have been clearly established in the minds of first-century dwellers in Palestine that this Abrahamic covenant was a matter of *continuing relevance,* that there were *contemporary benefits* to be gained by being associated with the patriarch, and that participation in the covenant relationship was a privilege to be cherished *for the present.* In these incidental references to God's covenant with Abraham there is no discernible sense from any of the parties that the Abrahamic covenant either had passed away or was to be understood as meaningful for only one particular generation or epoch of history. Granted, the unbelieving Jews made false use of the covenantal idea, seeking to limit its benefits to the nation of Israel, but this misunderstanding on their part does not negate the fact that they still considered the Abrahamic covenant as having abiding validity and ongoing significance for their own day.

Thus, the incidental uses of the Abrahamic covenant in the New Testament establish that covenant's ongoing importance to people in the days of Jesus and beyond.

(2) *Integral uses.* The second kind of reference to this covenant in the New Testament we might call *integral.* In these cases the Abrahamic covenant itself is in focus, not merely for the sake of illustrat-

ing or supplementing an argument, but as the *center and substance* of the argument itself. This is certainly what is in view in John 8:37–59, where Jesus picks up on the offhand comment by the unbelieving Jews (cited above) to argue a central point concerning His deity and authority and to expose the absurdity of the claims of His detractors. The Abrahamic covenant also appears as the *denouement* of the Magnificat of our Lord's mother in Luke 1:46–55. It is the organizing motif and central feature of Paul's argument for justification by faith in Romans 4. And it is the issue of discussion in Hebrews 7, in which the writer exalts the high priesthood of Christ over the Levitical priesthood. The primacy of God's dealings with Abraham must, the author argues, be allowed to serve as the theological context for the subsequent covenantal arrangements introduced at Mount Sinai.

It is in these *integral* uses of the Abrahamic covenant that we can gain a clearer understanding of the relationship between that covenant and the New Covenant, and, as a result, the place of the Abrahamic covenant—and the promises inherent in that covenant—in the life of faith today. We will look somewhat more closely at two specific integral uses of the Abrahamic covenant in order to lay a foundation for the conclusions that will follow.

We turn first to the Benedictus of Zacharias in Luke 1:68–79. In this passage the father of John the Baptist is celebrating in a song of praise his understanding of the meaning of the forerunner's birth. The day of salvation has dawned with the visitation of God among His people (vv. 68–69). This is that which the prophets spoke of concerning the Savior who would descend from David and, ascending his throne, bring deliverance and redemption to Israel. This, exclaims Zacharias, is what had been promised to the fathers. God is remembering His covenant, which He swore on an oath to Abraham (vv. 69–72). And this act of mercy and grace will mean deliverance and the freedom and ability to walk in holiness before the God of Israel. In the birth of John the Baptist all the fervent expectations and hopes of the people of God from the time of Abraham are breaking in upon the historical scene, heralded by the birth of him whose calling it would be to make straight the paths of the Lord.

It is clear that Zacharias makes the covenant with Abraham the key element of his song of praise to God. *In the coming and work of the Messiah, God will bring to fulfillment all that had been promised long ago to Abraham.*[3] Thus, the Abrahamic covenant was not being *eclipsed* by the new covenant; rather, it was *becoming* the new covenant, at last arrived at its fullness in the Person and work of the Messiah, as Paul would later imply in 2 Corinthians 1:19–20. As Fred H. Klooster puts it:

> The covenant which the NT calls "old" or "first" and contrasts with the "new" is *not* the Abrahamic; the "old" covenant which became "obsolete" was the Sinaitic (Hebrews 7–10). The "new" and "better" covenant is the Abrahamic Covenant now fulfilled in Jesus Christ. It continues to function as a strategic instrument of the Kingdom.[4]

We should expect therefore, on the basis of what we see here, that the blessings of that now-fulfilled covenant—the promises of God's covenant—would accrue to those who enter it through the Author and Finisher of the covenant, Jesus Christ (Heb. 12:2).

This is precisely the argument of the apostle Paul in Galatians 3, our second example. His burden in this passage is to show that the true heirs of what was promised to Abraham are *not* those who yet insist that mere physical identification with the patriarch, at the very least by means of circumcision, is what is required to inherit the blessings of God. Rather, Paul insists that *the promises are for those who have the faith of Abraham,* since faith is the true covenant obligation and not mere outward conformity to administrative rites or rituals. This faith comes by way of the Seed of Abraham, who is the means of blessing for all the nations, that is, Jesus Christ. As we trust in Him, we enter into His finished work, the work of covenant satisfaction and fulfillment, and we embark upon a lifestyle of claiming and enjoying the promises we have inherited as true sons and daughters by faith.[5] Ridderbos goes so far as to assert, "The promises right from the start were intended for and directed to those who are in Christ or of Him."[6]

Richard Longenecker summarizes the thrust of Galatians 3 in these words:

> Paul . . . argues that Christ is the "seed" in view in the Abrahamic covenant . . . and goes on to speak of Christ's own sharing in the promises of that covenant as Abraham's legitimate "seed" . . . he is invoking a corporate solidarity understanding of the promise to Abraham wherein the Messiah, as the true descendant of Abraham and the representative of his people, and the Messiah's elect ones, as sharers in his experiences and his benefits, *are seen as the legitimate inheritors of God's promises.*[7]

In the mind of New Testament writers, therefore, the covenant with Abraham is still very much intact, fraught with meaning and significance for those who have the faith of Abraham. Thus, the blessings of that covenant, now fulfilled in Jesus Christ, accrue to His followers as an estate of exceedingly great and precious promises, ready to be embraced and enjoyed, as I argued in the previous chapter.

Yet, surprisingly, this matter of our *appropriation* of those promises tends to escape the attention of most commentators. Rightly focusing on the central issue of justification by faith, most commentators neglect to discuss the implications of Christ's fulfillment of the Abrahamic covenant when it comes to realizing the blessing of God's promises in our daily lives. It is to some conclusions regarding this important matter that we now turn.

IMPLICATIONS

Four conclusions and one caveat derive from the understanding outlined above, namely, that the promises of God's covenant as originally proffered to Abraham and his offspring are of continuing relevance to the life of faith today. I will begin with the caveat.

Throughout the Gospel accounts it is characteristic of those whom Jesus described as "not knowing the Scriptures nor the power of God" (Matt. 22:29) to treat the Abrahamic covenant as having a strictly restricted application, in particular, as a covenant with the physical descendants of Abraham alone. The unbelieving Jews acknowledged neither the extent of God's covenant—that it incorporates great numbers of people from beyond the mere ethnic confines of the nation of Israel—nor the scope of what it promises—salvation by grace through faith in Jesus Christ. They had come to see themselves as guardians of the covenant, preserving its ethnic and legal purity lest it be grasped after by the ignorant masses or misappropriated by the uncircumcised (cf. John 7:49). They did not consider their calling to be that of serving to channel the grace of God to those around them. This may have been true in the dispersion, where we read of many God-fearers associating themselves with Jewish communities (cf. Acts 10:1–2), but it was not true of the Jewish hierarchy in Jerusalem.

Further, they allowed the name of Israel to become a byword among the nations, despised by Rome and a political plaything of the Seleucid puppets of Rome. The "great name" that had been promised to Abraham was for a previous generation. The only greatness that lay in the name of Abraham for the unbelieving Jews of Jesus' day was in the ways they sought to use that name to establish their own respectability and preserve their social standing in Israel. And the conditions of blessedness and freedom that had been promised to the patriarch they had transformed into a system of traditions and regulations used not to liberate the people, but to control them.

Thus it would seem that, to the extent that religious leaders today seek to restrict, in an unscriptural manner, the application that is to be made of the Abrahamic covenant—by either limiting it to a particular people or limiting the scope of what it promises—they show that their approach to that covenant is tainted with a misunderstanding of God's intent, if not the sin of unbelief. We must allow the fullness of God's covenant to envelop our faith, and we must not allow false theologies or misguided exegetical schemes to rob the people of God in Christ of all that He has accomplished for them as the Finisher of the Abrahamic covenant. Let us not be found guilty of being identified more with the religion of the Jews than the faith of the apostles when it comes to our understanding and appropriation of the abiding validity of the promises made to our father in the faith (Rom. 4). The promises made to Abraham have been realized in Christ, and they await our faithful and obedient appropriation in our everyday callings as the heirs of Abraham and the followers of the Lord of glory.

With this in mind four conclusions can be seen to derive from all that has been said.

(1) It is clear that *the Abrahamic covenant, as the New Testament teaches us to regard it, can help us to keep focused on the Christocentric nature of God's eternal plan and His revelation to His people.* As early as Genesis 12, according to the New Testament, God was beginning to detail specifics concerning His redemptive purposes and plan. And His will can be seen to have reached climactic expression in the Person and work of Jesus, as the New Testament makes clear. As we allow this understanding to guide our studies in the Old Testament, as well as our preaching and teaching from that section of Scripture, it can help to keep us from falling into some form of legalistic, moralistic, or merely allegorical use of that portion of God's revelation. The Christ who fulfilled the Abrahamic covenant was in view throughout the period of God's revealing His will to His people. In our study and teaching of the Old Testament, therefore, we should expect to find that what Jesus said concerning these texts is true, that they speak of Him (John 5:39). Such a focus will allow us to bring the Old Testament to bear on our walk with the Lord in practical and relevant ways.

The Old Testament, in other words, is not simply an interesting historical document leading up to the "strong meat" of the New Testament. Nor should we regard it merely as a source of moral or spiritual examples, or as a platform for vain hermeneutical schemes. It is the Word of God and shows us the purposes and progress of His covenant, pointing us ever to Christ and to the grace He offers as the sole means of knowing God and of the full and abundant life.

(2) *The Abrahamic covenant helps us to understand more clearly the full scope of the achievement of Jesus Christ.* The writer of Hebrews referred to our "great salvation" (Heb. 2:3). Paul wrote that God was able to do "exceedingly abundantly above all that we ask or think" (Eph. 3:20). Throughout the New Testament we are impressed with the magnitude,

the enormity, of what Christ has achieved on our behalf, for example, when we are told that He is putting the whole world under His feet for the sake of building His church; or when we are reminded that all things in the world have been given to us for the sake of serving Christ (Eph. 1:22; 1 Cor. 3:21–23). Yet all too often pastors and teachers, short on covenant vision and understanding, allow the people of God to settle for something less than that great salvation as their own personal experience of the Lord. In the light of God's exceedingly great and precious promises, now fulfilled in Jesus Christ, let us supply the people of God instead with an understanding of the faith that enlarges their vision, challenges them to greater undertakings of faith, and is able to give them peace, joy, and assurance in even the most troubling of circumstances.

Yet the promises made to Abraham and fulfilled by Jesus extend even farther than this. Jesus has made possible for us much, much more than we have yet come to know. Our duty—and our privilege—is to search the Scriptures daily in order to discover more ways in which those ancient promises, first spoken to our father Abraham, may be claimed and enjoyed in our lives today. As I argued in the previous chapter, we must work hard to understand, proclaim, and appropriate as much as possible of the fullness of life that Christ has gained for us, until the world around us begins increasingly to be leavened by our grace-filled presence, to take note of our good works, and to glorify our Father who is in heaven.

(3) In a similar way, *the Abrahamic covenant, as explained in the New Testament, helps us to know how we are to think about the life of faith and work of ministry to which we have been called in Jesus Christ.* We are able sufficiently to understand the promises as we see them having been partially fulfilled throughout the period of the Old Testament. We know what God requires of us and how His covenant works. We know God's promises to have been fully realized in and through the Lord Jesus Christ. And we hear the apostles heralding the day of our having inherited those promises as sons and daughters of God and as participants in His covenant.

We must ask ourselves whether and to what extent that which we have been promised in God's covenant is being realized in our own daily experience as the followers of Christ. Do we in our churches believe that God intends to make us a great people, and do we organize our ministries and plan and use our resources and facilities accordingly? Or are we content merely to take what comes our way, indifferent to the promise of greatness that captured the imaginations of generations of our forebears in God's covenant?

Or, again, do we in fact believe that we have been made recipients of a great name, that our opinions and convictions matter in the public square, and that they will be listened to by those around us as we seek to bring the grace and truth of God to bear on matters of social policy and personal morality? Or do we merely wring our hands at the decline of our social and moral consensus and seek for political hopefuls to restore us to a safer and smoother road, thus relying more on the promises of men than of God?

Do we encourage and exemplify a boldness in heralding the truth of God's Word, a boldness that clearly shows that we expect others will listen to what we have to say, and that some will be persuaded? Do we trust the Lord to supply all our needs according to His riches in glory by Christ Jesus, or do we fret and fume, whine and complain over our lack of this, that, and the other? Do we resort to prayer, fasting, and extended seasons of worship to find the strength we need in order to serve the Lord in our communities, or are we content with the programs, resources, and policies of the status quo in our churches?

If we truly understand that the Abrahamic covenant has been fulfilled in Jesus Christ and extended to us as the heirs of the patriarch, then we will begin more earnestly and consistently to look for ways of realizing those exceedingly great and precious promises for our daily experience in the life of faith. We will beseech God more fervently for grace to help in our time of need, and believe more consistently that He will never fail us nor forsake us as we follow in faithful pursuit of His glorious promises. We will never be content to be motivated and led by the puny promises of mundane living; instead, we shall hunger and thirst for the righteousness of God, seeking His kingdom and promises with all the strength of our being throughout all our waking moments.

(4) Finally, *the Abrahamic covenant provides something of a touchstone that can be useful to us in these days of its fulfillment as we endeavor to evaluate our progress in realizing the fullness of what has been accomplished for us in Jesus Christ.*

The church of Christ must not be content with an approach to life and ministry that seeks only to perpetuate the status quo indefinitely into the future. The Word of God invites us to adopt the kind of vision, purpose, goals, objectives, and mission that will allow us to know the fullness of the blessings and promises of God's covenant. The Abrahamic covenant provides a framework of promises that we may begin to take as expectations of what we hope to realize by the grace of God through our ministries and in our lives. These exceedingly great and precious promises may serve as guides to our planning and keys to our assessment as we determine our ministry activities, allocate our resources, and undertake our labors for the Lord. As more and more we observe progress in realizing these promises, we will have assurance that our labors are not in vain in the Lord, and thus have much cause to praise and glorify Him (1 Cor. 15:58).

The Abrahamic covenant—the promises of God's covenant as given to Abraham—rightly understood in its original context and in the light of New Testament revelation, proves to be a much more powerful, much more dynamic, and much more meaningful and relevant arrangement than is normally understood by Christians today. It is the task of the theologian and pastor to hold out that great salvation before the eyes of God's people, to call them to press on toward fuller realization of their high calling in Christ Jesus, and to help them see more clearly "the depth of the riches both of the wisdom and knowledge of God! How unsearchable are His judgments, and His ways past finding out!" (Rom. 11:33). Thus may we all begin to know with greater joy and effects the power that is ours for living in God's covenant today.

QUESTIONS FOR STUDY OR DISCUSSION

1. Have you ever heard anyone teach that the Abrahamic covenant was merely a temporal arrangement, limited to a particular time

or people? How did that person justify such a claim? Did you accept it? Why or why not?

2. In the light of this and the previous chapter, summarize your own thinking about the promises made to Abraham. How well do you understand them? Are they beginning to make any difference in your own outlook on life? In what ways?

3. God's promises are so many and so rich! In your own study of Scripture, how aware are you of the promises of God? How do you typically respond to them? Have these last two chapters affected how you will study the Scripture in the days to come? Explain.

4. How would you try to help someone understand the abiding validity of God's promises to Abraham? How would you try to keep from offending or alienating such a person even as you worked to persuade him or her that the promises made to Abraham are still valid for us today? What would you hope to achieve by doing this?

5. Review the goals you set for your study of God's covenant. Are you making any progress? Are you seeing changes in your outlook? Do you need to revise your goals in any way?

4

THE COVENANT
OF GLORY

. . . having predestined us to adoption as sons by Jesus Christ to Himself, according to the good pleasure of His will, to the praise of the glory of His grace . . .—Ephesians 1:5–6

The glory of God appears, by the account given in Scripture, to be that event, in the earnest desires of which, and in their delight in which, the best part of the moral world, and when in their best frames, most naturally express the direct tendency of the spirit of true goodness, the virtuous and pious affections of their heart.
—Jonathan Edwards[1]

The question arises as to why God would want to conceive and provide such a covenant relationship with men. What could He possibly gain from it, who, we are reminded by the apostle Paul, has no need of men nor of anything outside Himself (Acts 17:24–25)?

The answer may be simply put: He has given us His covenant because it pleased Him to do so for His own glory. God's motivation in creating His covenant and filling it with exceedingly great and precious promises for His people is so that He might be glorified. The glory of God is the end for which we and His covenant have been created, and it is the context in which, as Edwards observed, people express their relationship with Him and realize their fullest joy and satisfaction in the Lord.

Now that is easily enough said. Indeed, most readers will readily affirm the glory of God as the supreme end of all things. To the catechism question, "What is man's chief end?" we all reply, "To glorify God and enjoy Him forever." Understanding what is *intended* by "the glory of God," and especially what this means for us who desire to live within God's covenant, is quite another thing. This is largely because of our tendency more to *mouth* than truly to *understand the meaning of* the various words deriving from the idea of the "glory of God"—words such as "to glorify" God, which, the Westminster Catechism reminds us, is to be our chief end in life. It will be difficult for us to realize that chief end, and thus to enjoy to the full God's promises in His covenant, if we do not truly understand what this idea entails.

In this chapter, therefore, we shall examine the nature and meaning of the glory of God, looking at it from the perspective of Scripture and the covenant, and seeing how the glory of God in the covenant is supremely realized for us in the work of our Lord Jesus Christ. Only as we truly understand this matter of the glory of God, and of what it means for us to live unto His glory, or to glorify Him in all things, can we hope to set our lives on a course of true covenant fulfillment. The purpose of God's covenant is that He might be glorified in us, that is, in the way we understand, claim, and appropriate the promises of His covenant in our everyday lives. His covenant is therefore supremely a covenant of glory, and it is to the goal of understanding the implications of this that we now turn.

THE GLORY OF GOD

In the Bible the glory of God is not some vague or general concept of God's being exalted to His rightful place, receiving the praise of all creation and, especially, of His people. I suspect that when most Christians think of the glory of God this or something rather like it comes to mind. When we say, "Let God be glorified," we mean basically to let Him get the praise and honor for whatever it is we have in mind. When we sing, "To God be the glory / great things He hath done," we mean that we want Him to receive praise for, among other things, His glorious work of redemption. To "glorify God" is thus to praise, honor, and adore Him for His greatness and goodness, at least as this concept is typically understood among Christians today.

In other words, for most of us the concept of "the glory of God" is understood as a *liturgical* idea, involving the act of giving God praise for something He has done or something that He is, either through singing or in spoken words of prayer and praise.

The glory of God undoubtedly involves such practices. For, when we are singing the praises of God or otherwise raising our voices to exalt and magnify His Name, we are certainly acknowledging that praise and honor are due Him and are appropriate to His exalted being and state. But if this is all we understand concerning the glory of God, we fail to appreciate a rather more fundamental biblical notion of that idea, which is that *the glory of God is nothing less than the very presence of God among men, manifest and understandable, with compelling effects.*

Let's examine this idea more closely, and then we shall put forward a more thorough definition of the glory of God to guide the remainder of our study in this chapter.

That God's glory indicates His presence among people is clear from any number of passages. Consider, for example, Exodus 24:15–17:

> Then Moses went up into the mountain, and a cloud covered the mountain. Now the glory of the LORD rested on Mount Sinai, and the cloud covered it six days. . . . The sight of the glory of the LORD was like a consuming fire. . . .

Two observations concerning the glory of God are evident here. First, the phrase "glory of the LORD" referred to the presence of God upon the mountain. Moses was going up to meet with God, as he had been commanded, and the descent of God's glory upon the mountain was Moses' summons to appear before the divine presence. In other words, Moses knew to come up to the mountain when he saw the glory of God appearing on its summit. The presence of God's glory indicated the presence of God Himself, and thus, that the time had come for Moses to commune with Him on the mountain. The glory of God is thus the presence of God Himself.

Second, that presence took on a manifestly physical and recognizable form: "The sight of the glory of the LORD was like a consuming fire on the top of the mountain." Notice that the text says "*like* a consuming fire," not that the glory of God actually was a consuming fire. To the eyes of the Israelites it appeared that way, but that does not mean it actually was. The important point is that the glory of God, indicating the presence of God among men, took a recognizable, albeit greatly exaggerated, form, a form that left no doubt in the minds of those who witnessed it that the divine presence was its cause and controlling factor.

The same thing is evident when the glory of God came down to fill the temple at its dedication by Solomon (2 Chron. 7:1–3). In this passage we are told that fire came down from heaven and consumed the sacrifices that had been prepared, and that the glory of God also came down and filled the temple. We should note that the glory of God is not the fire, but it is something very real and very tangible that came down with the fire and seems to have been closely associated with it. The presence of the glory of God in the temple was so pervasive and powerful that not only could the priests not enter while it was there, but they and all Israel fell on their faces to the ground outside the temple. The fire was there and so was the glory of God. The people saw it, were forced to make room for it, and fell down before it, worshiping God.

So, as in the previous instance, God's presence was clearly indicated in some observable, albeit remarkable form or manner, such that His presence was acknowledged and He was worshiped as is His due. So remarkable, so exaggerated was the physical manifestation that all who observed it recognized its divine provenance and content. As a result, both at Sinai and before the temple, the people responded with awe, fear, reverence, and worship.

One final passage will allow us to set up a definition of the glory of God. On the mount of transfiguration, Luke tells us, the disciples beheld Jesus' glory as His features changed and His garments began to glow with a brilliant light (Luke 9:28–32). The presence of the divine voice in the midst of this glorious display served to confirm that God was, indeed, on the mountain with them, both in His divine essence and in the Person of our Lord Jesus Christ. For his part, Peter was ready to perpetuate this experience indefinitely, so great was his excitement and, apparently, his sense of fulfillment and satisfaction at being in this situation. As in the Old Testament examples cited above, the presence of the glory of God was unmistakably visible and excited a response of awe and worship on the part of those who saw it.

Now, on the basis of what we have seen in these three representative passages (and we could cite many other similar appearances of the glory of God in Scripture), let's try for a more complete definition of the glory of God: *the glory of God as seen by men is the manifestation of the very presence of God, expressed in the form of natural phenomena, supernaturally exaggerated, so as to leave no doubt as to the nature and source of the manifestation, and eliciting thereby appropriate responses on the part of people.*

This definition has three important parts. (1) *The glory of God, when seen by men, is a manifestation of the very presence of God.* Something happens or something appears (recall Edwards), the source of which can only be divine in nature and essence. It is the very presence of God among men and women. When God is being glorified, He is present, showing Himself to people—creating wonder, amazement, and fear—and especially inducing worship on their parts. However He shows Himself—whatever form His glory takes—it is in a recognizable phenomenon and expresses the presence of God among men.

Thus the glory of God may well reside in the praises of His people. That ordinary folk should suddenly break out into joyous and sustained choruses of thanks and praise to the Deity can perhaps only be explained by the fact that God is in and among them, inducing them to acknowledge His presence and to declare their love for Him in this uniquely Christian way.

However, to limit the glory of God to such a display is to misunderstand and to restrict the essential nature of God's glory and to deny a presence to God in more ordinary circumstances and situations, as we shall see.

(2) This divine presence, which is the glory of God, takes the form, when seen by men, of *natural phenomena, supernaturally exaggerated*. So clear yet so powerful is the manifestation of the divine presence that we can only say that what we are seeing is *like* something familiar. Since the phenomenon is so exaggerated in expression we know that it cannot be something merely ordinary or mundane. Rather, the very exaggeration of the phenomenon makes it apparent that somehow God is in it, expressing Himself through its operation or appearance, so that the phenomenon, while recognizable enough, is somehow *more* than what we normally experience when such phenomena are in evidence among us. The glory of God on Mount Sinai was not a consuming fire, but it was *like* a consuming fire, so that, while it roared and billowed forth great clouds of smoke, causing the people to fear greatly, nothing was damaged or destroyed. Jesus' features on the mount of transfiguration were *changed* somehow, but they were still His features. His garments *shone with a brilliance*, but they were recognizably His own garments and not some special spiritual clothing of which the disciples would have known nothing whatsoever.

We should expect, therefore, that God wills to be glorified among us in ordinary ways and by ordinary means, but with extraordinary, even supernatural emphasis, indicating the divine presence in and through those ordinary ways and means. Such everyday matters as loving another person, being patient in a trying situation, being kind to an undeserving individual, or speaking about religious matters may well be apt means by which ordinary acts may be supernaturally endowed with the presence of God unto His glory.

(3) The manifestation of the glory of God leaves no doubt as to the *fact of His presence, eliciting appropriate responses of awe, fear, reverence, and worship on the part of those who observe it.* The remarkable phenomenon that appears before us is not amenable to naturalistic explanations. What we see, or what we experience, is of such an extraordinary, albeit recognizable, nature, that we can only account for it by the very presence of God, and this induces us to *acknowledge* that divine presence in appropriate ways. In the presence of something so unusual, so striking, and so compelling, and knowing this to be the very pres-

ence of God Himself, we cannot help but respond to Him in fear and reverence.

So we may say that God is glorified, and the purpose of His covenant is realized, when it is clear to us and to all around us that He is in our midst, fulfilling His covenant promises, supernaturally manifesting His divine presence through otherwise ordinary means, in a way that testifies to His presence, power, and majesty, leading people to acknowledge Him as He truly is.

THE GLORY OF GOD AND GOD'S COVENANT

What then is the relationship between the glory of God and the covenant He has been pleased to enter into with men?

(1) *The glory of God is the end of His covenant.* It was that He might be glorified that God conceived, initiated, and sustains His covenant. Paul is abundantly clear on this in Ephesians 1:3–6:

> Blessed be the God and Father of our Lord Jesus Christ, who has blessed us with every spiritual blessing in the heavenly places in Christ, just as He chose us in Him before the foundation of the world, that we should be holy and without blame before Him in love, having predestined us to adoption as sons by Jesus Christ to Himself, according to the good pleasure of His will, to the praise of the glory of His grace, by which He has made us accepted in the Beloved.

Here we glimpse the essential nature of God's covenant, that He would bless a people of His own choice. The eternal nature of the covenant is also in view. This determination on God's part was decided and entered into before the creation of the world. We see its consummation in Christ, all the promises of blessing coming to realization in Him. And we understand that God's objective in this was "to the praise of the glory of His grace."

How was that glory to be expressed (or, to use Edwards's parlance, how would it *appear*?)? Let us simply note at this point that Paul seems to indicate a connection between the holy, blameless, and loving lives of His chosen ones and the glory that is ascribed to God. Unusual, spectacular manifestations of God's glory such as often appeared in the Old Testament are not the primary means whereby God will glorify Himself in His covenant. Rather, it is through the lives of His people that He intends to make Himself known, by ordinary means, supernaturally exaggerated.

The glory of God, that He should be manifestly and undeniably displayed before men, is clearly the end of God's covenant. He intends to be glorified as people come to realize more and more of His covenant promises. But the glory of God is more than simply the end of God's covenant.

(2) *The glory of God is furthermore the seal of God's covenant.* It is His mark, bestowed upon the initial entering of that covenant by one of His chosen beneficiaries. Here is how Paul expresses this idea in Ephesians 1:13–14:

> In Him you also trusted, after you heard the word of truth, the gospel of your salvation; in whom also, having believed, you were sealed with the Holy Spirit of promise, who is the guarantee of our inheritance until the redemption of the purchased possession, to the praise of His glory.

Here Paul tells us that, when we first came to faith in Jesus Christ, God gave us His Spirit and, with Him, the first "down payment" of His glory. Perhaps you are reflecting just now on the moment of your first beginning to believe in Jesus (as I am), wondering just what that first down payment of glory might have been. Some might wish to say that, when one truly comes to faith in Christ, he or she is overwhelmed with a sense of assurance, together with a new and deep-seated joy and faith. That may or may not be; if it is, however, as it certainly was with me, we may well acknowledge that this is a manifestation of the divine presence in us. The appearance of tears of joy, a suddenly peaceful countenance, or an irrepressible smile on the face may also be expressions of the glory of God, who was working in us at the very moment of our coming to faith, making His saving presence known in unmistakable ways.

But not everyone experiences such a manifestation of God upon first coming to faith in Christ. Others may wish to say that the evidence of God's glory at that initial confession of faith takes the form of some extraordinary manifestation of the power of God's Spirit, as when the first believers spoke in unknown languages on that first Christian Pentecost. Here is not the place to argue the merits of the case for or against the continuation of such extraordinary gifts of the Spirit. Certainly it will be clear, as even Paul suggests (1 Cor. 12:30, where the form of the question in Greek demands a negative answer), that not all believers can expect to have such an experience. We should, therefore, not make the mistake of insisting that the evidence of the Spirit's coming into our lives and beginning to express the glory of God in us—the mark of our having entered into His covenant—is necessarily associated with this or some similar phenomenon.

Instead, I would suggest something much more simple, yet, in its expression much more profound—and certainly universal to all who believe—as that initial deposit, that seal and mark, of glory which God expresses in us at the moment we come consciously to profess saving faith in Jesus Christ and enter into His covenant.

Paul tells us, in Galatians 4:6, that, on the basis of God having chosen us to be His children, He, at His appointed time, sent His Spirit into our hearts. The result is that we were enabled to address Him at last as our dear and loving Father, and to do so in intimate, personal, and truly meaningful terms (the Aramaic, "Abba," being somewhat the equivalent of "Daddy!"). We may have spoken of God as Father before, perhaps when saying the Lord's Prayer, or even acknowledged Him as having some kind of paternal relationship to all mankind. But never this intimately. Never this personally. Never so fraught with this much emotion and clarity of understanding. And what is most remarkable about this passage, as the Greek makes abundantly clear, is that *it is not we ourselves who thus cry out to God, but the Spirit of God in us crying out, using our voices to the end of glorifying God in our testimony!*

Here then is that first deposit of glory whereby God seals His covenant and marks us as His chosen ones. He sends His Spirit into our hearts. His Spirit enlightens our minds to the truth of the gospel, warms our hearts with a newly discovered love for God, empowers us to believe the offer of forgiveness, *and engages our wills and voices to declare the truth of who God is, the loving, saving Father of His chosen covenant people.* And not only does the Spirit use our voice to glorify God, thus evidencing the presence of God in us in a new and undeniable way, but He also, at the same time, speaks to our own spirits, confirming the truth of our profession and the certainty of our new relationship, assuring us that our sins are forgiven and that we have been adopted by the heavenly Father into His eternal and blessed household (Rom. 8:16).

What, indeed, could be a more glorious way of embarking on the adventure of faith in Christ, than to have God's Spirit Himself speaking in, to, and through us in one momentous action of confessing Christ? For in this confession we show that we have become holy persons—"set apart ones"—and have embarked upon a course of realizing the purpose of God's covenant whereby He is to be glorified. And, in thus glorifying Him, we, if we have truly come to know Him, discover a new hope and a new outlook on life that can, as we learn how to draw on the promises of God, increasingly make all things new in our lives.

The glory of God is the end of God's covenant, as well as its seal upon those first entering into it.

(3) *Moreover, the glory of God is the evidence of God's covenant.* It is the ongoing sign that we have actually entered into and are abiding within that relationship with Him, which is based on His gracious promises fulfilled for us in Jesus Christ. Here again is Paul (Eph. 1:9–12):

... having made known to us the mystery of His will, according to His good pleasure which He purposed in Himself, that in the dispensation of the fullness of the times He might gather together in one all things in Christ, both which are in heaven and which are on earth—in Him. In Him also we have obtained an inheritance, being predestined according to the purpose of Him who works all things according to the counsel of His will, that we who first trusted in Christ should be to the praise of His glory.

God's intention for us, once we have come to saving faith in Christ and entered into covenant relationship with Him, is that we "should [live] to the praise of His glory," that is, that our lives should give sufficient evidence of His presence in us to lead to God being glorified—acknowledged as present and responded to according to what is due Him—both by us and by those around us.

But how should we expect to see this? Do we expect our features to change, our garments to glow with a supernatural brilliance, or the likeness of a consuming fire to follow us wherever we go?

Of course not. However, in a way not dissimilar from these, God intends to show His presence in us through ordinary phenomena, with which the world is not completely unfamiliar, supernaturally exaggerated with a consistency and power that can only be accounted for by the presence of God in us. It will be in the kind of people that we are, in the way that we live day by day and in the things we say and do, that God will glorify Himself.

Things like the *fruit of the Spirit* (Gal. 5:22–23). Certainly there are to be found in this world such things as love, joy, peace, and so forth. But they tend to be fleeting, based on circumstances, ultimately self-serving, and not entirely satisfying. Yet people in the world have some sense of such things, and they desire them eagerly for their lives. In the Christian life growth in the expression of such fruit *is the normal pattern*. Where the Spirit of God is—guiding us into all truth, exposing our sins and giving us repentance from them, kindling in us greater love for God and man, transforming us increasingly into the image of the Lord—we can expect that increase and greater consistency of expression of the fruit of the Spirit will be the norm. We will begin to stand out as people not merely *in search* of such benefits, but *characterized* by them. More and more our desire, so that we might *be* to the praise of the glory of God's grace, will be to pursue such fruit, to root out their opposites and labor in prayer for the grace of God to bring forth His presence in us as opposed to the old person of sin and self-centeredness

(Eph. 4:17–24). And not only will we eagerly desire and earnestly seek the grace of God for such fruit in our lives, but we will more and more delight to see it in us, giving praise and thanks to God increasingly each day as we see the evidence of His Spirit at work within us, willing and doing of His good pleasure (Phil. 2:12–13).

The fruit of the Spirit, then, is perhaps the first place where we should expect to see the glory of God manifested in our lives. Second would be the *gifts of the Spirit* that He supplies us in order that we may serve others with the grace of God. Peter says:

> As each one has received a gift, minister it to one another, as good stewards of the manifold grace of God. If anyone speaks, let him speak as the oracles of God. If anyone ministers, let him do it as with the ability which God supplies, that in all things God may be glorified through Jesus Christ, to whom belong the glory and the dominion forever and ever. Amen. (1 Peter 4:10–11)

Devoting oneself to a life of serving the needs of others is hardly the norm in our dog-eat-dog world. We are so accustomed to the "every man for himself" mentality that it strikes us as strange and somehow quaint to find a person here and there who dedicates himself or herself to serving others. In the city where I used to live, a local television station would make a weekly award of a gold pin to an individual nominated by his or her peers for outstanding service to the community. In a city of nearly a million people, to find fifty-two people a year to celebrate for their selfless service was apparently no small task, since many weeks went by each year without an award being made.

But it is to be the *norm* in the Christian community that we, empowered by the Spirit of God, should diligently seek out opportunities for serving one another, using every gift at our disposal to address the needs of those around us, and thus revealing the reality of Christ dwelling in us. As it becomes apparent that what we do is not in our own strength, but in the strength of God's Spirit, our neighbors will be forced to acknowledge a presence in us that is altogether foreign to the larger community—the very presence of God. And this may be for some of them, as it apparently was for "a great many of the priests" in Jerusalem (Acts 6:1–7), the decisive factor in helping them come to a saving knowledge of the Lord.

The glory of God is the evidence of His covenant, as He brings forth the fruit of His Spirit in our lives and equips us for ministry with the gifts we need to serve one another in love. A third way in which the glory of God is evidenced in the covenant community is through *lives of moral purity*. Paul establishes the basis for such thinking in 1 Corinthians 6:18–20:

> Flee sexual immorality. Every sin that a man does is outside the body, but he who commits sexual immorality sins against his own body. Or do you not know that your body is the temple of the Holy Spirit, who is in you, whom you have from God, and you are not your own? For you were bought at a price; therefore glorify God in your body.

To glorify God—that is, to manifest His living presence—in our bodies we must flee immorality. This is a great challenge for believers today, when the moral consensus of the age is so tolerant of everything that affronts the majesty and dignity of God and the moral sensibilities of godly men and women. Alas, it seems to be a challenge that we are having great difficulty surmounting. And yet we must resist the world's attempts to squeeze us into its mold (Rom. 12:1–2 J. B. PHILLIPS) and stand squarely on the teaching of God's Word concerning issues of morality and ethics. We do not take our cues on such matters from the spirit of the age; rather, we must let the Spirit of God shape our thinking, reform our hearts, and bring our lives in line with God's expectations of a moral life. Only thus will His presence in us be clearly evident to all, and only thus will we know more of the truly moral, full, and abundant life for which He has called us into His covenant.

Such moral living will undoubtedly afford many opportunities for us *to bear witness to our faith in Jesus Christ*—yet another means by which the glory of God is manifested in us and our participation in the community of God's covenant is proved.

Further, bearing witness for the Lord requires the power of His indwelling Spirit (Acts 1:8) and can lead to many people giving glory and praise to God for His saving mercies (Acts 13:44–49). When the gospel is proclaimed with authority, clarity, and power by ordinary people, it is evident that God must be at work in them, enabling them to do so. Recall how the people in Jerusalem in Acts 2 marveled to see so many ordinary men and women prophesying with joy of the mighty works of God. This was the experience of the first Christians, and it has been the experience of faithful generations of believers in all ages. We have every right and reason to believe that it would please God to glorify Himself among the members of His covenant community today by their active, faithful, glad, and powerful witness to Him among their neighbors, associates, and friends. Indeed, his promise that we should be a blessing to all the nations would seem to make such witness bearing an essential component of our lives in His covenant.

Finally, the glory of God is manifested among the members of His covenant community by their *willingness to sacrifice freely for Him*. As Peter would glorify God through the sacrifice of his own life (John 21:18–19), so all believers are called, as Jesus showed us, to lay down their lives for their friends (John 15:13). The first Christians showed their willingness to sacrifice by giving up their possessions as need arose in order to care for others in the community (Acts 2:44–45; 4:32–37; 6:1–7) and to share with those far removed from their community when needs became known (Acts 11:27–30). Thus the glory of God was seen in the oneness they knew as the body of Christ. They were also willing to sacrifice the comforts of home—and even their own lives (Acts 7)—in order to stand firm for the gospel (Acts 8:1–4). Here they glorified God by emphasizing as a first priority their mission of extending the blessings of God to all nations. As the Lord Jesus glorified the Father by laying down His life, so the first Christians understood the need for sacrifices of their own—whether in building community or in pursuing mission—so that God might be glorified in them and His covenant purposes might be fulfilled.

Thus God's glory is integrally and intimately associated with His covenant. It is the end for which He created the covenant, the seal by which He initiates the covenant with His people, and the evidence of His dwelling among them. *Living in God's covenant is thus a call to seek His glory, to make our own lives available as arenas for God to demonstrate His living presence before the watching world.* We shall have more to say in a later chapter about what this requires of us in a postmodern world such as our own. For now, let us resolve no more merely to mouth words expressing some vague idea of the glory of God, but to call upon Him for the grace we need in order to know His glory at work within us, as He overcomes the lingering effects of sin and selfishness and sets us free in the Spirit and truth to live for Him with ever-increasing glory (2 Cor. 3:12–18).

THE GLORY OF GOD IN THE FACE OF JESUS

The knowledge of the glory of God that we seek and that brings such meaning, purpose, joy, and peace to our lives is supremely evident in the Person and work of our Lord Jesus Christ (2 Cor. 4:6). He is the very embodiment of God's glory and points the way for us, in surrender to His lordship, to glorify God in our lives as well. His moral purity, unbounded generosity, commitment to truth, proclamation of God's kingdom, and sacrificial death on the cross provide an outline of the life of glory that each of us is called to pursue (1 Cor. 10:31; 11:1).

But this involves more than merely disciplining our minds to ask, "What would Jesus do?" in each situation of our lives. Rather, it is to understand our utter necessity for His cleansing and forgiving grace, to confess our need of Him and cry out for His mercy and grace, and to seek daily to be filled with His Spirit, by whom alone we are able to live for God's glory in the whole of our lives. It is to discipline our hearts and spirits as well as our minds according to the means of grace—prayer, the Word, fasting, worship, and the rest—that He has provided us, so that in our times alone we are seeking to be like Him, just as in our lives in the world.[2]

It is, in short, to take the prayer of John the Baptist as our own, that every day Jesus Christ might increase in us, and that we in our sinful, old ways of living, may decrease more and more. Thus will the glory of God begin to be in evidence in and among us in such a way that the power and the reality of His covenant will be more apparent to us and to the people around us as well. They will see Jesus in us and in our congregations, and thus they may be more likely, like those Greeks who accosted Philip, to seek the Lord for themselves.

Questions for Study or Discussion

1. How do you think most of the Christians you know understand the idea of "the glory of God"? How do they seek to realize that great end in their lives?

2. Scripture indicates that, when people have actually *seen* some expression of God's glory, it affects them profoundly. Have you ever had such an experience? Explain.

3. God intends to glorify Himself in our everyday lives. In what ways would you like to see more of the glory of God at work in you in each of the following areas:

    a. the fruit of the Spirit

    b. the gifts of the Spirit

    c. a more moral life

    d. power for Christian witness

    e. a sacrificial life

4. Look at 2 Corinthians 3:12–18. How can you see that there is a direct relationship between time spent in the study of God's Word and the expression of His glory in our lives? Is your own use of the disciplines of grace—prayer, the Word, etc.—sufficient to allow God to manifest His glory through you? Explain.

5. Who are some of the people who, if the glory of God were more consistently and powerfully to appear in your life, would most likely be affected by that glory? What would you expect to see in them?

THE EVERLASTING COVENANT

He has remembered His covenant forever, The word which He commanded for a thousand generations.—Psalm 105:8

The covenants made with creation, Abraham, Moses, and David are all confirmed in Jesus Christ.—Willem Van Gemeren[1]

There is no escaping the fact that the Scriptures describe several different periods of covenant making between God and His people. God entered into covenant relationships with Noah, Abraham, Moses, and David, and He promised an era when a New Covenant would be established, which we recognize to have arrived with the coming of our Lord Jesus Christ.[2] Moreover, during each of these different periods of covenant making we note that something different is required of those whom God selects as beneficiaries of His covenant plan. Noah was to build an ark and repopulate the earth. Abraham was to move to Canaan and circumcise the males in his household. Israel was to walk in God's commandments. David was to prepare for the building of a temple for the Lord and to expect an heir who would be the second in an eternal dynasty of Davidic kings. In the period of the New Covenant, faith in Christ is what God requires of those who would enter into this special relationship with Him.

All this covenant making can be a little confusing. It may appear that God is capricious about His manner of relating to His chosen people, now requiring this of them, now that, now something else altogether. Further, and as a consequence, what He actually requires of us today might seem open to question. How can we know how much of what He required in the past is still valid for us today? Of course, we know we should not be building arks today, but how did Paul know that circumcision was to be left behind as an outmoded means of expressing our covenant relationship with God? And what about the Law of God today? What is its status for those of us who have come to know the Lord through faith in Jesus Christ? And should we actually be expecting a temple to be rebuilt in Jerusalem, and should we be encouraging contemporary Israeli powers-that-be to move in that direction?

These are not easy questions to resolve, but they can be huge in significance for living in God's covenant today. It all depends on the overarching *hermeneutic*, or method of interpretation, with which we approach the study of Scripture. Undoubtedly the most dominant school of biblical interpretation among evangelicals today is what is called dispensationalism, so called because it recognizes various covenantal dispensations of Scripture as providing critical benchmarks in the progress of God's revelation and of His redemptive plan. While contemporary dispensationalism is a far cry from the rigid Schofieldism of an earlier generation, and while dispensational thinkers today seem to be in a state of high flux over the best interpretation of their hermeneutic, still their approach to understanding the Scriptures dominates among evangelical churches. And, among the members of evangelical churches, a great many of whom have not kept pace with recent developments in dispensational thinking, the *effects* of a rigid dispensational approach to Scripture remain and are not always happy.

Chief among these effects is the sense of radical disjunction between the era of Law and the era of grace that rigid dispensational thinking tends to promote. For those steeped in a dispensational mind-set, the role of the Law of God in the life of faith is constrained by the New Testament. In practice this means that only nine of the Ten Commandments—the Sabbath injunction not being repeated in the New

Testament—and virtually none of the case laws, or, at best, only a handful, have any abiding significance for the Christian community. This poses a problem for Christian ethics, however, for without the case laws of the Old Testament to help us in further understanding the out-working of the Ten Commandments, we are left with a vague "ethic of love" to guide our practice: What would Jesus do?

Further, those still under the influence of rigid dispensational think-ing consider that the Old Testament has little to say about such cen-tral issues of church life as worship. Appeal to the Old Testament for principles to guide the church's practice in worship would appear to be unnecessary, if not counterproductive, for a great many contemporary evangelicals who look to the New Testament alone in such matters. And, not finding much in the way of guidance for worship there, they feel free to innovate in what can be highly pragmatic ways. Much of the debate animating the current bout of "worship wars" among evan-gelicals has its roots in this fundamental question of which aspects of the Word of God shall guide our practice in worship: the Old Testa-ment, with its emphasis on the majesty and holiness of God and the duty of His servants in worshiping Him, or the New Testament, with its concern for the spread of the gospel among all nations? Or should some combination of the two determine our practice in worship?

The problems posed by the lingering shadows of rigid dispensational thinking may be overcome when we take the perspective that, in Scrip-ture, God's covenant is one covenant, everlasting in nature, although expressed among His people according to different administrative modes, appropriate to the needs and circumstances of the time. Rather than seeing the Bible as carved up into several different eras of covenant making, with a different covenant replacing, supplanting, or largely undoing a previous one, we may observe that, throughout the Bible, what we have is one everlasting covenant—God's covenant—being unfolded to His people in a manner designed to enable them to know the benefits of its promises and to glorify Him according to the historical, cultural, and social circumstances in which they were called.

The everlasting character of God's covenant is attested to in many places, among them, Psalm 105:8–9; Psalm 111:5, 9; and Hebrews

13:20. In this chapter we want to take a closer look at the everlasting—or eternal—character of God's covenant and see how this perspective can help us to understand issues of covenantal continuity and discontinuity in the Scriptures and to lay hold of the contemporary relevance of the various covenants of Scripture to us today.

THE ELEMENTS OF GOD'S COVENANT

One of the ways we can see the unity of God's covenant in Scripture—its eternal character—is by the various covenantal elements that all the different covenants in Scripture have in common. These are essentially three.

(1) *All the covenants are of grace.* Each covenant of Scripture is utterly of grace and fully depends on God's design, timing, choice of recipients, implementation, sustenance, and fulfillment.

In none of the periods of covenant making is anyone other than God involved in deciding the terms of the covenant. God told Adam which trees he could eat, which he could not, and what the consequences of disobedience would be. God chose Noah from among the men of the earth, all of whom had fallen into disfavor with Him,[3] and declared the terms whereby He would save him and his family from the deluge to come. In His covenant with Abraham, God showed the patriarch where to go, declared the promises He would fulfill through him, and decided on circumcision as the temporal expression of Abraham's covenantal relationship with Him. God dictated the Law to Moses; He revealed His plan for the Davidic dynasty; and He called the terms of the New Covenant. In no case are any of the beneficiaries of any particular covenant invited to discuss the matter with God or in any other way to have input as to the nature, scope, or design of the covenant. God alone determines the design of the covenant. He decides the terms in each case. The covenants are all of God's grace in their design. They are all temporal expressions of the one, divine covenant.

The same is true with respect to the timing and beneficiaries of God's several covenants. He determines when they shall be initiated, with whom, and to whom they should ultimately reach. It is true that we often find God responding to the cries of His people, as for example, in Exodus 2:23–24. But we must remember, in this case, for example, that as early as Genesis 15:13, God had determined how long Israel would suffer in captivity and precisely when it would please Him to intervene on their behalf. The same is true with respect to each new period of covenant making. God rules over the timing and choice of beneficiaries. God is clear to Israel that there is nothing inherently appealing in them as a people that might have induced Him to enter into a covenant with them. Rather, they were perhaps the *least* appealing of all the nations of the earth when God condescended to show His love to them (Deut. 7:7–8). *That God acts at all, and toward any person or people whatsoever, is all of His gracious decision, design, and choice.* This is true in all the periods of covenant making, strongly suggesting that these are all expressions of one overarching covenant.

Similarly, in the implementation of His covenants, as well as in their sustenance and fulfillment, God acts alone. He brought Israel out of Egypt and settled them in the land of Palestine; He chose David, advanced and protected him, and elevated him to the kingship in Israel; He sent His Son to inaugurate and fulfill the promise of the New Covenant. No covenant would have begun between God and men, and none would ever have lasted or been fulfilled, had this in any way depended upon them. God's covenants are all of grace in these aspects as well.

In all these respects, since all the covenants—from Adam to the New Covenant—are entirely of grace, they may be seen as different expressions of one overarching covenant idea, an idea founded in the grace of God. Back of, or perhaps better, serving as the framework and guiding motif for each of the covenants of Scripture is a covenantal idea, originating in and executed by grace alone, which bears testimony to the fact that each of the covenants is but a temporal expression of a larger covenantal idea, God's covenant.

(2) *All the covenants require faith.* A similar uniformity in the covenants can be seen with the way in which men entered into the various covenants with God. Fundamentally, we may say that *each of the covenants of Scripture is entered into by faith.* Adam had to believe God that God knew better than he what course of conduct he should follow, and that God was able to bless or judge him according to what He had declared. Adam's failure was a failure of belief, of *faith*, before it was a failure of action.

Noah had to believe God: that He was going to do what He had said and that following the instructions of His Word was thus the best course of action for him.

Abraham is commended because he exercised the faith necessary to know the benefits of God's covenant (Gen. 15:6). He further demonstrated faith in God by going into his wife, Sarah, when all his experience told him that she was barren and they were too old to expect a child to result from any further intimate relations. He showed additional faith and trust in God by offering Isaac as a sacrifice to the Lord, as we have seen.

David believed God and arranged for his son to succeed him to the throne of Israel. Participants in the New Covenant believe that in Jesus Christ, the Son of God, they have the hope of forgiveness and everlasting life through His suffering, death, and resurrection.

All the covenants of Scripture share in this same element. They are all entered into—their benefits and blessings are realized—by the exercise of faith, trust in God and in the promises of His Word. So again it may be seen that all the covenants of Scripture partake of a larger covenantal character, which suggests that they are all part of a larger covenant, God's covenant.

(3) *All the covenants require obedience.* Finally, all the various covenants share in *the same requirement of obedience* on the part of those who are called of God to enter into covenant with Him. Responding by faith to the gracious initiative of God, the beneficiaries of His various covenants are expected to obey His Word, that is, to act in obedience to what He revealed to them concerning His particular re-

quirements for them. These are not always the same, and this is because, as we shall see, the covenant people lived in different times and places, and entered into God's covenant under different historical, cultural, and social circumstances. Some adjustment of the covenant was necessary to accommodate these differences; however, the fundamental requirement of obedience was the same for all. What God had spoken to them they were expected to do, for only thus would they prove their faith, demonstrate gratitude for His grace, and realize the promises of His covenant in their generation.

COVENANT ADMINISTRATIONS

In each of the eras of covenant making, different administrative requirements are provided so that the chosen people can enjoy the benefits God planned for them. We will examine these administrative elements of God's covenants from two perspectives, a microperspective and a macroperspective.

(1) *The microperspective: Adam.* Adam was given to understand that he would know the blessings of God by following three administrative guidelines. First, he was to fill the earth (Gen. 1:26–28). He and Eve were to bear children and to guide and teach their children so that they too would bear offspring, until all the earth was filled with a population of people created in the image of their first parents, that is, in the pristine image of God. Had Adam and Eve remained faithful to God's covenant, that worldwide race would have been a blessed and godly people, without sin or separation from God, and would have enjoyed all the benefits and blessings of God's covenant to the full. It is significant that, in Genesis 5:3, we are told that Seth is born to Adam and Eve in the image of Adam, which by then had fallen into the corruption of sin. Seth, like his brothers before him, was born in sin, as are all those who have descended from Adam and Eve.

Second, Adam and Eve were to subdue the earth and rule over it (Gen. 1:26–28). This entailed their cultivating the garden, so that they might bring out from their labors more of the goodness of God with

69

which He had endowed it. They were also to guard the garden against any intrusions that might tend to corrupt or thwart the divine plan (Gen. 2:15). As it happened, this was to be both an intellectual and a manual endeavor. Adam's naming the animals was a purely intellectual activity designed to impose more order on his environment, thus making subsequent work easier and more efficient, at the same time allowing people more fully to appreciate the diversity and wonder of God's creation. His work of pruning and cultivating the garden, while certainly involving the use of his mind, was primarily an undertaking of arduous, manual labor.

Third, Adam and Eve were to refrain from eating the fruit of the tree that was in the center of the garden. They were given to believe that this was the principal administrative component of the covenant God was making with them. Failure in this area would bring disastrous results, the nature of which could only be hinted at by the threat of death, an administrative stricture attached to this primary administrative component.

Had Adam and Eve remained faithful to this primary administrative component, the whole earth would have been populated by a godly race of people and subsequently transformed it into an Edenic environment, the entire world becoming the beautiful and "very good" place (Gen. 1:31) that Eden itself was. This blessing was kept from Adam, Eve, and their descendants, however, because of their failure in the first instance to obey what, on the surface, seems like the simplest element of covenant obedience.

(2) *The microperspective: Noah.* The covenant with Noah was to be differently administered. He was, first of all, to construct an ark, which would be the vessel of initial deliverance for him and his family, as well as for the creatures of the earth. Beyond that, however, other administrative components were added to ensure that Noah and his offspring would enjoy the benefits of God's gracious covenant (Gen. 9:1–7).

Second, the mandate to populate the earth, initially given to Adam and Eve, was continued with Noah. He and his sons were to have children so that the earth would be repopulated. Third, while they were given permission, for the first time in human history, to eat the flesh of animals, they were not allowed to eat the blood, for reasons that God would explain in a later generation. Fourth, the dignity of human life and the integrity of the image of God represented therein were to be preserved against violence. Capital punishment was to be administered against any who shed the blood of men unto death.

Fifth, as a further testimony of God's faithfulness, and of His willingness to bless His covenant people, God placed the rainbow in the clouds so that, whenever the threat of rain and storms appeared, they would not have to be afraid, but would know from this sign that God would preserve them and keep them unto Himself (Gen. 9:8–17).

Apparently the mandate to cultivate and guard the earth also remained intact from the covenant with Adam, for immediately we find Noah becoming a tiller of the soil (Gen. 9:20). His carelessness with the fruit of his labors, however, set the stage for Ham's act of violence against his father, occasioning the curse upon Ham's descendants (vv. 22–27). This act of disrespect on Ham's part seems almost tantamount to murder. We do not know exactly what he told his brothers about his father, but we can be certain that it was disrespectful, for, when Noah learned of it, he considered it sufficiently odious to condemn not just Ham, but the children and all other offspring who would descend from him.

Thus, in the covenant with Noah we note both the introduction of a new administrative element of God's covenant—the ark—and the continuation of elements from the previous era of covenant making. The ark, like the tree before it, was a unique element of administration, designed for a particular historical and social situation. As we would not have expected the tree to continue, neither should we expect the ark to do so. The elements of filling the earth and cultivating it, now modified and enlarged somewhat according to the new circumstances in which Noah found himself, remained intact in the covenant God made with Noah.

(3) *The microperspective: Abraham.* We have already examined the covenant with Abraham in some detail; however, we can make some additional observations about the administrative elements of this covenant as we find them in the microperspective. First, it seems clear that Abraham was to continue to multiply. He was to become a great nation. Thus, God expected him to have children and not to be satisfied with either an adopted heir or a child by someone other than Sarah (Gen. 15:1–4, 16; 17).

Second, Abraham was to work at productive labor to increase his well-being and provide for his offspring. Thus we see him becoming wealthy as a keeper of herds and the manager of a significant household of servants.

Third, Abraham was required to administer circumcision to the male members of his household (Gen. 17:10). This would mark them, among the many nations and peoples that lived in and around the land of Canaan at the time, as members of God's special people, symbolizing their "separateness" unto Him.

Thus, in addition to the continuation of previous administrative elements, one new element—circumcision—was added to the means whereby God would provide blessing to His chosen people. Circumcision was a new and important component in the way that God would administer His promises unto His glory with Abraham and his offspring.

(4) *The microperspective: Moses.* In the covenant made with Israel through Moses all these existing administrative elements were carried forward—having children, working the land, and circumcising the males of the household. By Moses' day, however, Israel was no longer merely a family unit, or even a tribe. They had become a numerous people comprising many tribes and families, and they were being taken to resettle, repopulate, and recultivate a land that had fallen into corruption under pagan peoples. They had become, in fact, a nation and, as such, would require rather more sophisticated means to maintain a right covenant relationship with God.

Thus, the Law of God was added—the Ten Commandments as the "constitution" or overall framework of law, the civil statutes as illustrations of how those commandments were to be carried out city by city, and the liturgical provisions that were intended to keep the people together in their worship of the living God. This Law, in its three-fold aspect, would provide the legal, moral, and spiritual administration within which the people of Israel would raise their children, make their way in life, and be a light to the nations (Lev. 18:4–5; Deut. 4:5–8).

(5) *The microperspective: David.* Further, the people of Israel were told that a day would come when they would ask for a king to rule over them. God did not begrudge them this, as, by the time it would come to pass, such an arrangement would be necessary for the nation so that they might continue to survive and thrive among the increasingly sophisticated and powerful nations around them. Yet, well in advance of their request, God was careful to set forth the requirements by which He would be willing to give them a king (Gen. 49:8–10; Deut. 17:14–20). That Israel seems to have had little, if any regard, for these requirements when they chose Saul as their king explains God's comment that they had rejected Him as their King in this action (1 Sam. 8:7). Yet he would provide for them a king according to His own requirements, whom the people would ultimately recognize and accept, namely, David.

The covenant with David was not really a different covenant. It was simply the outworking of an aspect of God's covenant that He had foretold many generations before. God had promised Judah that his descendants would have the rule over all Israel (Gen. 49:8–10), and that One would arise in his lineage who would also subdue all the nations under His authority. This One was called "Shiloh," which in the Hebrew means, "Him to whom it belongs." A kingdom was being promised to the descendants of Jacob and a dynasty to the sons of Judah. But that dynasty would end with the appearance of the One for whom the kingdom was intended in the first place, and then that kingdom would spread out beyond Israel to encompass all the nations. Of that kingdom we shall have more to say shortly.

The covenant with David (2 Sam. 7:8–17) was simply a restatement in more contemporary terms of what had been promised to Judah and foretold by Moses. The covenant with David, therefore, thus has its roots in the covenant with Abraham. David would begin a dynasty of kings, one of whom would rule on the throne of God forever.

(6) *The microperspective: Jesus Christ.* When we come to the New Covenant, first prophesied by Jeremiah (31:31–34) and fulfilled in Jesus Christ, we may note a dramatic change in the administrative elements.

First, faith in Christ as the Messiah of Israel and Savior of the nations is the sine qua non of covenant membership, for "without faith it is impossible to please [God]" (Heb. 11:6). Next, the evangelization of the nations is mandated (Matt. 28:18–20), thus effectively opening the covenant to Jews and Gentiles alike. Third, the covenant people are constituted as a community and called to give themselves to building the church—with its ordinances and offices—as the temporal focus of divine power and activity and the continuation, after a fashion, of the presence of Christ on earth. The administrative elements of filling the earth and ruling the earth, as well as obedience to the moral and civil components of the Law—with appropriate social and cultural interpretation, adaptation, and adjustment—are included in these, while circumcision drops away, for reasons we shall shortly examine, as well as temporal kingship (since Christ was now ruling from His throne in heaven, Ps. 2; Acts 2:22–36; Eph. 1:18–23). Singular elements of the religious laws of Israel also cease—especially those related to the system of sacrifices and the work of priests—since those had all been fulfilled in Christ (Heb. 7–10). New ordinances have been established—baptism and the Lord's Supper—which recall in greater vividness the work that Christ has done to bring the fullness of God's covenant to His people.

Thus, our brief examination of the administrative elements of the various covenants, considered from the microperspective, reveals a certain amount of overlap or continuity between the covenants, as well as a certain amount of discontinuity, owing to changes in historical and social circumstances. What we do *not* see are any clear lines of demarcation absolutely setting off one covenant from its predecessor, as though that former covenant had proved altogether weak and ineffective and was to be discarded *en toto* for something new. Rather, the picture is more like a rolling snowball, a basic shape that gathers greater form and bulk as it progresses, while certain aspects of it are buried or discarded as need be.

The macroperspective. We turn now to consider the administrative elements of the various covenants from the macroperspective. Here we may conveniently regard the covenants according to their Old Testament and New Testament expressions. In short, we may say that *the covenants of the Old Testament were administered according to shadows and externals*, while *the covenant in the New Testament is administered by fulfillment and internals*.

The New Testament teaches us to regard the administrative elements of the religious aspect of the Mosaic covenant as "shadows" of heavenly things (Heb. 8:4–5 ; 9; 10). That is, they were not themselves the *substance* of God's dealings with His people, but only the *means* whereby a *semblance* or *foretaste* of that substance—forgiveness of sin, for example—was mediated to them. As shadows they suggested in outline the reality that they represented, but they were not themselves that reality.

The same thing could be said for the administrative elements of the other covenant eras. Noah's ark was a means of deliverance through the flood, but it was only a shadow of the deliverance from sin that God would ultimately accomplish through Christ. The Davidic kings were, in many cases, able leaders and administrators, allowing the grace of God to flow to His people, but they were only foreshadows of the coming King—Shiloh—for whom the kingdom was ultimately intended.

Moreover, all these shadows have in common that they apply primarily to external matters—the sacrificing of animals, obedience to a king, building and taking refuge in an ark. Participation in these matters could in no way get at the real heart of the issue between God and His people, which is the condition of their hearts before Him (cf. Ps. 50).

Even circumcision as an administrative element of the Abrahamic covenant, for all the benefits it afforded the circumcised, was but a shadow of a fuller circumcision yet to come, the circumcision of the heart. For Israel's problem throughout the period of the Old Testament, the reason she was never able fully to enjoy the blessings of God's covenant, was that her heart was simply not in it. Even at what we might justly consider one of the high-water marks of Old Covenant activity—the preparation of a new generation to enter the land of Canaan and subdue it in obedience to God—we find the Lord lamenting their lack of a true heart for Him: "Oh, that they had such a heart in them that they would fear Me and always keep all My commandments, that it might be well with them and with their children forever!" (Deut. 5:29). But they did not have such a heart, and nothing in the covenant arrangements under which they were operating at that time was sufficient to give them such a heart. They could deal only with external matters, tangible expressions of their relationship with God, which, in and of themselves, could never mediate the full blessings of the covenant to the people of God (Heb. 10:4), but only anticipated further development and fulfillment to come.

Yet, even during this period, we see God pointing forward to a time when He would bring a fuller, more complete realization of His covenant to His people, in which *He Himself would deal with the problem of their hearts,* thus allowing Him to mediate His covenant to His people at greater depths of realization. As early as Deuteronomy 30:6 a circumcision of the heart is promised to God's people, a work that He will accomplish on their behalf. David, perhaps mindful of this verse, prays for such a cleansing in His psalm of confession. He asks God to create in him something that did not exist and that he could not effect for all his sincere repentance according to every then extant covenant obligation—a clean heart (Ps. 51:10). Ezekiel, in very dramatic terms, tells us that a time was coming when God would tear out the stony hearts of His people and give them a living heart of flesh so that they might realize the promise of His covenant (Ezek. 11:19–20). He later adds that God would give His own Spirit along with this new heart so that His people might walk in obedience to Him (Ezek. 36:26–27). Jeremiah adds to this the proviso of a New Covenant in which the Law of God would be *internalized* in the new hearts of His people, so that they would both know and obey Him from within, according to a work of circumcision that He would accomplish in their hearts (Jer. 31:31–34).

Thus, *with the coming of Christ and the completion of His redemptive work, this era of internals and fulfillment was inaugurated,* in which God works on the hearts of His people, sending His Spirit into their lives and adopting them as His own people, according to the terms of His New Covenant, namely, faith in Christ, who is graciously offered to the people of God's choosing. Under this aspect of the macroadministration of God's covenant, sins are forgiven, new life begins, and His people come under the lordship of Shiloh their King, who leads them from within, by His Word and Spirit, to love, obey, and serve Him. In this new dispensation of God's covenant the need for an outward sign of having been cleansed and accepted—circumcision—is alleviated; more appropriate signs and seals are provided—baptism and the Lord's Supper, which are both more inclusive in terms of race and gender, and which reflect more clearly the glory of the redemptive work of Him in whom all the promises of God's covenant are "Yes" and "Amen."

We should note that, throughout the various periods of covenant making activity between God and His people, when both at the micro- and macro-levels His covenant is undergoing changes, alterations, and adjustments according to the needs and circumstances of the people, that covenant yet remains His one eternal covenant. We can see this not only in the straightforward references to the eternality of God's covenant, such as were mentioned above, but in God's constant habit of referring to the covenant as "My" covenant, and the Scripture writers' use of the term "His" covenant to refer to God's activity on behalf of His people (cf. Gen. 6:18; Exod. 2:23–25; Deut. 29:10–29; Jer. 31:31–34; Luke 1:67–75; Rom. 4:9–16; etc.). It is a changing, even an evolving, covenant, to be sure, but it is at all times God's covenant, an eternal covenant of promise for the people of His choosing.

LIVING IN GOD'S ETERNAL COVENANT

What are the implications for us of the ongoing, eternal character of God's covenant as we see it in Scripture? In large part, this book is an attempt to unpack some of those implications. Here we shall mention five general guidelines that can help us to appropriate more of the fullness of the covenant as we shall be discussing it in subsequent chapters.

(1) Keeping in mind the *progressive* as well as the *eternal character* of God's covenant, we should expect in our own dispensation to be able to glean insights and guidance from previous covenant eras concerning our calling and duty as the people of God today. We are not limited to the pages of the New Testament to inform our lives in Christ. Rather, the riches and wisdom of each covenant era remain for us, so that we may plumb the depths and lay hold of the promises of God's covenant for our lives today.

Further, this aspect of God's covenant can guide us in thinking about how we shall experience this special relationship with God in the new heavens and the new earth. As a people, we do not spend enough time thinking about and looking forward to our heavenly existence for eternity. When we do, our thoughts are too often clouded by images from childhood of streets of gold, heavenly harps, and a home in the clouds. Yet we shall inhabit a *new* earth, which shall have been fused with a *new* heaven, where saints, angels, and other creatures freely mingle and interact before the eternal and glorious throne of God. Much of what we know as life in God's covenant here and now will continue, infinitely enhanced and made ever more wondrous, in the eternal state. For example, while we do not expect to raise families to fill our new environment, since in heaven there is no marriage, and since the number of God's elect will have all been gathered in, yet it seems quite likely that we will continue to be creatures of culture, making music, producing art, enjoying fruitful labor, establishing institutions, and so forth. How much more wonderful and glorious will such cultural endeavors be when the covenant comes to its full and eternal realization in the realm of glory! As we meditate on and anticipate this eternally happy state, our hearts will be filled with joy and longing, and we will be motivated in the here and now to more fervent preparation for that blessed eternal existence (2 Peter 3:11–13).

(2) We should be ever mindful of the *historical-mindedness* that the eternal character of God's covenant promotes. God's covenant is realized in history, in the circumstances and events of particular people, times, and places. The incredible flexibility of this unique relationship means that each generation of covenant people can learn from its predecessors, and must be careful to keep in mind those who will follow them. We live in the present, and are called to pursue our unique covenant calling in particular times and places (concerning which we shall have more to say in the next chapter). But, for the sake of even greater covenant prosperity in the present we must seek to learn from our forebears in the faith, both those in Scripture and those who have gone before us in history (Rom. 15:4; Ps. 78:1–8). And we must be ever mindful of the heritage of God's covenant that we will leave to the generations to follow us, as we labor diligently and with joy to prepare for our eternal home with the Lord, and with our heirs in the faith to follow (2 Peter 3:10–14).

We are but the latest expression of an ongoing stream of history in which God is creating a people for Himself. Let us not lose sight of the riches our ancestors in the faith have accumulated and bequeathed to us, and let us not fail to lay up for future generations blessings and wisdom of God to help them in their own day.

(3) The eternal character of God's covenant encourages us to *mine all the riches of His exceedingly great and precious promises,* understanding, claiming, and enjoying all that God has spoken throughout His Word for our own experience in His covenant today. For example, the promise of a great name that Abraham began to realize in his lifetime is available to us today, allowing and encouraging us to exert influence for God's grace and truth in ways that we might not at this moment think possible. How might we appropriate this promise to Abraham to help us in serving our churches and our communities, for example, as members of local school boards or civil governments? In what ways might we, claiming and acting on this promise, begin to give new shape to local institutions—museums, recreation councils, and

so forth—or bring more of a spirit of charity and justice to our communities? How might such a promise, sincerely believed and faithfully entered into, enhance our effectiveness as witnesses for Christ and apologists of the faith?

(4) The eternal nature of God's covenant calls us to maintain an *abiding love for God's Law*. The problem of antinomianism is rampant among evangelicals today, who glibly assert that they are "not under law but under grace" and go about in ignorance of the righteousness and perfect love revealed in the Law of God. It is no wonder that the evangelical community has little in the way of a powerful, living ethic to recommend as an alternative to the crumbling relativism of our secular age. Without a love for God's Law as the embodiment of His righteousness and the framework of His love, we have no hope of persuading our generation that the Christian life can be anything other than an emotional or psychological crutch for the otherwise feeble-minded and insecure. And they will continue to prefer their own feeble crutches to one that requires any form of submission to God (Ps. 2:1–3).

The Law of God, in the seed form, was present from the first days of creation, when the seventh day was hallowed as a day to rest in the Lord. It was further unfolded with Noah, when God forbade the taking of human life. Under Moses the Law of God came to its fullest verbal expression, while, under the New Covenant, it was perfectly fulfilled by our Lord Jesus Christ and is being written on the circumcised hearts of the people of God, where it serves internally to motivate them to love and good works. As we keep in mind the eternal nature of God's covenant, we will search throughout the various covenant epochs for insight and instruction concerning how we may show the righteousness and love of God through obedience to His Law today.

(5) Finally, the eternal character of God's covenant should stimulate us to *ever greater confidence in the Lord Jesus Christ*, who is the fulfillment of all God's covenant promises for us. We rejoice to rest in Jesus for our salvation, and to seek the comfort of His friendship in our times of need. But we must remember that He is the God of the everlasting covenant, and thus stands ever ready to mediate its fullest blessings and richest promises to us as we walk by grace through faith in

Him. Paul's declaration that God would provide all our needs by His riches in glory in Christ Jesus, or that he could do all things through Christ, is no idle boast or mere platitude (Phil. 4:13, 19). His confidence was in Christ crucified, resurrected, reigning, interceding, empowering, and coming again for His people, who would be enabled to do exceedingly abundantly above all that they could ever ask or think through Him (Eph. 3:20). The solidity, scope, majesty, and power of God's covenant testify to nothing so much as the greatness of Him who is its fulfillment and Lord. By keeping the full, eternal character of God's covenant in mind, our faith in Christ will be strengthened and enlarged, and our walk with Him abundantly enriched day by day.

God's covenant is an eternal covenant. It has its origins in the councils of eternity, from before the foundations of the world. It has endured through all the vicissitudes and foolishness of human history. It vibrates in the air around us even today. And it will stand forever in the new heavens and the new earth. We who have come to know Jesus Christ as Shiloh and Savior are the people of this covenant, called by God to live in its eternal power and presence unto His eternal glory and praise.

Questions for Study or Discussion

1. Which parts of this chapter strike you as new ideas? Which of your existing ideas do they challenge, and in what ways?

2. Can you distinguish between the *essential* elements of God's covenant and the various *administrative* components by which the blessings of God were distributed to His people in different eras? Is this an important distinction? Why or why not? Do we trust in the *administrative* components of God's covenant for our salvation? If not, what are they for?

3. Review the various administrative components of the New Covenant discussed in this chapter. In what ways can you see that these are being appealed to as means to the blessing of God in your own church? Are any of them lacking or in need of shoring up?

4. Ask these same questions about your own life. To what extent are you making use of the administrative components of the New Covenant in order to gain the blessings and promises of God? Where is your use of those components in need of repair?

5. Review the goals you set for your study of God's covenant. Are you making any progress? In what ways? Do you need to alter or adjust your goals in any ways?

6

THE PEOPLE
OF THE COVENANT

But you are a chosen generation, a royal priesthood, a holy nation, His own special people, that you may proclaim the praises of Him who called you out of darkness into His marvelous light.—1 Peter 2:9

I shall start, then, with the church, into whose bosom God is pleased to gather his sons, not only that they may be nourished by her help and ministry as long as they are infants and children, but also that they may be guided by her motherly care until they mature and at last reach the goal of faith.—John Calvin[1]

The purpose of God's everlasting covenant, the reason why He has extended such exceedingly great and precious promises to His people, is that we might live in such a way as to bring praise to the glory of His grace, as we have seen. This calling in God's covenant is how we are meant to live, what His promises do in and through us. His covenant is eternal and cannot be interrupted. It will realize the purpose for which He created it. By living in God's covenant, we fulfill the purpose for which we were created; we demonstrate and testify to the reality of the living God; we find the fullest and most complete satisfaction and joy in life; and we make ourselves ready for our eternal dwelling-place with God, which our Lord Jesus Christ is even now preparing for us (2 Peter 3:11–14; John 14:1–3). This is what we mean when we declare our purpose in life to be "to glorify God and enjoy Him forever."

Yet the pressures of living in a postmodern world can often keep us from realizing this purpose. We are distracted by obligations at work; caught up in the frivolity of the popular culture; lured away from the life of sacrifice and service to one of self-centeredness and self-indulgence; worn out and worn down by a myriad of activities and diversions, so that we have little time, energy, or inclination toward spiritual matters; and warned by the unbelieving world to keep our religion to ourselves as a purely private matter. The world tells us that our faith is irrelevant, our convictions intolerant, our lifestyle out of date, and our witness merely a matter of opinion. It invites us not to be so serious about our faith that we are unable to enjoy with them the pleasures of worldly living. It would have us join rather than condemn them.

In the face of so many distractions and such opposition many Christians have found it difficult to maintain a proper perspective on their walk with the Lord. They have actually begun to believe the claims and charges of the world, and to accept its invitations to a self-indulgent way of life. As a result, such Christians have kept their faith to themselves, both in how they live and what they say, at the same time they try very hard to be just "one of the guys" when it comes to everyday matters of work, friendship, and avocations. While endeavoring to sustain a meaningful faith in God, they have compromised with the perspectives, preferences, priorities, and practices of the world, so that the glory of God is hardly evident in them and, for all appearances, they are hardly any different from the unbelieving people with whom they associate. This is true of students as well as of adults, men and women in all walks of life and all across the country. Many have failed to heed the warning of Francis Schaeffer, who said that we must be wary of saying we believe one thing while we live as though the spirit of the naturalism of the age were in fact our guide,[2] for this will surely rob us of the reality of our faith. In so doing, many have compromised their true identity as members of God's community and cut themselves off from the glorious experience of living in God's covenant.

Which makes it all the more important that we understand as fully as possible how God sees us as His people, and what are the implications of how He sees us for living in His covenant today. The world tells us that the Christian community is a reactionary throwback, an asylum for the weak and insecure, not capable of being trusted to judge on matters of morality and public policy, and entitled to its views but required to keep them to themselves. We hear this stereotype in one form or another almost every day. Unless we steep our minds and lock our hearts into what God says about us, there is the very real danger that we will allow the world to pipe the tune for our dance of faith, and this will not only undermine the reality of our experience of living in God's covenant, but find us at cross purposes with that very covenant as well.

So in this chapter we are going to take a closer look at the *people* of God's covenant—who they are and how God sees them. Then we shall consider more carefully the implications of this divine perspective for living in God's covenant today. Unless we begin to see ourselves as disciples of Christ, and our churches as part of a larger expression of the kingdom of Christ, we shall never know the reality of living in God's covenant as He intends it for us.

A PEOPLE OF A NEW COVENANT

One of the great strengths that comes from living according to a covenantal perspective on Scripture and the life of faith is that it opens to us the glories of the Old Testament as a normative guide for our lives. At the same time, one of the dangers is that, overshadowed as this covenantal perspective is by a pessimistic and largely withdrawn New Testament hermeneutic, we too easily fall into the mind-set of unreality and defeatism that seems to characterize the experience of God's people in the Old Testament. Their problem, as God Himself identified it, was that they did not have a heart for Him (Deut. 5:29). Throughout the Old Testament, for the vast majority of the covenant people, their hearts were deceitful and desperately wicked (Jer. 17:9), and they could not find the way to love the Lord with all their hearts, souls, minds, and strength, or their neighbors as themselves.

Yet even as early as Moses the people were told to expect that a time was coming when God would "circumcise" their hearts, when He would cut away all the impurity that kept them from knowing and serving Him. At that time He would renew in them a living, growing heart, a heart governed by the inward power of the Spirit of God (Deut. 30:6; Ezek. 11:19–20; 36:26–27). We today who are the followers of Christ have come to know the joy of that "new heart" and are embarked upon a totally new way of life. Yet while we may have experienced that new heart and the new life that comes with it, we still tend to fall into unbelief when it comes to taking God's Word seriously for our everyday experience in Christ.

I was reminded of this not long ago when I was conducting a workshop on the role of elders for the officers of a local church. Beginning with Ezekiel 34 I showed them how Israel's shepherds had failed and, thus, would be removed by God from their callings. In their places He would send them David to be their shepherd—a clear reference to David's greater Son, our Lord Jesus Christ. Jesus, in John 10 and throughout the course of His ministry, defined the terms of shepherding that He desires for His people. Then He entrusted that work to the elders of the church, so that, through their ministries of shepherding, the church of God might become a renowned planting place and a source of blessing to all within and around it (Acts 20:28; 1 Peter 5:1–3; Ezek. 34:11–30).

During one of the breaks, I was taken aside by one of the elders, a pillar in the church, a man grounded in a dispensational hermeneutic and accustomed to being an elder according to a paradigm more characteristic of the secular corporate world than of life in God's covenant. He said to me, "T. M., what you are sharing with us is all good and clear, at least as you describe it. But you need to remember that we live in the real world, and in the real world such things as you are teaching are just not feasible." I replied, "No, my friend. We are not living in the real world if we deny the straightforward teaching of Scripture and default to the pressures and priorities of the world for living the life of faith. The real world is the kingdom of God and the covenant community that stands at its center. *And recovering the reality of the real world requires that we stop listening to those inner voices of defeatism, withdrawal, pragmatism, and conformity to the world, as well as those voices from without that are telling us to keep our place in society, and that we begin living according to the design and promises of God's covenant."*

For the fact is that we are a people of a New Covenant, a better covenant, indeed, the fullness of God's covenant, and in this dispensation we, trusting in God who has called us, shall be able to do exceedingly abundantly more than we ever thought or asked. It all depends on our understanding who we are in God's covenant community and what our churches are called to be, and on learning to live according to the promises of His Word and not the limitations of the world or of our own experience.

"The days are coming," God spoke through Jeremiah, when He would enter into a qualitatively new administration of His covenant (Jer. 31:31–34). This would not be the same kind of situation as under the Old Covenant. During that time the people of Israel, without a heart for God, repeatedly broke His covenant and fell into the ways of the surrounding world (v. 32). Without circumcised hearts, and lacking the indwelling power of God's Spirit, Israel concentrated on the *externals* of God's covenant and neglected the larger issues of a broken and a contrite heart (Ps. 51:17). They measured their success by the worldly prosperity of their neighbors and fell into pagan ways in a pragmatic attempt to keep peace with the surrounding nations and hold on to the prosperity they had managed to acquire. They went through the motions of the life of faith without the heart of gratitude, trust, and honor to God that is the wellspring of that life (Ps. 50:1–15). As a result, they failed over and over again, and each experience of failure sent them, not to seeking the Lord for grace to live according to His Word, but for more and more pragmatic ways and means of shoring up their defenses against the encroaching world.

Sound familiar? It should, for in many ways, the pattern outlined above describes the situation in our churches today, where our outlook and practice are informed more by the limitations and likings of the world than the clear teaching and bold hope of the promises of God's covenant.

We must remember, in the first place, that we are a people of a New Covenant, which itself is but the latest administration of God's eternal covenant. God Himself stands back of this covenant as its Designer, Administrator, and Guarantor. He will not allow His promises to fail! All the blessings of Abraham for all the glory that God desires are ours to realize, day in and day out, as we concentrate our hopes and dreams and daily walk in Him and in the promises of His covenant. "This world is not my home," we need to keep telling ourselves. Then we need to fortify ourselves—heart, soul, mind, and strength—with the outlook of our New Covenant relationship to God, trusting that He will do what He has promised by the power He possesses to make all things new in Christ.

This New Covenant experience is an *inward* experience in the first place. God has sent His Spirit into our hearts crying out through our own voices, "Abba! Father!" We are the sons and daughters of the King of kings and Lord of lords! He has torn out the heart of stone that confined our thinking and living to worldly ways and has given us a new heart of flesh, vivified and energized by His indwelling Spirit. Now nothing shall be impossible for us as we walk by faith and not by sight.

The challenge is to live according to our *new hearts* and not our *fleshly eyes*. As we look within, we find a new power at work, willing and doing according to the good pleasure of God, allowing us to see things as they *really* are in a world where God's kingdom, like a stone cut not by human hands (Dan. 2:45), is growing ineluctably to overwhelm every foe and all opposition to the divine plan for His people. That power becomes available to us, swelling our new hearts with love for God, filling our new minds with visions of kingdom possibilities, and charging our revived souls with new resolve and new strength to live according to God's covenant in the world.

The Spirit within our new hearts works with the Law of God to mold and shape us into the people God wants us to be. In the New Covenant God has written His Law on our hearts (Jer. 31:33), so that obeying Him is what we earnestly desire, following Him is what we live for. No more is the Law of God a standard of righteousness for which we strive in order that we might know the saving mercy of God, or fulfill some sense of religious duty or obligation. Indeed, the Law was never intended as such. Instead, we say with the psalmist, "Oh, how I love Your law!" (Ps. 119:97), and then, *in eager gratitude for the saving grace of God,* we go forth to show that love through heartfelt obedience in the whole of our lives, bringing forth the life of virtue, goodness, holiness, and loving service that identifies those who have the very character of God imprinted on their souls. We will have great love and patience with those fellow believers who accost us for our love of God's Law saying, "I'm under grace, not law." So we will encourage them to look at the glory of God in the face of Jesus Christ and see if they do not see reflected there the holiness of God's Law. Then we shall invite them to put aside their facile self-righteousness and join us in mining the depths of God's glory as it is revealed in His Law and in all the counsel of God, and to go with us into the world as a *new* people with a *new* agenda for life in our postmodern world.

In the New Covenant, moreover, we recognize that the touchstone of our common experience is the knowledge of God (Jer. 31:34). All those in whom God has wrought this circumcision of their hearts shall know Him; love, seek, and delight in Him; worship Him in Spirit and in truth; and go forth eagerly to serve Him by loving others as themselves. This knowledge of God—this living, intimate relationship with Him as our Father, into which we have entered by the grace of Jesus Christ—is the fountainhead of all we are and all to which we aspire in the New Covenant. Knowing Him, we look out on the world, as it were, through His eyes. We long to see His goodness brought out more and more in every nook and cranny of creation (Gen. 1:31). We ache for the lost who grope about blindly in the world, seeking some hope, some respite from looming despair. We go eagerly searching for the elect of God, calling them to hear their Shepherd's voice and follow Him into His fold. And we anticipate with great excitement our weekly times of gathering together to heap upon our God in worship the adoration and acknowledgments due to Him alone.

And we bask in the forgiveness of sins that He has accomplished for us through our Lord Jesus Christ (Jer. 31:34). This is the great truth that lies at the foundation of all our love for God and all our desire to be His covenant people: He has extended to us, most unworthy sinners, the grace that leads to forgiveness and salvation, and only because it pleased Him to do so for His own glory (Ps. 132:13–14). Like the psalmist in the eighth psalm we marvel that such a thing could be! But we accept it as so and daily strive to bring our lives in line with the purposes and promises of Him who has done such a marvelous work in our souls.

So while we glory in the treasures that we might bring forth from the Old Testament for living in God's covenant today, we do not fall into the mind-set of defeatism that seems so prevalent there. Rather, as members of the *new* dispensation of God's covenant, we long with all our hearts to rise to the fullest, richest realization of its promises. We listen not to the world, and not to the lingering voices within that seem ever to say, "It will never happen, never happen." Instead, we listen to God speaking to us from His Word, communing with our new hearts by His Spirit within, assuring us every day that greater things are yet to be if we can continue to walk by faith and not by sight.

We are a people of the New Covenant, and it is in the mind-set of that expression of God's covenant that we must learn to live, seeing our salvation in Christ as grounded squarely in the knowledge of God, love for His Law, and zeal to serve Him in loving obedience.

A People for God's Possession

As such we are not our own, as Paul reminds us (1 Cor. 6:19–20). We have been bought with the price of pure and holy blood, and we belong to God. He will define the specific purposes of what belongs to Him. As His bond servants, we must listen carefully to discern His expectations and to understand His agenda for our lives in His covenant today. That agenda unfolds for us not in the isolation of our individual walk with Christ, but in the corporate expression of our oneness as members of the body of Christ, the church.

The passage from 1 Peter that begins this chapter is an excellent place for us to turn in gaining a concise understanding of God's expectations for us as His covenant people. In this collection of images and quotations from the Old Testament we can see how God is importing very positive ideas from the previous period of covenantal dispensation into the present epoch, encouraging us to think in terms of Old Testament realities but with the New Testament expectations that accompany a circumcised heart and the indwelling of God's Spirit. We will want to make note of several aspects of this passage.

(1) There is God's declaration that *we are a chosen people*. Implied in this is the fact that our salvation, and, with it, all the blessings of God's covenant, are entirely of grace, and that they devolve upon us as members of a larger society of faith. The reason we have come to the knowledge of God, the forgiveness of sins, a heartfelt love for God's Law, and an unbreakable covenant relationship with Him is that it pleased Him to reach out to us, whom He had chosen to be His in Jesus Christ from before the foundation of the world.

Many people struggle with the doctrine of election, and I suppose that is understandable. It can seem rather arbitrary that God chooses some and bypasses others in gathering together a people as His church. This, however, is not the case. Arbitrariness is grounded in chance, whim, caprice, happenstance. Election is grounded in the goodness, holiness, justice, mercy, righteousness, and perfection of God. What happens in a merely arbitrary way can be neither good nor ill; it's simply the product of chance. What happens as the result of good, holy, just, merciful, righteous, and perfect counsel and planning can only be good, holy, just, merciful, righteous, and perfect in its outworking. The reason some have difficulty seeing this is not related to the *fact* of God's election; rather, it is evidence of *the noetic effects of sin*, of the difficulty we have in our sinful minds grasping sublime and holy truths.

Still, some protest, does not the doctrine of election make us little more than puppets in the hands of God? Let's try looking at it differently. Imagine that you are in danger of drowning, but that you do not yet know it. While swimming quite distractedly along the shore, you have begun to drift far out to sea, even though the beach still looks close enough to reach with relative ease. A strong riptide is building beneath you, which you cannot yet sense. Your arms and legs are feeling a little weary, but the water feels so good that you're not ready to come in just yet. And, even though you are beginning to have difficulty keeping your head above water, still, you keep saying to yourself, *I'm all right; I'll just stay out here a little longer.* Soon enough, however, panic will set in, your muscles will give out, you will begin gulping water, and the terror of drowning will overwhelm you as you realize you have no strength to extricate yourself from your dilemma or to avoid your inevitable doom.

Happily, a lifeguard is watching you from his tower on the beach. He has noticed your distress and, being familiar with the waters in the area, knows that a riptide is building beneath you. Many, many times he has helped people in a similar situation.

What would you like for that lifeguard to do? Would it help you at that moment, in your misguided self-confidence but utter helplessness, for him simply to get on the bullhorn and begin urging you to swim back to shore? Even if he were enormously persuasive, witty, and persistent, what good would it do? No, you don't want his advice, *you want his help!* You want him to apply his strength to your rescue, for your own strength is inadequate for the task. And, happily, he is pleased and able to do so, not because of any merit on your part—what have you ever done for him?—but simply because *he has chosen this work of saving people and you happen to be one in need of what he is so well qualified to do.*

The analogy has holes, of course, but at least it helps us to see that we are not so much puppets subject to the divine whim as drowning swimmers in need of saving grace. Because God has chosen to set His love on us in His way and time, the fact that He saves us—sending a preacher to tell us the Good News and His Spirit to open our hearts to Him—is simply the outworking of His good and perfect plan according to our need and His pleasure and power. Without His election we would never come into the purview of His observation, nor ever realize the saving application of His unmerited grace to our dying lives. God is obligated to save no one. All have sinned and fallen short of His glory (Rom. 3:23); all are condemned to die (Rom. 6:23). The fact is that the whole world is drowning in its self-confidence and ignorance. But in His mercy and grace, God has wondrously been pleased to save *some*. We are but the beneficiaries of His grace in being the objects of His electing love.

Such grace should fill us with confidence and hope and be an impetus for a life of serving God in gratitude for His choosing and saving us. Having elected us from before the foundations of the world, and having saved us by His grace at a point in time, it is inconceivable that He should ever let anything wrest us from His caring hand (John 10:27–29). We belong to Him, now and forever, and not because of anything we have done or might do, but simply because He has chosen to love and save us for Himself! Nothing can separate us from the love God has for us in Christ Jesus (Rom. 8:38–39). We are secure *in* Him precisely *because of* Him!

On this basis then, secure in the electing and saving grace of God, enveloped in His covenant, we become part of a people whose hearts are filled with gratitude and who go forth to serve Him every day.

(2) Moreover, Peter declares *our royal heritage*. We are a chosen people and a *royal* priesthood. We are the offspring of royalty. Our Father is the Head of the dynasty that rules over all creation (Rev. 4:5–11). His Son, our Lord Jesus Christ, has been made King of kings and Lord of lords (Ps. 2; Acts 2:36). We are His offspring. We are destined to share in His rule.

For the realization of this we do not await some distant ethereal future when we shall be assigned our own personal planet to govern, as some cultists do. Rather, we understand that this rule begins now. It involves our conducting our lives according to the just and good purposes of God's Word, as we grow in the knowledge of His truth and lean on His indwelling Spirit to help us govern our affairs according to His covenant constitution. This rule begins with such seemingly mundane matters as how we use *our time*. We are called to rule our time so that the wisdom of God may have its full course in our lives (Ps. 90:12), as we redeem time for the purposes of realizing God's promises and bringing glory and honor to Him (Eph. 5:15–17). Thus we will need time for the practice of spiritual disciplines, so that we may be prepared— heart, soul, mind, and strength—for redeeming the rest of our time throughout the day. We must guard against any of the time of our lives being usurped by foolishness or sin. We must "improve" our times, as Edwards puts it in various places, so that the time we are allotted each day is invested with the kind of attention to detail that enables us to draw on God's promises, and that brings forth a yield to the glory of God in our lives (Matt. 25:14–30).[3]

Further, we must learn to rule over *our bodies,* as Paul exhorts us in Romans 6. Moral purity, as we have seen, is a mark of God's covenant. We must not allow our members—minds, eyes, tongues, mouths, hands, feet, or any other of our bodily members—to become servants of sin. Rather, we must rule them, enforcing upon them the discipline of God's Word, restraining their sinful tendency to incline again to their former ruler—the law of sin (Rom. 7:14–23)—and reminding them of our new allegiance to Him who saved us from drowning. We must teach our members how to serve their new King and daily work to shape and form them into obedient servants. We are not, like many others, ruled by our passions, by mere whim or fancy, or by some false vision of mere fun, success, status, or prosperity. And we submit to no man if it seems that in so doing we must be disloyal to God. Rather, we rule our bodies, and everything in them, by the same power by which we have been begotten again, the power of God's Word and Spirit; and we daily seek His grace to realize the purpose of His rule in our lives.

We are called also to rule over *our daily affairs* as His ambassadors, setting our relationships, roles, and responsibilities in order before Him, doing everything to His glory and praise. Thus our family life, work, friendships, avocations, and all the other activities of our lives are to be subject to the justice, goodness, truth, and love that characterize the rule of God in Christ Jesus through our lives. And, in a larger corporate sense, we join together with others of God's royal priesthood to shape whole areas of culture and society according to the patterns and priorities of His Word. What Abraham Kuyper observed about the world in general is equally true of every area of our lives: "Oh, no single piece of our mental world is to be hermetically sealed off from the rest, and there is not a square inch in the whole domain of our human existence over which Christ, who is Sovereign over *all,* does not cry: 'Mine!' "[4]

We are a royal priesthood, called to rule, and not to be tyrannized by sin, the demands of the market, the whims of others, or the sinful tendencies of our own not-yet-perfected hearts. The sooner we begin to take up the scepter in every area of our lives and exercise dominion over them in the Name of the King of glory, the sooner we will realize more of the blessings and promises of God's covenant in the realities of our daily experience.

(3) In addition Peter reminds us that *we are a priesthood*. The function of the priesthood during the period of the Old Covenant—which Peter is appealing to by analogy here—was at least twofold. First, it was to facilitate the worship of God. The priests were to keep the sanctuary in order, to preside at all the sacrifices and every feast, and to enable the people to bring their offerings before the Lord in a decent and orderly manner. Thus, the first and most important function of the priests was liturgical, to oversee and maintain the proper worship of God among the people.

We are a people called to worship, but not merely in the sense that we gather once a week in a familiar corporate setting to observe divine service. Besides this we are called to ensure that our whole lives before the Lord are a service of worship to Him (Rom. 12:1–2), that is, that they are characterized by faithful sacrifice, constant praise and thanksgiving, and ongoing dedication to Him in every way. In this area of contemporary Christian experience, more than any other, the world has invaded the sanctuaries of our lives and entices us to honor its idols—success, leisure, status, temporal delight—and to conduct our daily service of worship according to priorities, protocols, and procedures of the world (cf. Ps. 74). Our daily worship of God has been rudely intruded upon and coarsely compromised by our involvement with the world, and, as a people, we hardly know where to start in taking back the sanctuaries of our lives for the service of God.

Certainly one place to begin is in recovering more of our lives for personal worship, especially prayer. It was the practice of God's people in both the Old and New Testaments, as well as during the first centuries of the church, to set aside set times of prayer during the course of the day. They made their lives run on a schedule that was interrupted

95

and reenergized at regular intervals by time devoted to God in prayer. In that time they refocused their lives, retuned their hearts, and reminded themselves of who they were and how they had been called to live. Recapturing some of our time throughout the day for the practice of prayer may well be the place to begin in discovering more intimately and powerfully what it means to live in God's covenant.

The second function of the priests related to the ministry of God's Word. Ezra is the classic example of a faithful priest in this, in that he "prepared his heart to seek the Law of the LORD, and to do it, and to teach statutes and ordinances in Israel" (Ezra 7:10). In a similar way every one who names the Name of Christ and has entered into God's covenant is called to the ministry of the Word of God. This means that we must study and practice it, and then teach, encourage, and evangelize others with it (2 Tim. 2:15; James 1:22–25; Col. 3:16; Heb. 10:24; Mark 16:15). Indeed, never have so many and varied opportunities existed for the members of the Christian community to learn the Word of God, take it to heart, live it out, and teach it to others. Yet, almost unbelievably, we seem to be unable or unwilling to rise to this challenge. The level of biblical ignorance among contemporary Christians is appalling. Our failure to incarnate the teaching of God's Word in our everyday lives is lamented by preachers and church leaders throughout the land. And our continuing reticence when it comes to evangelism betrays a measure of unbelief concerning the gospel that is a mark of shame on the contemporary church.

As God's priesthood we are called to the ministry of His Word, beginning in our own lives, then reaching out to everyone around us. To us it is given to embody and to proclaim the Good News of God's covenant victory in Christ, and to call others to enter more deeply into that glorious lifestyle with us. We shall never be able to know and enjoy more fully the joy, peace, and power of living in God's covenant without a renewed commitment to His Word—knowing His Word, bringing our lives into joyous conformity with it, and teaching and proclaiming its truth to those around us each day.

(4) Peter also remarks that *the followers of Jesus Christ are a holy nation.* We are a people who, like the citizens of any nation, have much

in common. We derive from the same national origins, share the same history, honor the same conventions, venerate the same heroes, keep many of the same traditions, and aspire to the same vision and hope. Our national character is to be one of holiness before the Lord as we strengthen the bonds that unite us (Eph. 4:3), cherish the traditions that have brought us into being (Ps. 78:1–8), and reach forward to the hope of our national heritage and calling in Christ (Ps. 2; Acts 1:8).

Or, at least, this is what being a holy nation would seem to imply. All too often the church of Jesus Christ is a house divided by theological differences, worship styles, levels of education, economic class, and innumerable matters of personal and ecclesiastical taste and agenda. We are like the German people in the sixteenth century, a people with one common ancestry and cultural identity, but no overarching sense of purpose and no unifying vision or polity, always ready to forge alliances against one another and for our own advantage as seems appropriate to us. We are a house divided, a people who have not learned the power of love to overcome every difference among us, or of holiness to allow us to put aside our selfish agendas for the sake of serving our brothers and sisters in Christ.

The Westminster Confession of Faith instructs the churches in its tradition concerning the character of God's covenant people as a holy nation (26.2):

Saints by profession are bound to maintain an holy fellowship and communion *in the worship of God, and in performing such other spiritual services as tend to their mutual edification; as also in relieving each other in outward things, according to their several abilities and necessities.* Which communion, as God offereth opportunity, *is to be extended unto all those who, in every place, call upon the name of the Lord Jesus* (emphasis added).

Here is the ideal of a holy nation at work. People worshiping together; ministering to one another across ecclesiastical and denominational bounds; sacrificing their own time and ease in order to meet the needs of their fellow citizens in the household of faith; working diligently together in their own communities to reach out to Christians elsewhere with the same love, care, and support that they give one another.

What a far cry from anything like this do we find among the churches of the evangelical community as a whole, or even among those of the Reformed tradition! Our attitude toward other Christ-loving churches is one of "every man for himself." We resent new churches that start up "too close" to our own. We heap criticism on those who worship differently than we do, or whose doctrinal views may not be the same as ours, or that we may even consider seriously faulty in some points. How little effort we give to bringing together the people of God's covenant throughout our communities for large-scale services of worship, collaborative ministry endeavors, and a common prophetic voice against the evils of our day.

We will never know what it means to live to the fullest in God's covenant until we begin to take seriously our calling, not just as individual believers or local churches within some particular tradition, but as a *holy nation*, raised up to articulate and pursue a common national vision, together, arm in arm, in every community in the land.

(5) Peter reminds us that *we are a people for God's own possession*. We are not our own; we have been bought with the price of God's own dear Son (1 Cor. 6:19). He has purchased us for Himself and has brought us into the light of His grace, that we should be to the praise of His glory who first believed in Him. We belong to God, and He has a specific purpose in mind for us: that we should proclaim by life and word the excellencies of Him who saved us and brought us into the exceedingly great and precious promises of His covenant, so that we might walk in light and know full and abundant life in Him.

Every reader must ask: Is this my purpose in life? Is this what motivates and drives me as I go out the door each day? Is this the standard by which I assess my life, allocate my resources, invest my time, talents, and energies? Or do I continue living as though my life were my own to do with as I please, and my church an isolated community with no larger connection?

We go to church and sing, "Take my life, and let it be / consecrated Lord to Thee." But then do we go out each week, in complete disregard of that pledge—dare I say, vow—and live as though our time, our treasure, and our talents and energy were our own to pursue our personal agendas in a materialistic and hedonistic postmodern culture?

As God's New Covenant people we are His, just as His covenant is His, to do with according to His good pleasure and for His glory—which also happens to be for the fullest, richest, most abundant and joyful life that we could ever hope to enjoy! But we must give ourselves daily in self-conscious submission to God's covenant, devoting ourselves afresh each day, and moment by moment throughout the day, to living in God's covenant according to His intentions and plans. Otherwise that loss of reality that Schaeffer warned about will invade our own lives, and they will seem no more real or meaningful than the shallow, empty lives of our unsaved neighbors and friends.

As God's New Covenant people we are a people whose hearts have been tuned to know Him and to love His Law. We have been incorporated into a vast nation of the followers of Christ. Our salvation is not intended merely to help us cope with life in the world. Our church is not just some spiritual "watering hole" in the vast secular desert, unconnected to the ocean of God's people all over the world. Living in God's covenant demands a radically new understanding of the life of faith and the mission of the local church. Our experience of that new reality will be something less than full, rich, and abundant, as long as we allow the world or our own preconceptions and preferences to tell us otherwise.

QUESTIONS FOR STUDY OR DISCUSSION

1. In what ways does the New Covenant differ from the Old Covenant? At the same time, how can you see that they are both part of the same eternal covenant of God?

2. Entering into God's covenant means that we have been given a new heart. How should we expect this to affect our outlook on life?

99

Our hopes and dreams? Our priorities and preferences? What can keep our hearts from rising to these New Covenant expectations?

3. To what extent does it appear that your life reflects the rule of God's kingdom in each of the following areas:

    a. use of your time

    b. use of your resources

    c. your relationships

    d. your work

    e. your avocations

4. In which of these areas would you like to see more of the power of God's kingdom at work, bringing the fullness of His promises to greater and greater reality in your life? What is the role of spiritual disciplines in helping you to realize this?

5. Surely one of the greatest obstacles to the church's witness in the postmodern world is that we are divided in many ways (cf. John 17:21). How might the churches in your community begin to overcome some of those divisions? What difficulties or obstacles might they anticipate? How could they work together to get beyond those difficulties and obstacles?

7

THE COVENANT
AND THE KINGDOM

But seek first the kingdom of God and His righteousness, and all these things shall be added to you.—Matthew 6:33

While all things are under the rule of Christ, it is his saving rule that constitutes his kingdom (Col. 1:13). The church is the heavenly polis on earth, the new humanity whose hearts are circumcised by his Spirit.[1]—Edmund Clowney

During a period of forty days following the resurrection the disciples sat enthralled as the Lord Jesus instructed them in the kingdom of God (Acts 1:1–4). Much of what He told them they had no doubt heard before—familiar parables, reminders and explanations of Old Testament prophecies, promises of the kingdom's inevitable growth and dominance from fairly inauspicious beginnings. Surely He taught them from the Psalms about His kingship and the promise that He would inherit the ends of the earth (Ps. 2); from Isaiah about His agenda of righteousness, justice, and peace (Isa. 9:1–7); and from Daniel about His kingdom's ultimate victory over all opposition and of their role in its unfolding (Dan. 2:44–45; 7:13–18). Probably more was added as well—new insights and understandings, clarification of their own roles in the kingdom, further development and elaboration of things He had been teaching them over the past three years. How wonderful it must have been for the eleven as they sat and listened to these powerful, exciting words!

Whatever Jesus said to them during those forty days, it took. As the moment of His ascension approached, the disciples were fairly frothing for the kingdom's arrival: "Lord, will You at this time restore the kingdom to Israel?" (Acts 1:6).

We can imagine their excitement as they began to gain a clearer picture of the biblical idea of the kingdom of God, an idea they would have been familiar with before their association with Christ, but which was enhanced and expanded during the period of His earthly ministry, and now was being greatly clarified and made more urgent. The idea of God establishing a kingdom among His people is a theme hinted at throughout the Old Testament, in places like Genesis 49:8–10, 2 Samuel 7:8–16, Isaiah 9:1–7, and Daniel 7:11–18. Jesus declared that His coming was in some sense the inauguration of that kingdom (cf. Matt. 12:22–29), so that, in Him, the rule of God foretold in the Old Testament was beginning to be established among men.

The kingdom of God was the centerpiece of Jesus' preaching and teaching. In His parables, sermons, and informal periods of instruction, Jesus challenged His hearers to observe a new power breaking out among them and beginning to work a transforming effect on the lives of men and nations. He called that power the kingdom of God or the kingdom of heaven. He spoke of the great worth of this kingdom, its inherent power, and its inevitable triumph over all the dark forces that were arrayed against it. He called His followers to repudiate their former ways of life and prepare to live under a new ethic of world-changing power. He claimed to be the Monarch of that kingdom, and it was this that ultimately brought the wrath of Rome down on Him. There could only be one king among men and nations, and Caesar had laid claim to that title.

Yet Jesus was King, indeed, although of a kingdom "not of this world," a kingdom that had its origins in eternity, drew its power from the throne of almighty God, and would turn the known world upside down for the cause of Christ in just a few years. The prospect of this thrilled the disciples. In their minds they could see themselves seated on thrones and judging the tribes of Israel, right alongside the Lord Himself. And they were eager for this to begin "at this time"

So central a role does the kingdom of God have in the ministry of Jesus Christ and the subsequent events of the New Testament, that we could very easily lose sight of God's covenant in all the excitement. Yet these are not two independent entities, serving separate purposes in some larger divine scheme. *The kingdom of God and God's covenant are part and parcel of the same dispensation of grace whereby God, through our Lord Jesus Christ, is fulfilling His ancient promises and bringing the present evil age to its conclusion.* These two mighty vehicles—His kingdom and covenant—work hand in hand to accomplish the eternal purposes of God in creating a people for Himself who will serve and glorify Him.

THE KINGDOM OF GOD

It will help us in understanding the relationship between the kingdom and the covenant if we can achieve a definition of the kingdom of God. Several passages of Scripture, in addition to ones we have already examined, can help us in this task.

Daniel 2:31–45 depicts the kingdom of God as a growing stone, cut without hands and thrown to the earth, which expands on the earth until it overcomes every earthly kingdom and domain. Daniel was shown that this kingdom would begin its inevitable domination of the earth during the reign of the kingdom of iron and clay depicted in Nebuchadnezzar's dream, the third world empire following that of Babylon, that is, Rome. From humble, simple beginnings that kingdom would grow and expand until every opposing factor was overwhelmed and the whole earth was dominated by its powerful presence.

In Psalm 2 the kingdom of God is announced against the backdrop of a world in rebellion against God, and poses a threat to the kings of the earth. It is inaugurated at the ascension of God's own Son to His throne of glory on Mount Zion. He is given the ends of the earth as His inheritance and is to rule over the nations with a rod of iron. All who embrace His rule will know life and peace; all who oppose it will be shattered when His anger flares up suddenly. Those who serve under the rule of God's heavenly King are thus charged with a mandate of declaring His rule and calling the nations to embrace the Son of God, lest they perish under His wrath.

Daniel 7:11–18 shows us "One like the Son of Man" who receives an eternal kingdom from the Ancient of Days and gives it to the saints of the Most High God. It becomes theirs forever, being bestowed upon them, as Peter tells us, by the outpouring of the Spirit of God from on high (Acts 2:33–36). As the Spirit begins to work out the progress of the kingdom in their lives and upon the earth, the righteousness, peace, and joy that bring glory and honor to God begin to appear in and among those in whom the Spirit dwells (Rom. 14:17–18). They are filled with a new power and go about to proclaim the excellencies of Him who has called them out of darkness into His glorious light (Acts 1:8; 1 Peter 2:9–10). The enemies of God are subdued, albeit not without considerable suffering on the part of the citizens of God's kingdom (Dan. 7:21–27); and the fruit of His kingdom increases on the earth, and the righteousness of His Law brings the blessings and promises of God's covenant to His people, and, through them, to all the nations.

Given this brief survey let me offer a definition of the kingdom of God in the light of our study of God's covenant. The kingdom of God is the *operative power* of God's covenant, the *driving force of His indwelling Spirit* by which God makes real the promises of His covenant and brings His glory to light among men. The kingdom of God is not so much a *place* as a *power*. It is the rule of God, exercised by the Lord Jesus Christ in the Person of the Holy Spirit and according to the promises of God's Word. This indwelling spiritual power enlivens God's covenant people, reorients their vision of themselves and the world, imbues them with a new sense of mission and purpose, and animates them to faithfulness and to being a blessing to the world. As Ridderbos says, the kingdom of God establishes the entire world "in the wide perspective of the realization of all God's rights and promises."[2]

Seen from this perspective the kingdom of God *is the supreme administrative element of God's covenant in its new dispensation.* As He comes to dwell among His people, the Spirit of God accomplishes the circumcision of their hearts, creates in them a hunger for the Law of God, thrills them with a vision of God's ultimate victory, brings forth the fruit of righteousness in them, and empowers them for witness to the Lord Jesus Christ. In the Holy Spirit God's covenant is both internalized and fulfilled, and God's rule—His kingdom—begins to unfold its glory in the midst of the nations.

THE KINGDOM AND THE CHURCH

But where does the church fit into this picture? We have already said that one of the elements unique to the era of the New Covenant is the calling incumbent upon the people of God to build the church. The coming of the kingdom might seem to distract from, or at least, compete with, this calling. In fact, it serves to make it a reality.

This is so, in the first place, because *the Ruler of the kingdom of God, our Lord Jesus Christ, has taken His place of authority over the kingdom as Head of the church.* He directs the work of His Spirit from His throne at the right hand of the Father, where, with all power in heaven and earth at His disposal, He serves as Head of the church, God's King established in Mount Zion (Matt. 28:18–20; Eph. 1:18–23; Ps. 2). Thus, He who governs and builds His church and He who rules over the power that makes God's covenant effectual in the new dispensation are One and the same. We can be sure that He will not rule or govern at cross purposes with Himself. The kingdom of God, the power that makes God's covenant fruitful in the new dispensation, necessarily works to the end of building the church, the body of Christ. When, therefore, God's covenant people take up the task of building the church—concerning which we shall have more to say in the following chapter—they may expect the power of God to fill them, carry them along, and make it so that their labors are not in vain in the Lord (1 Cor. 15:58).

In fact, we in the covenant community should be careful that our efforts are *primarily* focused on this end—building the church—since it is to that end that Christ our Head and King is marshaling His power at this time (Matt. 16:18). In our day of Christian political and social activism and parachurch proliferation, we may be enticed to believe that the work of the kingdom of God is going forth in other, more visible and ostensibly more productive arenas than that of the church. For many Christians the church seems passive, exhausted, and withdrawn from the real struggles of living in a secular and postmodern age. More relevant and powerful structures would seem to be necessary for realizing an agenda of righteousness, justice, and peace on earth.

However, we must not fall into the deception of thinking that the kingdom of God will come to its fullest fruition through political, social, or cultural activity in the first place, or through para-ecclesiastical agencies apart from the church. Such efforts and agencies certainly have their place in the work of the kingdom. Yet when we in the Christian community devote more of our time, energy, and resources to these activities than to the work of building the church, we run ahead of the Lord's agenda—or rather, outside it—and cannot expect the power of His Spirit to accompany us as fully as if we were devoting ourselves to our primary covenant task. However, when such efforts are kept within the sphere and focus of building the church, then we may expect to know the full measure of God's power helping us and prospering our endeavors. He who rules over us as Savior and King intends to build His church, not just a society where traditional or family values may flourish. Unless we keep this in mind, we run the risk of wasting our precious resources, time, and energy in efforts that Christ our King will not bless with the promises of His covenant.

We should further observe that, according to the Scriptures, *the church is the court from which the progress of the kingdom is advanced.* That is, it is from the church that God's power goes forth into the world, making all things new and reconciling all things to Himself through Jesus Christ. By her instruction, discipline, and witness, the church brings the new reality of kingdom life and the promises of God's covenant to the peoples of the earth. Christ, the Head of the church and Ruler of God's kingdom, establishes His rule first within His people and then outward, through the influence of their lives, into the surrounding cultures and societies and nations (Ps. 110:1–2).

Again, we may be tempted to think that the halls of national legislatures or judiciaries, the programs of para-ecclesiastical agencies, or other such secondary social and cultural arenas should be the primary focus of our labors and resources. But the teaching of Scripture is that God's kingdom proceeds through, and His covenant is chiefly realized within, the body of Christ, His church. All other such undertakings must be considered as strictly secondary to the King's agenda. They may well be useful for His purposes, but not if we seek to establish them as isolated outposts in the spiritual warfare, cut off from the nurturing bosom of the kingdom community and the work of building the church. They may make a short-term impact on enemy territory, but they will ultimately be overwhelmed, taken over, and turned against the purposes of Christ and His kingdom if they do not develop within and remain committed to the task of building His church first and foremost. The history of higher education in America, which began in the churches but, by the end of the nineteenth century, had been taken over by more secular interests, is surely stark testimony to what happens in such cases.

In the Gospel of Matthew Jesus made it very clear that the interests and concerns of His kingdom were to be devoted to the work of building His church. In the first fifteen chapters of that Gospel He plied His disciples with parable upon parable, teaching upon teaching, concerning the kingdom of God, building into their vision and hopes the prospect of an approaching powerful, growing reign in which they would have important roles. Then, in the great confrontation at Caesarea-Philippi, when Jesus asked the disciples who they said that He was, Peter answered, "You are the Christ, the Son of the living God" (Matt. 16:16). Jesus confirmed Peter's answer by telling him that he would have an integral—albeit temporary—role as a focal point on which Christ would build *His church*. We might have expected, given all the previous instruction concerning the kingdom, that Jesus would say, "My kingdom." Instead, He said, "I will build My church" (v. 18). This is the first mention of the church in Matthew's Gospel. Jesus said that His church would defeat all the schemes and powers of hell, which would be unable to prevail against it. He told the leaders of His church that they would have authority to open the gates of the kingdom of God to those who satisfied the qualifications thereof. The church that is to be built is to be, as it were, a center of administration for the unfolding of God's kingdom, possessing a power that overthrows the devil and incorporates God's people into His eternal covenant plan.

So it is clear that the power of the kingdom, in a primary sense, resides in the church and goes forth from the church to do the work for which the Lord has established it. Thus, if we are seeking an arena in which to know the power of God's kingdom, and, thus, more fully to realize the promises of His covenant, we must turn to the church. For the church, drawn by the grace of God into the promises of His covenant, realizes and expresses those promises in the power of the Spirit unto the progress of the kingdom of God. It is the kingdom of God, expressed in and through the church, that brings the fullness of God's covenant to fruition and accomplishes the purposes of His glory on earth.

Thus, kingdom, covenant, and church are all interrelated concepts under the authority of Christ and working together according to the will and purpose of God. The church, in this new dispensation in which we live, is the focal point of kingdom power and covenant promise, thus taking the place that the ark held in the time of Noah, the family of Abraham in the days of the patriarchs, and the nation of Israel throughout the bulk of the Old Testament (cf. Heb. 12:22–29).

IMPLICATIONS OF THE KINGDOM OF GOD

For the purpose of realizing the fullness of God's covenant promises, two primary implications derive from this understanding of the nature of God's kingdom and the relationship among covenant, kingdom, and church.

(1) *Seek first the kingdom.* We must learn to seek the kingdom of God as the first priority in all our lives (Matt. 6:33). This means simply that

we must desire above all else to *know the presence and rule of God* in every aspect of our lives, to *appropriate the power of God* so that we might truly live for His glory, and to *proclaim the rule of God* to every man, woman, and child with whom we have contact.

First, we must desire above all else to *know the presence and rule of God in our daily lives.* This means that we must seek the Lord, and seek Him earnestly (Pss. 63:1; 105:4). To seek the kingdom is to desire to dwell in the presence of the King, inhabit His court, hear His Word, and know the glory of His countenance smiling upon us (Ps. 84). This aspect of seeking the kingdom involves the spiritual disciplines by which we order and nurture our lives in Christ—those practices of prayer, Scripture reading and meditation, fasting, and so forth by which we learn to draw near to the Lord in order to know and love Him more. Without a vital and growing commitment to the practice of spiritual disciplines, we cannot hope to know much of the power of God's kingdom in our lives.

Yet, second, seeking the kingdom also speaks to the manner of our being in the world and the various ways by which we work to *bring every aspect of our lives under the loving oversight of our heavenly King.* All our relationships, roles, and responsibilities are given to us as trusts from the Lord, to be conducted according to His good pleasure and for the purposes of His rule (Matt. 25:14–20). Therefore, we must seek His guidance and strength in each of these, so that they might be brought under His authority and used for the purposes of building His church unto the glory of God (Eph. 1:22–23; 2:19–22).

For this, we must learn how to appropriate the power of God's kingdom for carrying out our callings in a way that will glorify and honor Him. This we do by faith.

Faith, the writer of Hebrews tells us, is the assurance of things hoped for, the evidence of things not seen (Heb. 11:1). That is, in the exercise of faith there is both an inward assurance that the things we have come to know are true and reliable, and an outward manifestation, expressed as obedience, of our confidence in the Lord, whom we cannot see. Faith comes to fruition in our lives as we grow in understanding of God's promises, take those promises to heart, and then begin to shape and direct our lives in such a way as to demonstrate to others that we believe God's promises to be reliable and sure.

Thus, for example, when the promise of God tells us that power is available through the indwelling Spirit to enable us to bear witness to Christ (Acts 1:8), we respond by studying further in order to understand the message we are to proclaim and to prepare ourselves to proclaim it to the people around us (1 Cor. 9:19–23). We want to believe that the gospel is true, that it is the promise of God for salvation to all who believe, that God will save His elect from among the lost as they hear the message of His Good News, and that He is pleased to use us to make that Good News known. As we study, therefore, we seek the Lord's grace to convince and assure us that the things we are reading are reliable and true, laboring in meditation and prayer to know with the certainty of faith that what His Word tells us is true. We want to be sure in our hearts as well as our heads that God is calling us to be His witnesses to the people around us, sending us to declare the message of Jesus in ways that will make sense to them. Finally, as we grow increasingly assured of these facts, we will begin exploring and initiating ways of acting upon them. We will begin to pray for the lost with whom we have regular contact, as well as others we might meet in the normal course of our daily life. We will start to reach out to the people around us, begin to get to know them, go out of our way to serve them in love, and look for opportunities to proclaim the news of Jesus Christ to them as often as we can.

As we act in faith in every area of our lives, we will find that the power of God's kingdom will work in and through us to bring the promises of His covenant to fruition in us and others, unto the building up of the church. *But we must take seriously the challenge of faith, that it is to be a way of life (2 Cor. 5:7) and not merely some kind of intellectual assent to theological articles or mere pious agreement with religious platitudes and practices.* Faith is proved in mind, heart, and life, as we grow in love for God and our neighbors and reach out in the confidence of God's covenant to be a blessing to everyone around us (1 Tim. 1:5; Gen. 12:1–3).

Third, seeking the kingdom requires that we proclaim its reality, *calling men and women—saved and unsaved alike—to submit themselves ever more completely to the gracious rule of Jesus Christ.*

The postmodern world is, consciously or otherwise, in all-out revolt against the Lord. It wants nothing to do with Him or His Law except insofar as identification with Him may be politically or socially expedient. The elite leadership of our society has charted a moral and cultural course that seeks to throw off the strictures of God's Law and relegate Him to a marginal role in the affairs of men. God's reply to this outrage is to send His people into the world, in the power of His Spirit and the kingdom lifestyle He expresses through them, to declare that His King is ruling from heaven, that He has been made heir of all the nations, and that it is in the best interest of all men to embrace His rule, accept His forgiveness, and begin to order their lives according to His promises and unto His glory (Ps. 2). The imminence of the kingdom, together with a call for repentance, was the first and consistent message of our Lord Jesus Christ (Matt. 4:17). It was the word that Peter declared to the assembled throngs in Jerusalem on the first Christian Pentecost (Acts 2:32–36). It was the message that turned the world upside down for Christ, and that occasioned the deaths of so many martyrs during the period of the early church. And it is the message that continues in effect and must be declared to a rebellious world by God's covenant people today.

We are truly seeking the kingdom of God when we are yielding our lives more and more to His sovereign, gracious rule, and when we are calling men and women to join us in honoring the King who has saved us by His life, death, and resurrection.

The kingdom of God is the operative power of God's covenant, the spiritual energy whereby God is building His church, calling out a people unto Himself and accomplishing the purposes of His glory. As His covenant people we are called to seek this kingdom earnestly, personally, and in our dealings with others, so that the exceedingly great and precious promises of God's covenant may become the happy possession of more and more people, as they unite in obedient faith to praise, honor, glorify, and live for Him.

(2) *Build first the church*. The nature of the kingdom and its function as the operative power of God's covenant mean that we must devote ourselves to building the church as first in our agenda of communal activities. We shall have much more to say about this in the next chapter. For now, let me simply observe that there is nothing more important, more urgent, or of more eternal consequence to which we may devote ourselves than laboring to help the body of Christ come to the fullest possible expression in our communities. When Jesus walked the earth, He was the epicenter of God's power, the locus of His kingdom, the bearer of His gifts, and the fulfiller of His promises. This should be no less true for the church today, which is the body of Christ in its communities. We are doing the work of the kingdom of God—and, hence furthering its progress and rule among the peoples of the world—when we are devoting ourselves to building the church of Jesus Christ.

Thus, members of the covenant community, who are also citizens of the heavenly kingdom, must devote themselves to building this church to its fullest possible expression, both in their local congregations and in their communities and throughout the world, devoting the main body of their intellectual, emotional, and material resources to the work of worship, disciple making, diaconal ministry, and mission. That members of the covenant community today have their loyalties so fragmented between such activities as work, school, recreation, leisure, and mere diversion, with so little in the way of focused energy or resources being devoted to building the church, is a great travesty and shame. That we invest our resources, energy, and time more in the work of para-ecclesiastical, cultural, or social endeavors—as good and useful as these may be—more than in building the church merely indicates how impoverished our understanding of Christ's kingdom and agenda has become. Moreover, that we have such a skewed understanding of the meaning of "church growth" and that, as a result, there is so little evidence of the presence of healthy, growing churches in most of our communities, is equally scandalous.

Here there is a need for a serious refocusing of our efforts. The resources, time, and energy of the people of God's kingdom are being diverted and dissipated in all manner of well-meaning but ultimately fruitless undertakings. Meanwhile, the church is languishing in comfort, complacency, and compromise with the demands and ways of the world. Only deep-felt repentance and true spiritual renewal will be able to turn our focus away from earthly aspirations to our heavenly calling as the covenant people of God.

THE KINGDOM HAS COME—LET THE PLUNDERING PROCEED

Second Kings 7:1–16 records the familiar story of the leprous beggars who, upon discovering that the Lord had put the Syrians to flight, began to help themselves to the spoils hastily abandoned in the besieging army's camp. Piqued by their selfish greed, they decided to report their find to the beleaguered Samarians:

> Then they said to one another, "We are not doing what is right. This day is a day of good news, and we remain silent. If we wait until morning light, some punishment will come upon us. Now therefore, come, let us go and tell the king's household" (v. 9).

So they reported to the king of Samaria what they had discovered, and, once the report had been confirmed, the desperate people of the suddenly delivered city rushed upon the spoils to relieve their distress. In the process, the king's unbelieving chamberlain was trampled to death by the stampeding throngs. The prophet Elisha had declared in advance that the city would be relieved and prosperity would return to Samaria once again, only to be mocked by the chamberlain. Those who heeded the report enjoyed the blessings of God's grace, while the one who balked at the prophet's word was condemned to death.

Life in the kingdom of God is like this. God has foretold a time of great growth and expansion, when righteousness, justice, and peace would obtain, and His people would have power to declare the Good News of the new era to the whole earth. Those who believe the report are even now rushing ahead to plunder the former holdings of the

113

prince of this world, and are finding the blessings of God and the promises of His covenant on every hand, while those who hesitate in unbelief condemn themselves to less than the full and abundant life Christ has promised.

In Matthew 12:22–29 Jesus announced that His ability to cast out demons signaled the arrival of the kingdom of God. The time had come, the ancient prophecies were being fulfilled, and Jesus Himself was leading the effort to plunder the holdings of the now-bound strong man:

> But if I cast out demons by the Spirit of God, surely the kingdom of God has come upon you. Or else how can one enter a strong man's house and plunder his goods, unless he first binds the strong man? And then he will plunder his house (vv. 28–29).

We in the covenant community, the church of our risen Lord Jesus, should understand that the ancient prophecies of kingdom arrival and advance have been fulfilled. The enemy has been routed, and the treasury of his former holdings lies bare for the taking. All who believe the Word of Christ will rush forward out of their former captivity to the things of this world and, in the power of God's kingdom, will plunder the erstwhile domain of the devil, taking everything captive for the kingdom purposes of Christ.

They will redeem their time, taking back every moment that was given over to the purposes of this evil age, recovering and redeploying them for the work of Christ and His kingdom (Eph. 5:15–17). They will redeem their bodies from lethargy, sinful self-indulgence, mere worldly pleasures and diversions, and every harmful thing and offer themselves as living sacrifices to their risen Lord (Rom. 6:6–14; 12:1–2). They will tend the weed-infested gardens of their lives, plowing under the thorns and thistles of worldly pleasure and sowing the seeds of righteousness, justice, and peace in every corner of their lives (1 Cor. 3:5–9). And they will rush out to the whole of creation—all their relationships, roles, and responsibilities, as well as all the institutions and undertakings of life together in society—taking every thought captive and making it obedient to Jesus Christ (2 Cor. 10:3–5). As Robert E. Webber has written of the life of Christian discipleship, "We need to emphasize the cost of discipleship, the absolute claim of God over our entire life, the necessity of a faith that issues forth in obedience, and our belonging to an alternative culture shaped by the kingdom of Jesus."[3]

Do we expect the devil merely to sit by and let this plundering go forward without a fight? Not at all. He is like a roaring lion and would devour as many of us as he can (1 Peter 5:8). But he is a defeated, routed, and chained foe (Col. 2:15). He can be resisted; he will flee from us as we call upon the Name of the Lord; and the Lord will crush him under our feet in just a little while (1 Peter 5:8; James 4:7; Rom. 16:20). We may be wounded, buffeted, knocked about, and troubled in the fray, but we will be victorious in the end, and throughout every day that we devote ourselves to the cause of Christ and His kingdom.

For the Christian, every day should be like Christmas. We should bolt out of bed in the morning and rush downstairs to lay hold of the many excellent gifts the Lord has left for us, unwrapping them with eager expectation, delighting in them one by one, and making good use of them all day long for the work of building the church of our Lord. Thus do we enter into the power of the kingdom of God that is even now unfolding and surging all around us. And thus do we appropriate and enjoy the abundant blessings of the promises of God's eternal covenant.

QUESTIONS FOR STUDY OR DISCUSSION

1. Imagine that you woke up tomorrow morning in an entirely different country, one you had never visited before. You had to get work, establish new friendships, and find a way of making yourself at home in this new domain. How would you proceed? Do you think it would be helpful to go out into that new country insisting that "I'm an American, and in America, this is the way we do it!" Why or why not?

2. Have you woken up in the kingdom of God? Has God brought the power of His rule to bear on your heart, making you a new cre-

ation in Christ Jesus? Will it help you, as you try to understand and live within this new realm, to keep holding on to the things of this secular world as though they were the things that really mattered? Explain.

3. Jesus said, "The kingdom of God is within you" (Luke 17:21). The powerful unfolding of that kingdom begins in our hearts and works its way outward to every area of our lives. This suggests that we need to pay earnest attention to growing our hearts for the Lord, and this is the particular challenge of the disciplines of grace. How would you rate your involvement in the disciplines of grace—Bible study, prayer, fasting, worship, solitude, and the like—at this time? Is it sufficient to ensure that the kingdom of God will transform your heart and help you to know its power in every area of your life? What would you like to see different about your practice of the disciplines of grace?

4. Would you say that your church has a "kingdom orientation" toward its community and the world? Why or why not? What would a congregation look like that was oriented like that?

5. Is every day of your life in the kingdom of Christ like Christmas? Why or why not?

THE CHURCH, THE COVENANT COMMUNITY

I will build My church, and the gates of Hades shall not prevail against it.—Matthew 16:18

Christians must recover the primacy of being a Christian community. It means that the primary question we must ask is, "What does it mean to be a citizen of the local and global church?" This question must precede the question, "What does it mean to be a good citizen of the United States?"—Robert E. Webber[1]

As we have seen, God's covenant brings into being a unique people among all the peoples of the earth, a people chosen by God, designed for rule, assembled for worship, and sent into the world to declare His excellencies. Drawn into and filled with the power of His Spirit, they are citizens of a new kingdom, a kingdom not of this world, and must not allow themselves to be bound by the limitations or agendas of this world, but are determined on a course of glory and honor to God. In the eternal plan of God as it is expressed in His covenant, He is pleased to assemble His people in communities, scattered throughout the world, organized into gatherings large and small, which are the various congregations of the church of our Lord Jesus Christ. The church—and particular churches as expressions thereof—is yet another of the unique administrative elements of God's covenant in its new dispensation, and it is intended as a dramatic counterpart to the secular cities of lost men and women.

We may note three characteristics of the covenant community by way of introduction to its unique nature and mission. (1) We observe God's intention that *His community should contrast starkly with the surrounding world*. The Scripture uses various images to draw out this contrast: darkness and light, flesh and spirit, self-centeredness and self-denial, death and life. The covenant people are called to be different, to stand out, to bring the light of God's truth and the power of His grace to bear on the darkness and sin of unbelief by their character as well as their words. They are instructed not to allow themselves to become conformed to the surrounding world, but are to be transformed and renewed so that they might shine like cities set on a hill, beacons of newness and hope in the midst of a dying age (Rom. 12:1–2; Matt. 5:13–16). As Douglas John Hall puts it, Christians

> must stand off from the liberal middle-class culture with which we have been consistently identified; rediscover our own distinctive ontological foundations and the ethical directives that arise from them; and allow ourselves, if necessary, to become aliens in our own land.[2]

Given this calling to distinctiveness, it should strike us as curious, if not sad, how much like the rest of the world the members of today's covenant communities have become, and how hard we seem to work at showing and assuring the world that we are not much different from them.

(2) *The covenant community is uniquely a community of the Spirit.* The church is called into being by God's Spirit; is filled and taught by Him; receives gifts and power from the Spirit; bears His fruit; pursues His mission; and is kept by the Spirit unto the Lord forever. The presence of God's Spirit, with His heavenly and God-honoring orientation, is the very source of our uniqueness as a people. He gives us our new agenda, guides us in the stewardship of our abilities and resources, and moti-

vates us to service and mission for the glory of God. There is no explaining the church's uniqueness apart from the fact that we are a community of the Spirit, dependent more on *unseen resources* for our calling and hope than on the things and practices of a materialistic age.

This being so, it is difficult to explain our contemporary dependence on material resources (buildings and budgets) and our captivity to structures and procedures (committees, programs, projects) and our fascination with definitions of success (numbers, self-actualization)—things that have their origin more in the world of commerce than in the Scriptures.

(3) *The church is a community of wondrous diversity.* We are many members in one body; possess many gifts, yet for one overarching purpose; and know many callings, although we all serve one Lord. The mountain of the Lord's house is a mountain of many peaks, as the psalmist says (68:18), with many faces and hues, and stretching like a continuous range around the whole earth.

Why, then, is the covenant community so separatist in its ways? Why do we divide ourselves along denominational lines? Why do churches in local communities have so little contact with one another? Why do we not worship together as a larger body in our communities? Why do we not undertake ministries of care or outreach together? Why do we generally regard one another with a jealous, even distrustful eye?

All these anomalies suggest that, while we in the covenant community of the Lord have understood some things about His intentions for us as churches, we have missed or misunderstood many of the larger issues that make us a distinctive people. Instead of allowing our life in the world to be guided and shaped by the unique demands of God's Word and the powers of His Spirit, we have too often taken the world as our model, patterning our life in community after its expectations and ways. As a result, we are failing to realize our full potential as a community separated unto the Lord.

Thus it would seem that recovering an understanding of the unique foundations, mission, and power of the church will help us to reclaim some of our distinctiveness as a community, and enable us to experience more fully what it means to live within God's covenant in today's world.

119

The Foundations of the Covenant Community

The recovery of our distinctiveness as a community must begin at the foundations. For, unless we build from a solid base, we cannot expect to grow as the Lord purposes and to become the "joy of the whole earth" that God intends us to be (Ps. 48:2). Four planks make up the foundations on which we may hope to realize anew our unique character as the covenant community of the Lord.

(1) *Prayer*. No one disputes the importance of prayer in the life of the believer or the covenant community as a whole. But how much prayer? Of what sort? And in what kinds of contexts?

Living in God's covenant demands a life of prayer of every member of the covenant community. Prayer is perhaps the single most distinctive attribute of one who has entered into covenant relationship with the Lord. While we shall dwell most of all on this plank, this is not the place to address the matter of our individual labors of prayer.[3] Instead, I would like to make some general observations about the discipline of prayer as it pertains to the church as a whole, and as we see these demonstrated in the first covenant community in the book of Acts.

First, we note that the first community of Christians was founded on and grew by *corporate prayer*. In Acts 1 we find the people of God, only 120 souls at that time, united together in prayer for a period of ten days, waiting for the promise of God and the beginning of the new era of covenant dispensation. We do not know the details of this gathering, only that they continued together in uninterrupted prayer for an extended period as they awaited the stirring of the Lord in their midst. Doubtless people had to go to work, take care of their families, and attend to a myriad of other duties and responsibilities. However, the meeting of prayer continued throughout a ten-day period, providing a continuous offering of praise, thanks, and intercession to the Lord.

With but a few extraordinary exceptions, churches today know little or nothing of this discipline. Our times of united prayer are restricted to poorly attended mid-week meetings and the uniting of our hearts under pastoral leadership during our services of worship. Such intermittent and passive prayers are hardly what we might expect of a people who are called to seek the Lord earnestly and continuously.

Another aspect of corporate prayer in the early church comes into view. After the pouring out of the Holy Spirit, we find the people of God assembling not only in public but in private homes for the work of prayer (Acts 2:42–46). It is important to note that the Greek indicates it was "the prayers" that God's people were pursuing, suggesting that there were set times for prayer in which the people withdrew from their worldly pursuits to focus on their heavenly calling. Such is borne out by the example of Peter and John, in Acts 3:1, who were on their way to the temple at "the hour of prayer" when their progress was interrupted by the healing of a lame man.

It was the practice of saints in both the Old and New Testaments to set aside times throughout the day to retire for prayer. The psalmist claimed to observe seven such seasons a day, while Daniel returned to his room for prayer three times during the day (Ps. 119:164; Dan. 6:10). The apostles seem more to have followed the psalmist, as we find Peter praying not only at 3:00 (Acts 3:1) but also just before noon (Acts 10:9), suggesting that he adhered to the practice of praying at 6:00 and 9:00 in the morning, then at noon, 3:00, 6:00, and before retiring thereafter. This practice of observing set hours of prayer continued into the period of the early church, as James F. White has shown.[4] When the early Christians faithfully attended to "the prayers," we can believe they were observing those hours of prayer, in some cases at the temple, others in private homes, and still others as best they could in the fields or at their places of employment.

The first covenant community was thus saturated with corporate prayer. Following the example of the 120, and submitting to biblical precedent, the early Christians pursued an ongoing meeting of God in prayer by observing the hours of prayer. In our day, when we have so much allowed the world to "squeeze us into its mold," to echo the memorable phrase of J. B. Phillips (Rom. 12:1–2), such a disciplined, continuous approach to prayer seems impractical, if not impossible. Yet the numbers of Christians who are discovering ways of devoting themselves to just such a practice is on the rise today, and we should be encouraged by their example to seek the Lord more continuously by finding ways that we, too, might observe the hours of prayer. This will surely have the effect of setting us off as a distinct people among our secular contemporaries.

Second, the prayers of God's people seem to have been *focused on the book of Psalms*. How else to explain the apparently spontaneous use of Psalms 146 and 2 in the corporate prayer that the people raised to God in their defense in Acts 4:23–31? How could they have so suddenly and wholeheartedly—"with one accord"—fallen in with such a prayer were it not their private practice to let the psalms guide them in their individual disciplines? Again, in Acts 1:15, we find Peter suddenly interrupting the prayer meeting in the upper room to call for a replacement for Judas. Why did he feel it was so urgent to do this at just this time, when they were in the midst of an intensive period of waiting on the Lord? Could the explanation be that they were praying through the psalter, and when they came to Psalm 109 it struck Peter as important to carry out the requirement of this text before going on?

Today we are used to relying on our own devices in our prayers— prayer lists, prayer cards, prayer formulas, our own memory, and so forth. But God has given us His own prayer list to guide our prayers, the psalms, and generations of Christians prior to our own found these to be a richer source of guidance and substance in prayer than anything they might have been able to come up with. We might begin to regain some of our distinctiveness as a community today if we could learn to pray the psalms with greater consistency and power, allowing God's prayer list to guide us as we come before His throne of grace.

Third, the covenant community of Acts prayed *with intensity*. They were earnest, devoted, determined, and passionate in their prayers. We see this in the use of the Greek, *homothumadon*, literally "with one passion," in Acts 1:14, 2:46, and 4:24. These were prayers from the heart, prayers with conviction. We can imagine much impassioned pleading with God, tears of joy and expectation flowing down the people's cheeks, many crying out with intensity before the Lord for His will to be made known in the midst of His people. These were hardly the reticent, reserved, "take your turn" kinds of prayers that we are familiar with in seasons of corporate prayer in our churches today, where only the predictable few ever feel inclined to join in.

What a contrast from the dispassionate, formal prayers we are used to hearing in our churches today, or the neatly scripted offerings to God that so many congregations have gone to in an effort to make the liturgies as smooth and professional as possible. It is hard to imagine that there would have been in the prayers of these first Christians any of the triviality—"Lord, we really just praise You," "bless us, Lord"—that characterizes so many of our prayers today. Theirs were prayers filled with passion, out of hearts circumcised and strengthened by the indwelling Spirit of God. Oh that such passionate prayers might erupt among the members of the covenant communities of the Lord today!

Prayer was central to all the important developments and routine practices of the early church. We find the covenant community turning to prayer at critical moments in its experience. During times of crisis and need, in the face of persecution, and before the beginning of significant new ministries (Acts 6:7; 12:5; 13:1–3), the members of the first covenant communities resorted to the foundation of prayer, keeping their focus before the Lord as a community and devoting themselves and their needs to Him. And we can believe that these prayers were just as passionate, just as frequent, and just as saturated with the promises of God's Word as those we have examined above.

We will not know the power of covenant distinctiveness until we begin to recover this most important plank in our ecclesiastical foundation. Prayer is the basis upon which everything in the life of the church goes forward. *Without more prayer, more passionate and corporate prayer, and prayer more in keeping with the guidelines of God's Word, we cannot hope to regain our distinctiveness as a kingdom of priests unto the Lord.*

(2) *The Word.* The second plank in our foundation as a covenant community is the Word of God. Not only in their prayers, but in all other aspects of life as well, the first Christians were devoted to Scripture and to living out the commands and realizing the promises of God's covenant Word. We see them, for example, in Acts 2:42ff. "devoted"

(NIV) to the teaching of the apostles. What can this mean? Certainly we can expect that they were *faithful in attendance whenever the apostles were opening the Word of God*. They met to hear the Word both publicly and in private homes (cf. Acts 20:20). But they also took the Word of God to heart, thinking it through and embracing it as their very life (Acts 17:11). They allowed the Word of God to shape their outlook, inform their hopes, bring them to repentance from sin, guide their daily walk, and transform them increasingly into the very image of Jesus Christ. They appealed to the Word for strength during their times of crisis (Acts 4:23–31). They did not have Scriptures of their own, so their times of being together before the Word must have been just that much more important. They knew what Jesus meant when He said, "The words that I speak to you are spirit, and they are life" (John 6:63).

They heard the Word, and *they proclaimed the Word* (Acts 4:31; 6:7; 8:4). They earnestly desired that others know what they were experiencing as true and life-changing. Their approach to the Word of God was not one of seeking some happy or comforting thought to help them cope with the trials and pressures of life, nor merely of satisfying some supercilious need for doctrinal precision. To them this was a Word to be heard, embraced, loved, and lived, and the first Christians did so passionately and faithfully.

The Westminster Larger Catechism captures something of the spirit with which these first Christians approached the Word of God in its answer to question 160, "What is required of those that hear the word preached?"

> It is required of those that hear the word preached, that they at-tend upon it with diligence, preparation, and prayer; examine what they hear by the scriptures; receive the truth with faith, love, meekness, and readiness of mind, as the word of God; meditate, and confer of it; hide it in their hearts, and bring forth the fruit of it in their lives.

We live in a day when the "famine of hearing" that Amos foresaw has settled on the church like a pall (Amos 8:11–14).[5] We have much preaching and teaching of the Word, but little of the kind of hearing that the Westminster divines prescribed or that the first Christians actually knew. No wonder we do not stand out like a city set on a hill. If we are to regain our distinctiveness as the covenant community of God, we need to recover our passion for the Scriptures, as well as our determination to live to the fullest within the parameters and promises of His covenant Word.

(3) *Godly leaders*. Also supporting the foundation of the covenant community in the dispensation of the New Covenant is the plank of godly leadership, men who were bold in the Lord, trusted Him to guide and care for His people, and labored sacrificially to ground the community in the promises of God's Word.

That this is a work of the Holy Spirit is clear from Acts 2, when Peter, of all people, as we might think, in the power of the Spirit, was thrust forward as the spokesman for the new era and preached powerfully and forcefully in the streets of the very city where, only a short while before, he had denied any knowledge of or relationship with the Lord Jesus. Immediately we see the apostles swinging into action, teaching and caring for the new community, making sure that all are as grounded as fully as possible in prayer and the teaching of the Word. They were men devoted to prayer and the Scriptures, unwilling to let anything distract them from this central calling (Acts 6:2). They were bold and uncompromising in their witness for Christ (Acts 4:8–13; 6:8–10); firm and effective in dealing with difficulties and challenges within the community (Acts 5:1–11; 6:1–7); and eager to help in raising up more leaders to serve the growing church (Acts 6:1–7).

The apostles clearly understood and wholeheartedly embraced the promises of God's covenant, and they were not shy about impressing the demands of the lifestyle of faith on the people under their care. They knew how to appropriate by faith the power of the kingdom and Spirit of God. They were focused on Christ, the King and Savior of the church, and resolved on the task of strengthening and expanding the church, no matter the cost to them personally. They risked imprisonment and even death to serve the cause of God's covenant as He was unfolding and expanding it in their midst. These were single-minded, courageous, creative, and self-sacrificing men, and God honored their faithfulness in ways of which we today know almost nothing.

(4) *Responsible members.* These three initial planks—prayer, the Word of God, and godly leadership—inspired the fourth, that of responsible church members. Those who entered the covenant community during this first season of the growth of the church did so knowing that they would play an integral role in the realization of God's promises. We see them spending time together, in public as well as in one another's homes (Acts 2:46). We can only speculate on what happened during those times, but, as seems clear, they were given to growing in love for one another, staying alert to one another's needs, and working and praying together to incorporate new members into the community of faith.

These first members of the covenant community *cared for one another in sacrificial ways,* freely giving of their possessions in order to meet the needs that were becoming apparent in their midst (Acts 2:44–45; 4:32–35). The thought of clutching their material possessions, or allowing these to become the driving force in their lives, was far from their understanding of what their kingdom calling required. *They encouraged one another* in the life of faith, in prayer and attendance on the Word and worship of God. They stood ready to *carry the message of the gospel* wherever God might send them, and did so faithfully when the door of opportunity was opened to them (Acts 8:1–4). They were pious, generous, eager students of the Word, devoted to worship and prayer, and zealous in their witness for Christ. The first Christians were a people who had been dramatically transformed by the coming of God's kingdom and the outworking of His covenant in their lives. It is no wonder that more and more people continued to be drawn to the church, given the experience and example of those who had come to Christ.

That first covenant community seems, indeed, to have realized the promise of Psalm 48 and Micah 4:1–5. They were the joy of those around them and carried the Word of God to their neighbors with such zeal and conviction that multitudes streamed up to the house of the Lord to learn from Him.

The lesson seems clear for the churches of the Lord today. Building a healthy, growing church does not so much depend on how we *market* ourselves as on *the kind of foundation* we lay for our lives together in the Lord. Until prayer, impassioned teaching and hearing of the Word of God, courageous and sacrificial leadership, and responsible church membership become the foundations of our own efforts to build the church, we can hope for but temporary and superficial results at best.

The church does not exist to put at ease the citizens of this world, and must not seek to appeal to them on terms designed neither to threaten them nor shake them from their zones of comfort. The call to repentance, piety, sacrificial living, submission to godly leadership, and a life of mission is a drastic, even revolutionary challenge to postmodern men and women. As Robert E. Webber observes, to prospective church members "we need to emphasize the cost of discipleship, the absolute claim of God over our entire life, the necessity of a faith that issues forth in obedience, and our belonging to an alternative culture shaped by the kingdom of Jesus."[6]

Compromising or postponing such a call, or substituting for it an invitation merely to explore the life of faith, presented in a relaxed, folksy, and entertaining manner, is not only to deceive potential seekers concerning the demands of covenant living, but actually to misrepresent the nature of living in God's covenant. That would make it appear not much different from what seekers are familiar with, except a little safer and friendlier under the benign gaze of an all-loving heavenly Father.

If we want to build a covenant community such as we see in the first chapters of the book of Acts, then we must do so intentionally, making certain that, at every step, and in the life of each member, the foundations of covenant living are clearly and firmly laid.

127

THE MISSION OF THE COVENANT COMMUNITY

We may speak of the mission of the covenant community as being bidirectional. It is focused both inward, on the community itself, and outward, on the world.

(1) The *inward focus* of the mission of the church was designed to ensure that churches would grow in strength and purity for the long term. This required, in the first place, that *church members take seriously their callings* as active members of a growing body, that they recognize and begin to develop their gifts for ministry, and that they seek eagerly and earnestly to serve others in the body as expressions of their love (1 Cor. 12:7–11; John 13:1–15).

The idea of church membership as most believers pursue it today would have been altogether unknown, perhaps unthinkable, to those first Christians. That life in God's covenant could consist of nothing more than weekly attendance at a service of worship, together with some meager giving and various kinds of self-interested identification with the community, was neither the way covenant living was presented nor the way it was understood in those early years. Those who came to faith in Christ were called to recognize Him as Lord, as the Master of their lives and Sovereign over all they were and had. He was free to do with them as He wished, having purchased them at the price of His own blood. For their part, they were to devote themselves to knowing Him, communing with Him, sitting under His chosen leaders so that they might be equipped for service, and living faithfully and sacrificially in order that the whole body might be strengthened by the contribution of each member.

When we compare the all-too-often complacent and comfortable congregations that characterize the church today, we are astonished. Indeed, it staggers belief, to see the lengths these first members of the covenant community were willing to go in order to realize the exceedingly great and precious promises God held out to them in the body of Christ. What depths of piety and spirituality they demonstrated! With what spontaneous, generous, and sacrificial love did they give of themselves for the greater good! How bold and insistent they were in the proclamation of the gospel!

Where are the followers of Christ today who will renounce the world and forego their comforts in order to strengthen the weak and needy among them? Where are church members today who are willing to risk safety and well-being for the sake of the kingdom of God? Where are the wealthy believers who will open their homes, not merely for fellowship or Bible study, but as meeting places for the church? Where are the men and women, young and old, who will sacrifice everything for the sake of making the gospel known to the world?

Yes, the first Christians had their problems, squabbles, disputes, and misunderstandings. Yet so readily did they put aside their differences and give up their comfortable lifestyles in order to work together for building up the body of Christ that they laid a foundation and provided an example that enabled subsequent generations of believers to stand firm together in the face of intense persecution and turn their world upside down for Jesus Christ.

The second aspect of the inward dynamic of their mission relates to *their quest for purity in the church.* The situation involving Ananias and Sapphira, related in Acts 5:1–11, is but one example of the way believers held one another accountable for integrity and forthrightness before the Lord. These first Christians understood the need to encourage and admonish one another (Heb. 10:24; Col. 3:16). They submitted to apostolic instructions about not allowing their petty disputes to compromise the purity of the church (Phil. 4:1–7). They sought out godly men to lead them, not merely those who were most successful or attractive according to the world's way of thinking (1 Tim. 3:1–13). And they submitted to such leaders for the sake of the unity, purity, and growth of the entire community (1 Cor. 16:15–16; 1 Thess. 5:12–13; Heb. 13:17).

By comparison, the spiritual shallowness and moral complacency of today's churches is a shameful legacy for the generations who will follow us in claiming the covenant promises of God.

(2) The *outward focus* of the mission of the covenant community relates to its calling to *take the gospel to the world.* The first Christians

understood that this required them to be ready witnesses for the Lord. They accepted the challenge of mission, even to the point of giving up the comforts of home, work, and familiar surroundings in order faithfully to proclaim the Good News of Jesus to others (Acts 8:1–4). So powerful, articulate, and consistent was their witness for the living Christ that it earned them the epithet, "Christian," among their neighbors in Antioch (Acts 11:19–26). In that city, so highly visible were the members of the covenant community, in both their love for one another and their witness for Christ, that, when Barnabas arrived from Jerusalem to check out the reports of kingdom activity there, he could actually *see* the grace of God at work among them (Acts 11:23).

These first believers not only took up the responsibility for being witnesses for Christ, but *they eagerly and generously supported the work* of carrying the gospel to places beyond their immediate communities (Acts 13:1–3). Paul felt no qualms whatsoever about calling the churches on various occasions to join in the work of foreign missions, whether they were established churches he had never visited, such as at Rome, or fledgling congregations still without pastoral leadership, as on Crete (Rom. 15:22–24; Titus 3:13). And the evidence is that the churches responded generously and sacrificially, such that the spread of the gospel continued unabated throughout that first generation and beyond (2 Cor. 4:15).

To look at churches today one could almost get the impression that "mission" means raising and spending money on ourselves, with a little left over for work in some distant land. Little evidence would suggest that mission is the calling of each church member, or the priority above all others of the churches as a whole. Mission agencies and parachurch organizations do the work of mission today, while local churches grudgingly contribute to their efforts from the leftovers of their resources, after they have made certain there is enough to staff and fund the programs and facilities they have chosen to meet their own needs. We have lost or redefined the meaning of "mission" in our churches today, failing to see that we have been blessed of God so that we might be a blessing to all the families of the earth (Gen. 12:1–3). We cannot expect to realize more of the glory of God's covenant promises in our midst until we begin to recover the urgency of mission that characterized the first covenant communities of the Lord.

THE POWER OF THE COVENANT COMMUNITY

It is a constant complaint of contemporary church leaders that the body of Christ has become marginalized, unable to exert social or cultural influence for the gospel of Jesus Christ.[7] The downward moral drift of our society and the continuing erosion of our treasured institutions and values suggest that their complaints are valid: we are not a people who are turning our world upside down for Christ. Instead, we have been told by the world to go stand in the corner and be quiet while they go about the serious business of trying to make the world safe and prosperous. And we have dutifully and shamefully complied.

How different was the experience of those first covenant communities. Their reputation for effecting dramatic change throughout society preceded them by the time the gospel arrived in Thessalonica (Acts 17:1–9). So powerful was their ministry there that the people "turned to God from idols" (1 Thess. 1:9), so completely and convincingly forsaking their pagan ways and practices that word of what had begun to happen among them sounded out throughout the Mediterranean world (1 Thess. 1:5–8). Acts 19 records how large numbers of Ephesians destroyed their occult books, occasioning so much concern among the local idol makers that a near riot ensued. The witness to Christ that these first covenant communities faithfully bore was backed up by dramatic evidence of changed lives. They no longer ran with their unsaved friends in the old, familiar haunts of sin and degradation (1 Peter 4:3–4). Increasingly they learned to use their tongues to edify and console rather than to destroy (Eph. 4:25, 29; 5:4). Their homes became places where love and mutual submission were abundant (Eph. 5:21–6:4). They undertook their work, however tedious or arduous, with praise and thanksgiving to God (Eph. 6:5–6; Col. 3:22–23). Some even set their slaves free as brothers and sisters in Christ (Philem. 15–16). And everywhere, constantly, and with everyone, they manifested a confidence and hope that provoked many to inquire of the reason for their joyous outlook on life (1 Peter 3:15). There could be no doubting that a new power had begun to be unleashed among those who were united in the covenant community.

At bottom, this was the power of love, love for God and for neighbors, the fruit of faithful instruction and obedience (1 Tim. 1:5), love that overcame obstacles and fears to create communities of mutual service and heartfelt devotion to God. Nowhere is this more evident than in the account of the provisioning of the Greek-speaking widows in Acts 6.

Here was a major challenge to the covenant community. A problem had arisen that had the potential to split the community along ethnic or economic lines. Surely the onlooking skeptics said to themselves, "Now we will see how empty and baseless are their claims to be in possession of power from God."

Yet the problem was met and resolved peaceably, in an orderly and loving manner, and the Word of the Lord continued to increase, and great multitudes were added to the church.

Even more astonishing is that we are told that "a great many of the priests were obedient to the faith" after this incident (Acts 6:7). These priests had heard the Lord, and they crucified Him. They heard the disciples and warned them to keep quiet about their faith in Jesus. No doubt they had seen many of their former parishioners go over to the covenant community, and had listened with doubting and jealous ears to their testimonies of new life in Christ. But now they saw something they had never seen or experienced before under their own ministries: a whole community, lovingly attending to the needs of its desperate members, without grumbling or complaining, willingly and sacrificially, as they continued worshiping and growing together. This must have been the straw that broke the backs of many of them, causing them at last to understand that no such thing can happen apart from some supernatural presence and power. This kingdom the apostles had been proclaiming must have been real. Surely God's covenant had begun to be fulfilled, and this Jesus they heralded was Lord and Savior indeed.

In a day such as ours, when churches would rather split than resolve their disagreements in the loving power of the Spirit, and when we allow doctrinal, liturgical, or other differences to separate and divide us, we need to recall what Jesus said about the importance of pursuing oneness in the Lord. Cyprian, bishop of Carthage in the middle of the third century, wrote to preserve the unity of the church against a narrow group of exclusivists who insisted that their view of a particular issue was the only correct one. His words echo those of Christ and stand as an admonition to us yet today:

> The Church also is one, which is spread abroad far and wide into a multitude by an increase of fruitfulness. As there are many rays of the sun, but one light; and many branches of a tree, but one strength based in its tenacious root; and since from one spring flow many streams, although the multiplicity seems diffused in the liberality of an overflowing abundance, yet the unity is still preserved in the source.[8]

Our ability to nurture and experience the unity of the Spirit in the bond of peace, as difficult as that may be to realize at times (Eph. 4:3), is the key to our effectiveness as witnesses for Christ. When the world sees our oneness—our loving forbearance, mutual encouragement, sacrificial ministries toward one another, joint commitment to the essentials of the faith, and observable participation together in worship and ministry—it will believe that the Jesus we proclaim has indeed been sent by the Father for the salvation of men. We have Jesus' own Word on it (John 17:21).

It is to the great shame of churches in the Reformed community, and especially those which profess adherence to the Westminster Confession of Faith, that we, of all the churches of the Lord, are historically most prone to promote separateness from those who do not adhere to every jot and tittle of our peculiar doctrinal distinctives. For, as we have seen, the Confession teaches us concerning our larger participation in the community of faith,

> Saints by profession are bound to maintain an holy fellowship and communion *in the worship of God and in performing such other spir-*

itual services as tend to their mutual edification; as also in relieving each other in outward things, according to their several abilities and necessities. Which communion, as God offereth opportunity, is to be extended *unto all those who, in every place, call upon the name of the Lord Jesus* (26.2, emphasis added).

Note the requirements of our communion: worshiping together, ministering to one another's edification, relieving one another in outward needs. And note well the single qualifier for pursuing this communion of the saints: that it is to be extended to all those who call upon the Name of the Lord Jesus Christ, regardless of how strange, deficient, or, in some cases, wrong their doctrinal views or practices may otherwise be. Calvin argued that we must hold fast to the fundamentals—which he defined as "God is one; Christ is God and the Son of God; our salvation rests in God's mercy; and the like"—without allowing differences in our views of the nonessentials to create schism among us. He recognized that "among the churches there are other [besides the fundamental] articles of doctrine disputed which still do not break the unity of faith."[9]

Perhaps he should have written, "*ought* not break the unity of faith." Reformed Christians, confident as we are of our doctrinal precision and perspicacity, ought to be the most aggressive and most tolerant in pursuing such communion with other churches. We are the members of God's covenant community with the clearest and most profound convictions, and, as Paul Tournier reminds us, "Tolerance is the natural endowment of true convictions."[10] What does our characteristic *intolerance* say about the degree of our "true convictions," much less about our love for the body of Christ and our commitment to our own doctrinal standards?

The early Christians understood that they had to work together to iron out their doctrinal differences and reach fundamental agreement on the essentials of the faith (Acts 15). They also participated in the nurture of a worldwide communion of churches that readily and generously came to one another's aid in times of need (Acts 11:27–30, etc.). The power that called them together also bound them together, and spoke volumes to the watching world concerning the reality of God's kingdom and the beauty of His covenant.

The covenant community today will never be a force for change or a power to be reckoned with so long as we persist in our course of ecclesiastical self-interest and indifference—even hostility—to other communions that are different from us. Jesus Christ broke down the dividing walls that separated the members of His first covenant communities (Eph. 2:14). Why are we so eager and so persistent in discovering new dividing walls and erecting them with such resolute determination against others who call upon the Name of the Lord Jesus? The power of love must flow over, around, and through all such barriers to enable us to pursue oneness in the Lord as we work out our love for Him and for one another in the power of the Spirit and according to His Word.

The church of Jesus Christ—His covenant, kingdom people—is called to nurture a oneness that will declare to the watching world the reality of the Spirit's power and the Savior's love. For this to occur we need to reassess our priorities and commitments. We need to return to our true foundations, rediscover Christ's mission, and work together to demonstrate the power of love in more energetic and creative ways. Only thus will we be able to persuade the world around us that what we profess about new life in Christ is really true.

QUESTIONS FOR STUDY OR DISCUSSION

1. How would you assess the state of the spiritual foundations of your church—prayer, the priority of the Word, etc.? On what do you base your assessment? How would you describe the state of these things in your own life?

2. In what ways is your church involved in the mission of the Lord? What does that involvement require of the members of your church? Would you describe their participation as active, spontaneous, a first priority, and effective? Why or why not?

3. What kinds of the things tend to get in the way of Christians making the pursuit of Christ's mission their first priority? Why do

we allow this to happen? How can we begin to recover the priority of mission in our churches?

4. What about the churches in your community? Do they express the oneness of Christ in any ways? Why or why not?

5. It seems clear that the world around us is not becoming more and more "Christian." Why do you think this is so? What would it take for the churches in your community to become the "joy of the whole earth" to your lost neighbors and friends? What should your role be in helping to encourage that?

the local militia drilled, gaining familiarity with the use of firearms, learning the discipline required to defend the town, standing review by their officers, and reinforcing their commitment to one another for mutual assistance and defense.

Worship in the covenant community is in some respects like a bivouac on the community green. We come together to submit ourselves to review under the loving scrutiny of our Sovereign General. We study and practice the use of the weapons of our warfare. We receive our marching orders concerning how we must carry on the conflict in the week ahead. And, by encouraging and affirming one another, we strengthen the bonds that unite us and deepen our resolve to stand together in the battles that lie ahead, confident that our General will never fail us, that His kingdom will know no end, and that we shall ultimately prevail.

Worship equips us for the spiritual warfare none of us can escape, and helps us more than any other aspect of the life of the church to be prepared to serve the Lord "in season and out."

This is not the place for a thorough investigation of the subject of worship.[2] Rather, my purpose is to provide some general comments concerning worship that can help us to see how it fits into God's covenant plan and so that we may assess our own practices of worship in order to determine the extent to which they are in conformity with God's desires for us. For the remarks that follow we will allow the Lord Himself to teach us, as we find Him instructing the covenant people on the subject of worship in Psalm 50.

THE GOD WE WORSHIP

There has been a tendency in recent years to make God smaller and more intimate than is perhaps healthy. As Robert E. Webber notes,

The recent emphasis on sensitivity, community, and getting to know one another, which certainly has its good qualities if developed within the total framework of the nature of the church and of the Christian's relationship to God, often leads to "warm fuzzies." Suddenly, God is no longer "the Holy One of Israel"; God is no longer the God of judgment, whose holiness inspires fear and awe, but just our buddy, our pal, our friend.[3]

We encourage people to come to our churches to find a place where they can "feel right at home," "have their needs met," or "become part of a caring family of God." They will be loved and received, we assure them, because God is love, and He wants us to come to Him just as we are, warts and all. "You'll find a friend in Jesus," we tell them. Thus our way of introducing them to the Lord lays a foundation in their minds of how to think about Him *that can color all their interest in and experience of church life from that point forward.*

In Psalm 50 God makes it abundantly clear to His people that, while He certainly loves them and holds them in high regard, He is not a Deity to be trivialized or trifled with. He is able to summon all the earth to attend to His business (v. 1). He is the Perfection of Beauty, rising up in the midst of His people (v. 2).[4] He comes to meet His people in devouring and purging fires (v. 3). He assembles the hosts of heaven to witness as He does business with His people (v. 4). He comes to them as Judge (v. 4).

This is a terrifying picture of God as immense, almighty, absolutely holy, and resolved on a course of judgment against all offenders. Hardly the picture of God that we tend to hold in mind or present in our seeker-friendly efforts at outreach. *Yet this is the way God presents Himself to His people.* This is how *He* wants them to think about Him as they come into His presence for worship. He wants them to tremble under His might, bow before His holiness, and shrink under His judgment and power. He wants them to "rejoice with trembling" (Ps. 2:11) before Him. If they do not fear Him, do not tremble before His awesome power and dread His perfect judgment, how shall they be able to appreciate the grace and mercy He has shown them in His covenant? If they do not understand what they have been rescued from—His terrible wrath against their sin—how shall they be sufficiently grateful so that they may serve Him with willing hearts as redeemed sinners? If they are not terrified at the prospect of His judgment, what will motivate them to implore others to be reconciled with Him? If they do not see Him as sovereign over all created things, how shall they learn to trust Him for their daily needs?

What a tone to set for coming before the Lord in worship! Today, when most of our worship services begin in chatty conversation, snappy praise tunes, or myriad and often trivial or humorous announcements from the pulpit, we need to recover a clear view of the God of the covenant as we come before Him in worship. We do not come together so that He might enter among us and do something nice or comforting or encouraging to meet our needs. We come together as the covenant people of the God who spoke the world into being and upholds it by the Word of His power; who washed out the peoples of the earth in the wrath of the flood; who delivered His own people by mighty acts of redemption from the mightiest nation on earth; and who brought back His Son from the dead for our justification and life. We need to see God in His awesome power and might and tremble before Him, even as our hearts fill with joy to be assembled in His covenant-keeping presence once again.

This should speak to us subjectively as well as objectively as far as worship is concerned. Subjectively, God's self-revelation in Psalm 50 demands that *we prepare our hearts and minds to come before this kind of God in worship*. What do we think about as we are getting ready for church, as we drive or walk there, and as we enter the sanctuary to prepare for our meeting with Him? Are we fixated on our own needs, on who's wearing what, or some other mundane and trivial matter? Or do we set our minds and hearts to contemplate the exalted God, the almighty Father who chose us, the Son who has redeemed us, and the Spirit by whose power we have been brought into covenant relationship with God? How we prepare for worship will in many ways determine what we experience in worship. If we go expecting to meet with God as He reveals Himself in His Word, we shall be much more likely to know His presence and be filled anew with awe, wonder, and love for Him throughout the service that follows.

Objectively this gets at how *we begin our service of worship*. What is going on in the sanctuary prior to worship? Are people allowed simply to mingle and chat, laughing and greeting one another as they take their seats or wander about the hall? Or are they encouraged to enter quietly and prepare in silence to meet with God? Of what do the first elements of worship consist? Are they designed to put the worshipers at ease or merely accommodate latecomers? Or have they been specifically chosen to set a tone for worship consistent with the awesome person of Him into whose presence the congregation is about to come?

I shall never forget my experience of worshiping in one Presbyterian church in Virginia some years ago. Without a preliminary word the pastor and musicians began to lead the congregation in songs of praise and adoration to God, songs that, as I recall, emphasized the attributes of God and various ways that He had shown His lovingkindness to His covenant people. As we stood to sing, there were no hymnals or songbooks, no overhead projector, nor any other printed expression of the words. Yet the congregation—mostly young couples and their children—moved easily from one song to the next without hesitation or stumbling. I later learned that these "songs of ascent" had been recorded (by permission of the copyright holders) and distributed on cassette to all families, who were taught to work together to learn them and to use them in their times of family worship as well. Doubtless many of these families played these cassettes or sang these songs as they prepared to come to church.

Then the pastor stepped to the pulpit and read the call to worship: "Oh come, let us worship and bow down; / Let us kneel before the LORD our Maker" (Ps. 95:6). At that, every person in the room—except one—fell on his or her knees on the floor, *and stayed there* while the pastor invoked the presence of God's Holy, life-giving, worship-enabling Spirit among them. I looked around (after I also knelt) and saw no frivolity among any of the people of any age. Everyone seemed sincere and spontaneous in devotion to the Lord. While I do not recommend this practice as normative for all churches, it does say something, I think, about the care with which the leaders of this particular church instruct their people to prepare for and enter into the worship of God. Each congregation of God's covenant people needs to review this aspect of its worship, for it will have such a strong bearing on everything else we do in our time together before the Lord.

WORSHIP OUR HIGHEST CALLING

Immediately upon coming into the presence of God the people are reminded of the fact that *worship is our highest calling from God*. To what other activity, for example, does God call all His people together at the same time (Ps. 50:5)? Note how this call to worship carefully delineates its object: "My godly ones" (NASB); "Those who have made a covenant with Me by sacrifice." Worship is for those who have entered into God's covenant through the sacrificial blood of Jesus Christ, and who sincerely follow Him in the life of godliness. God seeks such people to worship Him.

Indeed, it seems almost that God is offended by the presence among His people of those who have no such relationship with Him. Verses 16–22 of Psalm 50 are specifically directed to those who show no evidence in their lives that their profession of covenant relationship to God—whether in the songs they sing or in the prayers or confessions they make in worship—has any legitimacy at all. He is clearly angry with them, warning and rebuking them, pointing the finger and threatening them for their cavalier approach to the life of faith. "What right," asks the Lord, do such people have to take His covenant on their lips in such ways as these?

So important is the work of worship that God has taken care to prescribe the forms that we are to use in approaching Him. We are not free to worship God any way we please, as the sons of Aaron tragically discovered (Lev. 10:1–3). Rather, God has made known to His people what forms they should use in worshiping Him. These include offerings, songs of praise and thanksgiving, confessions of faith, prayers, and the proclamation of His Word. In approaching the people in Psalm 50 God comes to judge them, and His judgment is directly related to their practice of worship. But not their use of the prescribed forms. Concerning these God says, "I will not reprove you" (v. 8).[5] Apparently, in the outward forms and elements of worship, God's people were in complete conformity to His requirements. This was not the reason for His judgment against them, as we shall see.

That worship is the highest calling of the church can also be seen in that God comes personally to reprove His people for their failure in this work. We often hear God denouncing His people for failing to carry out their duties in such areas as, for example, the giving of alms. But in no other area do we see Him convoking an assembly of the entire church in order to take them to task for failing to worship Him as they ought. We need to recognize that there is a right way to worship God, and that failing to adhere to this way brings our church into serious jeopardy with God. While He may not come to meet with us, as is depicted here, He may withhold His covenant blessings and promises from our congregation until this most foundational of our covenant callings is more in accord with His pleasure.

Finally, we should be impressed with the high calling that worship has in the covenant community by a consideration of the fact that God scrutinizes our worship carefully. As we shall see, He not only considers whether the proper forms are being used, but whether our hearts are truly engaged and our lives outside of worship lend credence to what we are doing when we are assembled before Him. We may not always take worship seriously. It is all too easy to go through the motions of a familiar liturgy, singing well-worn hymns, allowing our minds to drift during prayer or the sermon, and giving but a pittance of our earnings to the work of the kingdom. In all these things we may, by our regular attendance and (albeit meager) participation, consider that we have rendered our due to the Lord.

But we need to remember that He looks much more deeply into our involvement in worship, seeing it from the inside and in the context of our entire lives. If worship is that important to God, perhaps it should begin to be so for us as well.

Worship in the Covenant Community

Then what is God looking for in worship? He makes His desires plain in this wonderful psalm of Asaph. (1) He is looking to see that *the prescribed forms for worship are all properly in use.*

There is a logic to worship, and this logic includes the use of prescribed forms in a reasonable arrangement, such that our coming before the Lord honors Him properly and allows us to fulfill all that this work requires of us. I have sat through too many services of worship in churches of all kinds of denominations in which this or that prescribed element of worship is omitted, inserted at an illogical place, or given less prominence than it deserves. In many churches, for example, immediately following the opening hymn, the congregation unites in the Lord's Prayer, which, while it contains an opening word of praise to God, is primarily a litany of requests. Does it seem logical, immediately after coming into God's presence, to begin plying Him with *our* wants, imploring Him to meet *our* needs? Would that not seem better suited to a later place in the service?

Some churches omit any confession of sin. In others the prayers are shorter than we might expect, or too narrowly focused. Some churches take the offering after the sermon, as though, having heard what God has to say to us, we will now decide how much that word was worth!

(2) We need to keep in mind that *worship is primarily a matter of our pleasing God, and not the other way around.* That God can be pleased with the worship we offer Him is clear from Psalm 50:23, where we are told that we can, indeed, honor the Lord, and to such a degree that He is willing to unfold more of the riches of His salvation to us. Think of it! Puny creatures such as we, whose lives are no more than mere breath, who are sinful throughout and spend most of our conscious moments in crass self-seeking (Pss. 8:3–4; 39:5; Rom. 7:18–19)—miserable creatures such as we can actually honor the God of heaven and earth! Astonishing! Unbelievable! Yet, wondrously true! *This* is what we should be striving for in our worship. To exalt the Name of God. To pour out our hearts in adoring praise and thanks to Him. To hang on His every Word, give all that we can to the work of His kingdom, and bear our souls in resolute trust before His throne of grace.

Yet how many of God's covenant people actually do this? Is it not more often the norm that people come to the service of worship, not primarily for what they have prepared to pour into it, but for what they hope to get out of it? For too many, worship is looked at as a time when

God is expected to do something for them. The duty of worship leaders, choirs, and pastors is to put on a good enough show to send us away satisfied, content, feeling good, or, at least, not offended. When we sense that our service is not delivering the goods, we begin to tweak or adjust it, updating here, dropping this, reviving that, shortening in another place, or trying to add more congregational representation here or there. We are like the proverbial fanatic who, having lost sight of his goal, simply redoubles his efforts. The sooner we get it in our minds that worship is not primarily for *us*, but for *God*, the greater is the likelihood both that we will actually honor God with our worship and that we ourselves will be richly blessed as a result.

(3) We need to see that *worship is primarily a matter of the heart*. While external forms matter, and while we should make careful study and prepare diligently to ensure that the proper forms are present in our worship, without hearts fully engaged and committed to God, those forms will be less than meaningless. Indeed, they could become a source of God's chastening upon His people, as in Psalm 50.

In verses 14 and 15 this "inward" aspect of worship is made clear. First, *worship requires a heart of gratitude*. God calls such thanksgiving a "sacrifice." It should cost us something—thoughtfulness, time, spoken words, renewed commitments, even the denial of our feelings (if we do not feel thankful). Indeed, the Scriptures call us to give thanks in everything and at all times (Phil. 4:6–7; 1 Thess. 5:17–18). The ideal seems to be that we *devote ourselves constantly* to giving thanks to God, day in and day out, in all our activities, for all our concerns, in every situation and circumstance into which the Lord brings us. After we have spent a week in such continuous thanksgiving, we then come together with the rest of God's people and rehearse our thanks and praise before Him together. The atmosphere of worship should be so filled with praise and thanksgiving, in so many different ways, from so many different people, that there should be no doubt in anyone's mind that this is our primary reason for being together. With such heartfelt expressions of thanks, God will surely be honored and pleased.

Second, we note that *God calls us to pay our vows to Him*. Remember all the vows you have made to God? Marriage vows—for better or for worse, for richer or for poorer, to love, cherish, and honor till death us do part? Church membership vows—to study to preserve the purity and peace of the church, to support her work and submit to her leaders? And all those private promises you made to God in rash moments of gratitude or desperation?

God takes our vows seriously. Solomon tells us it is better not to vow than to make a vow we have no intention of fulfilling (Eccl. 5:4–5). Vowing falsely or in a merely perfunctory or pragmatic manner, or failing to carry out our vows, are indications of a heart not fully committed to God. Such a heart makes God angry and can lead Him to sow confusion, chaos, disruption, distress, or disappointment into your life until you get your act together and bring your heart into line with His (Eccl. 5:6).

As we gather to worship, God is scrutinizing our outward behavior in the light of what He sees in our hearts. And, if we are not fulfilling our vows, He is less than honored by whatever we may outwardly be doing for Him.

Third, God can see that our hearts are fully committed to Him *when He is our first line of appeal in times of trouble or distress* (Ps. 50:15). How do we typically react to trials, disappointments, sudden emergencies, or pressing needs? Many people start by either complaining, worrying, getting angry, or casting about for some quick fix of the problem. Their hearts, you see, are wired to look to their own resources and wiles in order to restore their suddenly disrupted sense of peace. God says our hearts will be right when we turn first to Him, and when we call upon Him—asking, seeking, knocking, importuning Him at all hours and by every means—and when we look to Him to meet all our needs according to His riches in glory by Christ Jesus. When our hearts are truly dependent on Him, He will meet our needs. This does not mean that He will meet them in the way that we might have hoped or expected. But, in some altogether perfect and perhaps surprising way, God meets the needs of those who trust Him from the heart, allowing them to know His perfect peace and overcoming joy in the midst of every situation and circumstance of life.

During our worship, God is looking to see if we trust Him. If we do not give Him the tithe that He requires, either because we have spent most of our money on ourselves or we fear we might not have enough money to meet our needs, how can He see that our hearts are fully trusting in Him? To Him it will no doubt appear that we are trusting more in money than in Him. If we do not concentrate during the sermon, asking God to make His Word clear and to show us how to apply His truth to our own lives, how will God see that we actually trust in Him and His Word? In all the forms of worship God is looking on the hearts of His people in order to see if they trust in Him and will call upon Him for all their needs.

Fourth, the inward aspect of worship is seen in *how we are to respond to God's covenant care of us*. God intends that we should "honor" Him (v. 15 NASB). The Hebrew verb here has the sense of "being heavy" or "weighty." It is the same root from which the words "glory" and "glorify" come. We honor—or glorify—God when we make His presence heavy or weighty to everyone around us. We honor God by the manner of our lives, by the words we speak, and by the interests and passions we pursue. Honoring God is nothing other than glorifying God, which is the reason for which He has called us into His covenant in the first place. Honoring or glorifying God must begin in the heart, or it will be merely superficial, whatever form we try to give it. Truly to honor God at all times, in every situation, and before all people, is the goal of our covenant calling. But it must come from the heart.

(4) A final aspect of worship in the covenant community is disclosed in this psalm. We have seen that worship uses particular forms, that it is focused on pleasing God, and that it is above all an inward or heartfelt labor. The fourth element of covenant worship is that *it seeks the salvation of God* (v. 23). God desires to bestow His salvation on His people, to bring them to redemption through Jesus Christ and to deepen their daily experience of His saving and sanctifying mercies (John 17:17). Worship is the primary arena in which we may drink more deeply of God's salvation, have our vision and grasp of it enlarged, bask more wondrously in its radiance, prepare more dili-

gently to lay hold of it, rejoice more completely in the reality of it, and learn to appreciate more fully and consistently its final outworking in glory.

Worship among the members of the covenant community must therefore be decidedly Christocentric and Trinitarian. Jesus Christ must be the focus of our worship. Worship should rehearse all aspects of His saving work—incarnation, obedience, sacrifice, death and resurrection, session and intercession, return. Worship should invoke and draw on the power of God's Spirit to make that salvation real. It should praise and honor the Father who designed this saving plan and is unfolding it to us in His kingdom. Preachers must preach Jesus, no matter what the text or topic of their sermon might be, relying on the Spirit of God to work the Father's transforming grace into the lives of their hearers. And we must go away from worship with new insights into God's promises, new hope for a greater experience of His saving mercies, and new plans for living in His covenant during the week to come as obedient servants of King Jesus.

God desires for us to know more of His glorious salvation. When we worship Him according to His forms, in a manner designed above all to please and honor Him, and out of hearts filled with gratitude to and trust in Him, we can be sure that He will open up the riches of His grace in ever more glorious ways to the community of which we are a part.

WORSHIPING GOD IN HIS COVENANT

Some final words of application are perhaps in order here, since, undoubtedly, much of what has previously been discussed will be new or different for most readers. How may we begin to worship God in His covenant as He intends?

(1) We must strive as a people to *become more informed* about the meaning, nature, and practice of corporate worship. Few churches teach their people to worship. Few worship leaders teach *as* they lead in worship. In the churches of God's covenant community we seem to believe that worship is more *caught* than *taught*. Where did we get such a foolish notion? If we are to learn to worship God, and if we

are consistently to worship Him as He desires, we shall have to devote ourselves *in an ongoing manner* to the study of worship. This we can do through Bible studies, Sunday school classes, sermon series, books, and other resources. But it must become a burden of all the members of God's covenant community to learn to worship Him as He intends.

Suppose there were suddenly a dramatic overhauling of the tax system in America, with annual updates and renewals, *and with the promise that, if we were sincere, careful, and diligent in paying our taxes, we would actually get back much more than we ever put in!* Which of us would not head down to the bookstore to get the first edition of this new plan? We can envision study groups organizing in every community to help citizens get as much as possible of what was coming to them. Newsletters and Websites would spring up everywhere. The air would be filled with excitement; we would sign up for courses under tax gurus in order to learn how most to benefit from this new system that, yes, would take some effort to learn, but that promised so much if we were faithful and diligent.

Compare this with our approach to worship. Enough said?

(2) We need to work harder at *making sure that our services of worship are as complete* as they should be. Worship planners and leaders need to prepare carefully each week and to include in each service the forms of worship that God is seeking in an order that makes sense according to the purposes of worship. Worship services should be reviewed by those who planned and led them in an effort to ensure that what was carefully planned was faithfully executed. It is very easy to overlook, omit, minimize, or simply avoid some aspect of worship—confession of sin, say—because we just had a feeling we might offend someone, the announcements went too long, or we didn't want to cut into the time allotted for the sermon. Do this often enough, without taking the time to review the service of worship, and soon you will begin leaving it out in your planning altogether. After all, you will reason, we haven't done this for a number of weeks now, and nobody seems to have noticed. Let's just leave it out altogether.

You can be sure that God will notice. Study to know the forms of worship that are pleasing to God, and consider how to arrange them in the most logical way in order to help worship be a true dialog between God and His people that progresses in a decent and orderly manner (1 Cor. 14:40). Your worship will be richer and more God-honoring to the extent that it is more faithful to God's requirements.

(3) We must *carefully examine the state of our hearts in worship*. In my experience there is nothing more conducive to serious self-examination in worship than silence. Yet the trend in worship services today is to fill up all the time with some kind of activity—music, testimonies, skits, talking on the part of leaders. Little time is given for the people of God to sit in silence before Him as He searches their hearts and leads them to examine the condition of their souls before Him. There are plenty of opportunities to introduce time for silent meditation, prayer, or reflection in the liturgy: as part of pastoral prayers, preparation for offerings or the preaching of the Word, response to the preaching. Our problem is that we simply are not willing to take the time. Keep it moving, don't let it drag, keep them focused—this seems to be our attitude toward the liturgy. Yet if in worship God's people have come to do business with Him, to commune with Him, hear Him, and be transformed by Him, surely they will need some time in that concentrated context for His Spirit to minister within and among them in extended periods of silence.

(4) Finally, we should work to *make sure that our worship of God leads to mission in His name*. If in worship we have come to express our love for God, in obedience to the great commandment, then our response must be to go forth into our daily lives to show His love to our neighbors as well. Thus we will fulfill all that the Law and the prophets require of us (Matt. 22:34–40). Many elements of the service of worship can be brought to bear on this challenge. The prayers, offerings, selection of hymns (particularly the hymn of response to the sermon), confessions of faith, and, of course, the sermon itself all lend themselves to pointing the congregation beyond the walls of the church and this season of joyful gathering to a dying and needy world around us. In worship God shows us His salvation and enriches our experience of His grace (Ps. 50:23). He does this in order that, as Paul says, the grace we have experienced will spread through us to

more and more people (2 Cor. 4:15). Thus will our calling in God's eternal covenant realize its end, as the nations and peoples and families of the earth are blessed by God through our ministries to them (Gen. 12:1–3). And thus will His kingdom make progress and His church be built as we wait for the return of our glorious Lord from heaven.

Let's not allow the worship wars to wear us out or divide us as we seek to recover a clear understanding of what *God* is looking for in our worship. By focusing on Him instead of ourselves or the lost people of our community, we are more likely to settle on an approach to worship that will help us to express our distinctiveness as His kingdom people, and draw us more fully into His exceedingly great and precious covenant promises.

QUESTIONS FOR STUDY OR DISCUSSION

1. On a sheet of paper, write out a typical order of service for your church. Beside each element, write a brief sentence explaining what this part of the service of worship intends to accomplish.

2. To what extent is it apparent in your church's worship that all three of the Persons of the Trinity are in view? How is that expressed during the service?

3. Why do you suppose God puts such emphasis on the *inward* aspects of worship—our hearts? How can you tell when your heart is fully engaged in worship? What kinds of things tend to get in the way of that?

4. How would you assess your own understanding of the purposes and elements of worship at this time? If you were present in the congregation that first heard Psalm 50, which of the lessons of that psalm would speak most pointedly to you?

5. How can Christians encourage one another to a deeper and more meaningful approach to worshiping God? What might church leaders do? What can we do for one another?

10

COVENANT LIVING IN
A POSTMODERN WORLD

Therefore, since Christ suffered for us in the flesh, arm yourselves
also with the same mind, for he who has suffered in the flesh has
ceased from sin, that he no longer should live the rest of his time in
the flesh for the lusts of men, but for the will of God.—1 Peter 4:1–2

A POSTMODERN CREED

I believe in Matter the Indestructible Source,
    Fount and Substance of the great Cosmos,
And in Chance, its ultimate correlative, our Governor,
    which was conceived by nothing,
    appeared from nothing,
    was deified by frightened men,
    then, cast aside, was dropped and buried,
    and descended into ignorance.
    Yet in the Enlightened Time it rose again
    and ascended to prominence and rule, indivisibly bound
        to Matter the Indestructible Source.
    From there Chance will come to judge and destroy life
        and hope.
I believe in Whatever Works for Me,
    the freedom of the self,

the brotherhood of the like-minded,
the impossibility of sin,
the destruction of the body,
and the coming age of cold and dark.
Whatever.

As I approached the young couple walking toward me, I was fairly certain this conversation would not go very far. He was tall, dressed all in black, and pierced with rings and studs in as many places of his face as would permit. His hair was spiked and green, and he staggered along, leaning on his companion. She wore a buckskin jacket and black jeans, and had the wan look of someone who had not eaten a healthy meal in many days.

"Excuse me," I began, "would you be willing to help me out by answering a few brief questions on a questionnaire?"

They looked at each other for a moment, then he managed to say, "Sure, why not?"

I explained that I was in the neighborhood taking questionnaires trying to determine people's understanding of and attitudes toward the Bible.

At that she giggled a bit. He stared at me blankly, and I took that as a sign I should proceed.

"OK, then. First, how would you describe your own level of interest in the Bible?" I gave them four choices. They selected "Not at all interested."

"Can you think of anything that might lead you to become more interested in the Bible?"

He affected a stupid grin and said, "Yeah, sure, like if somebody *paid* me to read it." She looked at him with a silly gaze and giggled all the more, steadying him as she did.

I continued on through the exercise until the questions began to be rather more pointed. "What do you understand the Bible to teach concerning who Jesus is?"

At that, suddenly, his eyes rolled back in his head and he mumbled, "Oh, man, I think I'm going to be sick." She stifled a laugh as they turned away and ambled back down the street in the direction they had come. End of questionnaire.

Readers of this book will not often encounter people like this young couple for the purpose of engaging them in a conversation about the Good News of Jesus Christ. But the elementary principles that made this couple so detached, indifferent, self-absorbed, giddy, and flip are at work among people in all levels of our society. These principles—radical self-interest, a carefully chosen group identity, escapism, dedication to living only in the moment, and indifference to issues of ultimate truth—have become the traveling papers of more and more people in our society. Together they express a revolt against the rigid rationalism, blind optimism, massification, and materialism of what is perceived as a dying modernity. They are the ragged banners of postmodernism, which amounts to nothing so much as a widespread, semispontaneous, multifaceted declaration of independence against the disillusionment and despair of the modern age.

It is in such an age as this that this generation of God's covenant people is called to serve Him in His kingdom and through His church. But unless we understand the peculiar nature of the postmodern outlook, we shall have great difficulty making our message clear or helping many of our contemporaries find a secure and happy home within the framework of God's covenant and the family of His people.

Our day calls for mighty men and women, like the mighty men of David. There are giants to be slain, hordes to be resisted and overthrown, lost ground to be recovered, failed hopes to be revived. We have much work to do, and we will need the strength, wisdom, and grace of God to do that work effectively in such a time as this. Most of all, we need a new generation of the sons of Issachar, those mighty men of David of whom it was said that they "had understanding of the times, to know what Israel ought to do" (1 Chron. 12:32).

As we come forth from the worship of God to prosecute our mission in a postmodern world, we must make certain that we understand what we are up against, as well as what that requires of us who would see the advance of God's kingdom and know the fuller realization of His covenant promises. The challenges of covenant living in a post-

157

modern world are great, indeed; however, the opportunity for seeing many people come gloriously and hilariously to a saving knowledge of Christ has perhaps never been greater.

We cannot here go into much detail concerning this strange new worldview that has begun to settle in on our society. That would take another book.[1] Instead, I hope to mark out the broad parameters of postmodern thinking, explain some of its primary characteristics, and then outline some of its effects on our way of life. After that we will look at a comparison of the gospel of postmodernism with the gospel of Jesus Christ and, finally, make some observations concerning what we as God's covenant people should do in order to preserve our uniqueness and make our calling and convictions clear to a postmodern generation.

UNDERSTANDING POSTMODERNISM

Let's begin with a definition: postmodernism is a multifaceted and loosely organized response to the perceived failure of the modernist ideal, which promotes radical individualism characterized by passion and pragmatism. I want to examine this definition in more detail.

(1) *Postmodernism is multifaceted and loosely organized.* We find this worldview being expressed in every nook and cranny of society—schools and universities, the world of business and industry, government, popular culture, literate society, the arts, advertising, even the world of sports. Everywhere you look you are being told to follow your intuitions, be the most that you can be, color outside the lines, pursue the angle that works for you, do what feels good, find your own path, tell your own story, throw caution to the wind, and hope for the best. In the words of John Denver's song, "Sweet Surrender,"

> There's nothin' behind me
> And nothin' to bind me
> To somethin' that might have been
> True yesterday.

It is impossible to point to one particular place or institution that is responsible for the widespread dissemination of postmodern sentiments. Rather, these ideas have arisen over the past generation from all kinds of sources and spokesmen. We may point to some precursors of postmodern thinking—Nietzsche and Heidegger, for example—and numerous contemporary voices—Derrida, Foucault, Rorty, Fish, et al.—but the impetus for postmodernism is more far-flung than this, too much so to be organized or coordinated in any meaningful way. Rather, postmodernism is like the weeds in my garden. Nobody sowed them there, and I'm not exactly sure where they came from. But they spring up all over the place, are of an astonishing variety, are even lovely at first, but threaten to destroy everything that is good and wholesome and worth working for.

(2) Postmodernism is a response to *the perceived failure of the modernist ideal.* Modernism is the worldview that animated Western societies and much of the rest of the world for the past 250 years. To the postmodern mind the promise of modernism has proven to be empty, even dangerous, and society needs to be liberated from these fatal shackles.

Against what, precisely, is the postmodern mind reacting? Four aspects of modernism seem especially to be in the postmodernist's sights.

The first of these is the idea of progress. Fueled by evolutionary thinking and the astonishing achievements of the scientific revolution, modern man began to believe that society and the nations were on an ever-improving path of technological, economical, and political progress, moving closer to the ideal world of peace and prosperity for all. In order to hasten the day of this eschatological vision, modernist thinkers and leaders developed advanced means of production, manufacturing, communications, transportation, financing, education, and social reform, hoping these would better prepare the world for their utopian vision.

Instead, these convictions resulted in two world wars, the Cold War, political stasis and stagnation, educational tomfoolery of an advanced degree, the decay of the great cities, economic inflation, a growing gap between the rich and the poor, economic oppression among underdeveloped peoples for the sake of capitalist gains, political corruption at all levels, and a host of related ills. Postmodernists, in revulsion at the tragic outcomes of the modernist dream, decry all such ideas of progress—whether they are in the form of overarching philosophical, political, or religious ideas ("metanarratives"); increasing materialism; or political power as the last best hope of mankind. The postmodern outlook does not want to think about the future or where it might be going. We live one day at a time, and the main point of each day is not progress toward the future but peace in the present, whatever it takes.

Second, postmodernists rebel against the depersonalization that the modernist idea of progress brought with it. In order to achieve the modern eschatological hope, it became necessary to create assembly lines, mass education, a consumer society, and a powerful media to entertain, inform, and shape the people in the modernist outlook and hope. Brazilian educator Paulo Freire referred to this tendency as "massification," the effect of which is to create unthinking, uncritical, merely passive and responsive human beings. He describes the effects of massification in the world of manufacturing:

> In our highly technical world, mass production as an organization of human labor is possibly one of the most potent instruments of man's massification. By requiring a man to behave mechanically, mass production domesticates him. By separating his activity from the total project, requiring no critical attitude toward production, it dehumanizes him. By excessively narrowing a man's specialization, it constricts his horizons, making him a passive, fearful, naïve being. And therein lies the chief contradiction of mass production: while amplifying man's sphere of participation it simultaneously distorts this amplification by reducing man's critical capacity through exaggerated specializations.[2]

It should be rather easy to see how this tendency translates into such areas as education, popular culture, and the practices of political campaigning and social engineering.

160

Against such massification the postmodernist celebrates individuality, unbounded choice, and complete liberty of conscience. No one should be the lackey of anyone else, forced into some mold or process not of their own choosing, slaves to a clock or a bottom line, good for nothing except to fill a role in the great economic engine of modernist, materialist society.

Third, postmodernism reacts against the tyranny, injustice, and oppression that are the inevitable byproducts of a progressivist outlook and a massified society. Whether these take political, economic, moral, cultural, or psychological form, they are all to be rejected in favor of the free and unfettered individual who has been liberated to find his or her own way in life without fear of having to please anyone else.

Finally, postmodernists reject the primacy of place given to reason, science, and tradition as the best ways of coming to know what is best for ourselves and our society. Science has led us to technological and political disasters, the pillaging of the earth, and the fear of nuclear weapons. Reason can be used to justify any tyrannical or oppressive scheme. And tradition is a weight from the unenlightened past that needs to be deconstructed, reinterpreted, and either discarded or reserved for merely personal use.

In reacting to the perceived failure of the modernist ideal and its progressivist, materialist, rationalist outlook, postmodernism promotes *passion and pragmatism* as central to making one's way in life. Anything that anyone sincerely believes and is honestly able to stand for must have some measure of truth to it. Hence, postmodernism encourages a pluralistic view of truth, insisting that there are many ways of knowing and many paths to happiness and peace. Each person is responsible to discover the path that works for him or her, and then to pursue it with all sincerity of heart, keeping in mind at the same time the pluralistic prerogatives of everyone else.

By promoting an epistemology of passion and an ethic of pragmatism, postmodernists hope to give everyone freedom from modernist restraints to find their own way in life, define their own happiness, chart their own course, and hack their own path. No more mass conformity to some overarching eschatological idea. "Nothin' behind me / And nothin' to bind me / To somethin' that might have been / True yesterday." In reacting to the perceived failure of modernism and its threat to individual identity and freedom, postmodernism seeks to liberate the individual into a world defined by his or her passions and governed by a commitment to "whatever works for you."

But postmodernism is more than just an outrage against the status quo. In place of the views, ideals, and hopes of the modernist ideal, postmodern thinkers have substituted their own agenda and protocols for helping us make our way in life.

CHARACTERISTICS OF POSTMODERNISM

I want to expand briefly on five principal characteristics of the post-modern ideal. Some of these may be traced to one or a few individual sources. Others have simply coalesced out of the intellectual atmosphere to produce a growing consensus of like-minded individuals. I will not make any attempt to provide source documentation for these five characteristics, as my purpose in this section is only to summarize elements of the postmodern worldview in an effort to expand and clarify the discussion begun above.

(1) The first hallmark of the postmodern ideal is *radical individualism*. Each individual is a law unto himself and must be allowed to fashion his existence out of his fondest hopes and dreams, keeping in mind the constraints of living in society and the individualist prerogatives of everyone else. Since there is no absolute truth, and no overarching metanarrative to guide us in life, each of us has to make up his or her own story, find a group that will enable us to actualize that story, then live out our story to the best of our ability.

The problem with this, of course, is that not all are willing to keep in mind the constraints of living in society or the individualist prerogatives of everyone else. So if their story requires them to lie, cheat, steal, or kill in order to achieve happiness, they will feel quite justified in doing so and will find ways to rationalize ("spin") their behavior should they be accosted by indignant victims or an outraged public. Then they themselves will become quite indignant and outraged that anyone would dare to question their freedom to do whatever they thought was right for them to do (and thus, by implication, nobody else's business). Witness the spectacle of the presidential scandals of a recent administration.

(2) Postmodernism promotes a *"deconstructivist" view of truth*. To put this simply, nothing is what it seems; everything is what you make it. Any "text"—to use deconstructionist language—whether a book, painting, event in history, and the like—conveys only so much meaning as the radically free individual chooses to assign to it. There are no universal standards of meaning that apply in every place and time, and the original intention of the author of a text is of only limited use in helping us to discover our own meaning in the words or deeds with which we must deal each day.

Even individual words and ideas have no objective meaning. Everything is up for grabs. When, during the impeachment hearings, President Clinton quibbled about the meaning of such terms as "sexual relations" and "is" before his congressional interrogators, he was revealing the postmodern mind at work, challenging the notion of fixed meanings, asserting the right to redefine terms, and standing firm on his radically individualist ethic.

(3) Postmodernism prescribes a kind of *pragmatic relativism* as the guide to personal and social ethics. Essentially, this means that each of us is free to do whatever we want, as long as we make sure that whatever we do does not inhibit our ability to keep on doing whatever we want. We may like to steal from others. But the present state of society suggests that such behavior is frowned upon. Perhaps this may change in the future. For now, if we are going to steal, we had better be very, very good, or our ability to actualize our ethical preferences and priorities may be seriously constrained.

(4) Or *we should consort with others* who also find meaning in life by stealing, and who can help us to actualize our chosen way of life in a safe and reinforcing context, as, for example, in the film, *Gone in Sixty Seconds*. In order to get help in our difficult quest for a meaningful experience, we must find a group to identify with that can serve to af-

firm our chosen ethic and help us to realize it, at least in part. Our group becomes a society within a society where we can dress like we want, spike our hair and color it green, and pierce every square inch of our body without fear of condemnation or reprisal. Even if our group is just two individuals—like the Columbine shooters—we must be able to find sufficient reinforcement and affirmation to help us take whatever bold stances or drastic measures our chosen ethic may require.

This idea of *group power* is the fourth characteristic of postmodernism. With no overarching metanarrative to guide a society, it is up to smaller groups of individuals to create their own stories. These may be ethnic groups, biker groups, groups of political activists, environmentalists, rock music devotees, or any other type of microsociety that may be formed to help like-minded members find a context in which to pursue their stories. Everything in life and the larger society comes to be seen through the lens of the group's story or worldview. Things that might seem important to the larger society—such as traditions, heroes, and so forth—can conveniently be reinterpreted or simply forgotten within the group, according to its own chosen understanding or need. The current debate over the role of Afrocentric instruction in America's schools is an example of this. Afrocentrists undoubtedly have valid concerns to bring forward for the education of America's children. But when they reinterpret the facts of history—making ancient texts say what they want them to say (deconstructing those texts)—or when they leave out people traditionally regarded by the larger society as of significance for the sake of exalting lesser players on the larger social stage, their group interest runs the risk of unraveling the threads and cords that hold society together.

(5) The final characteristic of the postmodernist outlook is what we might call *sensuality*, or, the primacy of feelings. We have already touched on this. Essentially this is an appeal for such things as sincerity, passion, intensity, experience, and so forth as our primary guides to life. We should not spend a lot of time thinking about things. Instead, we should go with our gut feelings. And we should not allow others to confine, define, or restrain our feelings. That would not be authentic.

That would not be postmodern. The key to happiness is satisfying emotional experience, however and as often as that may be attained.

These five characteristics—individualism, deconstruction, pragmatism, group power, and sensuality—are certainly not the whole of postmodernism, but they lie somewhere very close to its core. Taken together, these principles raise enormous questions and pose huge challenges for our society.

Postmodernism *sows epistemological confusion* into the social order, subverting truth as we have known it. This can be seen, for example, in the growing pressure to liberate school children from any exposure to the Ten Commandments, substituting instead an ethic of "values clarification" as the only viable norm.

Consequently, postmodernism *clouds the issue of what is ethically permissible* in society, deconstructing traditional ethics and values and making every person a law unto himself.

In the process, postmodernism *debunks the authority of tradition*, thus putting in doubt the political views of the Founding Fathers, the meaning of law, the artistic heritage of the Western world, the reliability of religious creeds, and the guidance of parents.

Similarly, postmodernism *undermines notions of beauty and goodness*, making everyone an artist who wishes to be, sanctioning anything and everything in the name of art, and relegating to the dustbin of history the artistic heritage of the race.

Postmodernism *invites social anarchy* to the discussion of public policy, positing the possibility of many and varied moral and social norms and making passé cherished traditions of order, justice, and legality.

And postmodernism *opens the Pandora box of spirituality*, elevating every religion to the throne of heaven and making every individual a priest or priestess on his or her own terms.

These are the kinds of challenges that we in the covenant community will have to deal with in the days to come. There is no avoiding them. They press in on us on every hand. Yet as discouraging or even frightening as postmodernism might appear, there is much we can learn from it about the needs of people in our postmodern world. As Eddie Gibbs has written, "Despite the ultimately self-destructive tendencies of nihilistic postmodernism, Christians need to appreciate the valuable contribution it makes in criticizing modernism, rather than defensively assuming a denunciatory stance."[3]

Unless we understand the times in which we are living, we will not be prepared to take the appropriate actions that will allow us to continue growing in the grace and knowledge of the Lord, laying hold of His rich and glorious promises, building the church, and furthering His kingdom on earth.

THE GOSPEL OF POSTMODERNISM AND THE GOSPEL

It will be of help to us to compare the message of postmodernism point by point with the Good News of Jesus Christ. That way we will at least be able to see more clearly the many and stark differences. As we understand these differences and keep them in mind, we may find that we are better able to love postmodern men and women and to communicate our covenant faith to them in a way that will help them better to understand us.

We will approach this comparison from the perspective of five vantage points: the foundational principle, the concept of the ultimate, the understanding of the chief end of life, the means to that end, and the end of all things (eschatology).

(1) *The foundational principle.* Where do we take our stand in facing the postmodernist with the Good News of Jesus Christ? What is our starting point and touchstone? It is simply this: God speaking to us in His Word. Members of the covenant community believe that God has revealed Himself in His Word, the Bible, and that we are called to bring the whole of our lives under the guiding light of Scripture. We stand on the Word of God and bring every aspect of our lives under its scrutiny for teaching, correction, reproof, and training in righteousness (2 Tim. 3:15–17). We cannot *prove* that God is speaking to us in His Word; however, as the Westminster Confession of Faith points out (chapter 1), the Bible has many good and remarkable credentials recommending its divine provenance, and we believe that the

Holy Spirit of God confirms His voice to us as we approach the study of Scripture in receptive faith.

The postmodernist's starting point is also a faith perspective, no less than ours. He believes, although he cannot prove it, that he must take his stand in life on passionate pragmatism, trusting in gut instinct, strong feeling, intuition, or pure desire, and seeking the best way to actualize his personal story. "I gotta be me," he will say in the face of our saying, "I stand alone on the Word of God." He cannot prove to you that his foundation is reliable and sure. He can only say he hopes so, and that he believes in it passionately and devotes himself diligently to realizing his dreams and desires by every means at his disposal.

Thus it will be clear, from the beginning of our conversation, that our postmodern friends and we look out on the world and the great questions of life from very different points of view. Each of them involves an element of faith; however, from that point on, they part ways radically.

When looked at in this way, it is clear that the confrontation between God's covenant community and the postmodern world is supremely a contest of faith, not unlike that which took place between Elijah and the prophets of Baal (1 Kings 18). Because neither of our perspectives recognizes the ultimate authority of reason, and because neither of us would, even if we did, be able to satisfy the demands of the reason of the other, we will seek to "prove" the truth of the covenant way of life in an entirely different way. Not that we will set reason aside; however, we will not allow reason to be the final arbiter in deciding the question of which view—that of God's covenant or that of the postmodernist—is ultimately more reliable and true. Instead, we will, like Elijah, seek to establish a context or a setting in which God will be free to demonstrate His own existence and claims, powerfully and beyond any shadow of doubt. More on this in a bit.

(2) *The question of the ultimate.* The second point of comparison relates to the question of what is ultimate, or, as Francis Schaeffer might have said, *ultimately ultimate*. For us as members of the covenant community, God is ultimate. There is nothing beyond Him, nothing else

167

like Him, and everything that exists is completely dependent upon Him. He made everything and is infinite and eternal in His being and attributes. He alone is *ultimately ultimate*, and everything that is finds its meaning and purpose in His light.

For the postmodernist the only ultimately ultimate thing is the passionate self, that inner drive or desire that provokes, incites, entices, guides, and moves the postmodernist to action. We may need to push and probe a bit here in order to help the postmodernist see that he is a servant to his self. He lives to define himself, promote himself, actualize himself, help himself, indulge himself, and celebrate himself. The satisfaction of self defines the path of devotion for the postmodernist. He lives to serve himself, as a casual examination of his checkbook and date book would reveal, for he can think of nothing more ultimately ultimate than the fulfillment of his every dream and desire.

Our conversation about the gospel will thus begin with our explaining the God we know, love, and serve. We will invite and, by our gentle questioning, help the postmodernist to explain his own understanding of what is ultimately ultimate; and we will realize, as we listen, that what we are hearing is a reflection of what lies in the heart of the person talking. He is explaining his deepest desires and heartfelt passions and showing us that he is devoted to them above all else. Against his expressions of desire we will want to paint as clear as possible a portrait of God, showing Him to our postmodern friend in all His majesty, holiness, power, greatness, goodness, mercy, and love, being especially careful to indicate ways in which God might be seen to be in fact the fullest and richest realization of our postmodern friend's hopes and dreams.

(3) *The chief end of life.* The third point of comparison builds off this and seeks to identify the chief end of life. Obviously, if we have some sense of the ultimate, we will have some understanding of the chief end of life, and it will be related to that which we have identified as ultimate. For the member of the covenant community, the chief end of life is to know, enjoy, and glorify God, as we have seen. To delight in God and to seek Him; to worship, celebrate, honor, and exalt Him; and to

serve Him in every area of our lives—for the members of the covenant community the chief end of life consists in this.

For the postmodernist the chief end in life is to know, enjoy, and glorify the self, which is only saying the same thing that we say, although the object of the postmodernist's attention is rather smaller. Certainly our postmodern friend will not frame his response to our inquiry in these kinds of terms. But, as we listen carefully to how he answers, we will find that he is, in fact, saying nothing more or less than this. We might like to ask our postmodern friend why this should be so important to him. Why not, upon coming to know the self, rather seek to suppress and destroy it, as, say, in some kinds of mystic traditions? Why not decry the self and hunger for some other-worldly existence that can only be realized through suicide? Would not he himself agree that certain kinds of self-actualization ought to be suppressed? Given that such things as *self*ishness, *self*-interest, *self*-assertiveness, and the like often lead to unhappy social outcomes, could not a case be made for *suppressing* the self instead of *actualizing* it?

We might also like to ask our friend whether he is willing to allow his view to be embraced and enjoyed by all. If so, then do we not run the risk of legalizing the activities of psychotic monsters who may gain political, social, or technological power from time to time? If not, then does he mean to suggest that there is some larger standard above the self to which the self must submit? And what might that standard be? And how does our friend know that standard to be reliable and sure?

(4) *The means to the end.* The fourth point of comparison gets us to the heart of the matter. This relates to the means by which we hope to realize the chief end of life. The member of the covenant community will testify to the grace of God in Jesus Christ overcoming and forgiving his sin, delivering him from the fear of death, liberating him into the newness of life, empowering him to know the Ultimate God and to pursue his life end, and filling his daily experience with purpose, joy, peace, and hope.

Our postmodern friend can only respond to this question by discussing his own agenda and plan, what he is doing each day in order to maximize the satisfaction of the self. We will want to encourage him to talk at length about his activities, the many and varied ways that he, by a passionate pragmatism, seeks to satisfy the demands of the self. We will want him to reflect on the degree of satisfaction he is actually achieving and whether he suspects that this satisfaction is lasting or fleeting. We may wish to raise the specter of unknown or uncontrollable factors from beyond his immediate experience that might threaten or frustrate his dreams, and ask what contingency plans he has in place for such things as theft, serious illness, fickle friends, economic downturn, or other such things. Our purpose will be to help him see that his plan for achieving his hopes has no transcendence to it (or, at best, only an ill-defined and, therefore, uncertain transcendence), depends entirely on his own energy and wit, and is subject to powers and circumstances beyond his control. We will want, in so doing, to accomplish two things: first, to help him see the *inadequacy* and *uncertainty* of his scheme, and, second, to point out to him that those who are in Christ are able to overcome in spite of any or all contingencies en route to an eternal blessedness that begins even in this life.

(5) *The end of all things*. Finally, we broach the question of the end of all things. Where is life going? The member of the covenant community will talk in excited, hopeful, glorious tones of the new heavens and new earth (see the next chapter). The postmodernist can only talk about vague hopes of self-fulfillment; however, he will be forced to admit that, beyond self-fulfillment self-destruction awaits, either in the dust of the grave or in the nondistinct and all-absorbing "all-soul" of much New Age religion. The Christian holds out an eschatology of hope; the postmodernist clings to an eschatology of wishful thinking. As Peter reminds us, it may well be the tenacity and exuberance with which we cling to and express our hope that will make our witness of interest to our postmodern friends (1 Peter 3:15).

As we engage our postmodern friends in conversations on spiritual matters, we will want to keep this comparison and some of these questions in mind. Before the postmodernist will be willing to listen to what we have to say, three things will need to take place. First, he will need to see in us and in the covenant community a way of life that is radically different from what he knows or has experienced anywhere else. Second, he will need to be involved in relationships with individual Christians, so that his view of the covenant way of life will be reinforced from various quarters. And, third, he will need to have his own confidence undermined and shaken to the extent that he is willing to look beyond his familiar framework to consider new possibilities for beginning to make sense of his life.

This last requirement we have touched on in the preceding section and will return to shortly. For now, I want briefly to consider what we in the covenant community will need to do in order to demonstrate the uniqueness and consistency of our way of life, and to begin getting to know some of the postmodern people around us for the sake of extending the blessings of God's covenant to them.

COVENANT LIVING IN A POSTMODERN WORLD

The contemporary evangelical church is embarked upon a project of demonstrating to the watching world that we are a community among whom they can feel right at home. In as many ways as possible, evangelical churches are retooling their programs and practices to make our postmodern neighbors feel comfortable in our midst, to help them to feel as though the church is a place where they can realize their hoped-for but elusive self-fulfillment. In our worship, the kinds of programs we offer, the language and tenor of our preaching, even in our ecclesiastical architecture and décor we are saying to the postmodern world, "Come and see. We're not that different from you. We like what you like. You'll find nothing threatening or fearful here. Come and be a part of a community of people on a journey together to God."

This tack is, I believe, profoundly mistaken and misguided.

We need only consider, as we have already, a few of the many ways that the Scriptures contrast life in God's covenant with life in the lost world to see that God intends His people to be dramatically different from the prevailing sentiments and lifestyles of the surrounding age:

171

dead, alive; darkness, light; blind, seeing; natural man, spiritual man; lust of the flesh, lust of the Spirit; love for self, love for God and neighbors; hardness of heart, circumcised hearts; callous minds, renewed minds; lording it over, serving in love. We are called to be different, that we might no more cater to the lusts of men but fulfill the will of God instead. And though our determination to be a distinctive people may expose us to ridicule, scorn, and hate, we must arm ourselves with this purpose and be prepared to suffer as Jesus did. For we may well hope, by so doing, that we will rightly represent our Savior as His body and members thereof, thus enabling Him more readily to draw into our fellowship those others of His chosen race whom He is calling to Himself in our day.

What does this mean for us as we consider how we must carry out our covenant calling in a postmodern world?

(1) It means we must *become more devotional* in our approach to life. I do not say "more spiritual." Many of our postmodern contemporaries are more spiritual than we, giving themselves with greater fervor to unknown and unseen deities of their own devising, blissfully ignorant that they are playing into the hands of demons who delight in nothing so much as blinding men to the truth of God. Rather, we must cultivate a more devotional way of life. That is, our daily lives must be more evidently rooted and grounded in God and His truth, and we must be more manifestly involved with Him in all our activities.

Postmodern man is looking for authenticity and passion. This is the banner under which he marches and which he will respect and admire. When our postmodern friends look at us, do they see us as authentically rooted in our relationship with God and passionately committed to knowing, loving, and serving Him? How conspicuous and intense is our practice of spiritual disciplines? Is it evident to our contemporaries in the workplace, neighborhood, or school that we are conscious of living before the face of God in all we do, and at all times? Do we seek the Lord throughout the day or merely in the privacy of our homes in the morning or at night? Is our conversation seasoned with the salt of praise to God, wonder at His grace, and wisdom from His Word? Are our joy, peace, and boundless hope evident in all we say and do? Do our lives shine as lights in the darkness? In short, is it clear to one and all that we share the testimony of the psalmist, "You are the God of my salvation; / On you I wait all the day" (Ps. 25:5)?

A more devotional life is a life more intensely focused on God at all times. It derives from a rich and frequent exercise of spiritual disciplines; is evident in our plans and priorities; and comes to expression in our conversation, comportment, and common activities. There must be no misleading our postmodern contemporaries into thinking either that the life of faith is but a part of who we are, a mere category of our existence, or that it does not speak to and prepare us for joyous, powerful, hopeful living in every area of life. We must begin to work harder at becoming a more devotional people.

In Bach's "St. Matthew's Passion," that majestic tribute to the suffering of Christ, whenever the part of Christ is sung, it is accompanied, on all but one occasion—when He is alone on the cross—by an aura of violins, which give shimmering testimony to Christ's devotion and to the presence of God's grace with Him at all times. Just so must our devotion to God be evident to our postmodern contemporaries, not in some contrived or trivial manner, but flowing naturally and richly out of the reality of who we are as devoted members of the covenant community.

(2) We must begin to *cultivate a more missional outlook* on life. Postmodern man is a man on a mission. He works hard, plays hard, relaxes hard—all in a feverish effort to realize his goal of self-actualization. He has little tolerance for laziness, lethargy, or languorous living—unless, of course, these are his mission in life. If we want to identify with our postmodern contemporaries and reach them for Christ, we shall have to show ourselves equally committed to a focused, purposeful life. We shall need to present ourselves as a people with a mission.

Of course, God's covenant intends precisely this: that, being blessed of God, we should strive with all our might to serve as channels of His blessings to the rest of the world. Every waking moment, every relationship, role, and responsibility must be entered into for the purpose of glorifying God and bringing His rule to bear in our lives. We must begin to see that each one of us has been assigned a mission field in which we are to labor as faithful servants, diligently investing our time, talents, and energies in the work of pleasing God and cultivating a harvest for Him.

Sadly, for too many members of the covenant community, "mission" is what "missionaries" do, or what our church undertakes in some specialized program for the very few. We are happy to pray for those who are involved in mission, even to give some of our precious resources toward their support. But we have little sense that our own lives—in our neighborhoods, communities, places of employment, schools, and everywhere else—should be devoted to mission. To our postmodern friends I fear that we appear fragmented, perhaps even schizophrenic, when it comes to the place of faith in our lives.

The mission of the church is to make known the kingdom of God and to call the world to submit to the King, so that they might know the blessings of His forgiveness, peace, and love. Along the way we must be good stewards of all our responsibilities, working with our hands, caring for our possessions, raising our children, and doing our duty as citizens. But too often we see these activities as our primary callings in and of themselves, without any concern for the role they should play in the mission of the church. Church is one part of our lives, and all these things are something else altogether unrelated.

The Scriptures, on the other hand, call us to labor in all these areas as servants of Christ, seeking the glory of God and proving His will for us by lives wholly devoted to the task of making Him known (Col. 3:22–24; 1 Cor. 10:31; Rom. 12:1–2). Thus, we must learn to see the activities and arenas of our lives as staging grounds for mission, our assigned venues and duties for carrying out our kingdom calling in the Lord—our personal mission fields. We do not need to head off to distant shores in order to carry out the purposes of mission. Rather, we need to go wherever we go, doing whatever we do, in such a way that all will see and know that we are at all times enthusiastically and wholeheartedly engaged in endeavors of eternal significance, serving the Lord in the whole of our lives (Matt. 28:18–20; 1 Cor. 10:31).

This is a call to excellence, diligence, thoroughness, cooperative endeavor, service to others, confidence, ebullience, and hope in all we do.

There is no room for mere self-indulgence, petty backbiting or complaining, or just getting by. Whether we are students or homemakers, professional or blue-collar workers, volunteer coaches, charitable workers, or are engaged in any of a myriad of other occupations, let us be seen to be a people on a mission for the Lord, eager to please Him and to serve our neighbors with every ounce of our strength, every fiber in our bodies.

This applies to our churches as well. Instead of investing so much of our time, resources, and energy on activities centered at the church building and designed only for our own benefit, let us begin to push the life and ministry of the church out into our neighborhoods and community. Through house church and shepherding ministries, diaconal activities, reading and study groups, neighborhood outreaches, and other kinds of activities, churches with a clear sense of mission will begin to find ways of establishing a visible, serving presence throughout their communities. Thus they will truly be the church even while they are not actually "at church." Such a manifest sense of mission cannot fail to capture the attention of our postmodern generation.

(3) In order to reach our postmodern neighbors and friends the church today must *learn to be more relational.* That is, we must take the initiative in getting to know others, taking a keen interest in them, bringing them into our lives, serving them, and letting them know by every possible means that we love them as people made in the image of God.

How easy it is to settle into our own little groups and cliques, just like our postmodern contemporaries. There we feel comfortable, safe, and among friends. But life in God's covenant should mirror the life of Him who fulfilled that covenant, leading us, like Him, to seek out new people and to show ourselves genuinely concerned about them.

Our personal mission fields are the place to start. Jesus called us to make disciples (literally) "as you are going" (Matt. 28:18–20), that is, in the normal contexts of our everyday lives, the places we go week in and week out. Our mission fields are filled with people we see all the time. Many of them we do not know at all, some only by name. In a postmodern world, where men and women are prone to settle into their own groups and leave everyone else to the depersonalizing tendencies of lingering modernism, we have an opportunity to show the love of Christ and to shine like lights as we do so. Taking the time to get to know people, asking about their backgrounds and families, entering into conversations with them, providing affirmation and encouragement, and otherwise showing them the attention of a God who surrounds them with lovingkindness day by day will open wide doors of opportunity for us to carry out our mission in ways that sophisticated and expensive church programs cannot.

Here we must pray for the gift of hospitality, cultivate our conversational and listening skills, and study to "be a Barnabas," encouraging and comforting people in every way we can.

At the same time, sponsoring church activities and events in the neighborhoods and throughout the community—back-yard Bible clubs, social activities, study and prayer groups in the workplace, neighborhood care projects, and the like—will put us in touch with new neighbors, allowing us to show them the living presence of the body of Christ in ways they cannot see merely by driving past our church on a Sunday morning.

(4) The church in the postmodern world needs to *become more ministerial*, that is, more committed to serving others according to their needs. This is implied in what we have said in the two previous areas (mission and relationships). Our mission is to make Christ known to our neighbors. In order to do that we have to get to know them, to let them see that we are genuine and sincere and motivated by nothing but love. In such a context we will begin to discover their needs, whether for friendship, help with their children, or just someone to talk to. We will see ways that we can begin to come alongside our neighbors to encourage, affirm, and help them, showing the love of Christ to them at the same time that we are seeking to tell them about His love in the gospel.

Churches who wish to serve their neighbors will begin to make some of their resources available to meet emergency needs in their communities. Perhaps they will discover ways of using their facilities as centers of community activities. Churches can take the initiative in welcoming newcomers to the community; honoring community members for their service; providing family counseling services; offering after-school care for children; conducting community work projects; and a host of other services that will say to the community that we are here for them and for their families.

(5) Our churches need to *become more communal*. Jesus said that we must labor to maintain our oneness in the body of Christ, for this would be the key to our being able to persuade people that He had actually been sent from the Father (John 17:21). But Paul told us this would be no easy task. We would have to work hard to maintain the unity of the Spirit in the bond of peace (Eph. 4:3). As we have previously seen, it is all too easy to leave this important work undone.

This exhortation to unity applies not only to individual congregations but to all the evangelical churches in a given community. We must find ways of spending more time together, making visible our oneness in Christ and learning to delight and to serve together in Him. As it stands, too much of our time is fragmented into worldly interests and concerns—work, recreation, leisure, sports, entertainment, and so forth. Except for Sunday mornings, churches hardly have any consistent, visible time together to strengthen and celebrate their unity in Christ. And it is almost unheard of that local congregations should ever join together for worship, fellowship, or common ministry activities.

So we should not be surprised when we see the world turning away from Christian faith in increasing numbers. We are neglecting the very thing that will attract them most—our unity in Christ. If we could begin to concentrate more—to "work hard," as Paul's words could be translated—on cultivating our unity as members of the body of Christ, we might begin to see our postmodern friends responding to us more favorably. Postmodernists are eager for community. They will be more likely to take seriously our claims about the power of the gospel when they see its power to mold us into a loving, caring, celebrating, and serving community.

(6) If we would capture the attention and the imaginations of our postmodern friends, the church needs to *become more liturgical*. We are not helping the cause of Christ by bringing our worship of God

down to the level of the mundane, evaporating out all mystery and carefully protecting our hearers from anything strange, offensive, or even a little fearful. We must not lead our postmodern friends to think that God is just like them (Ps. 50:21). They need to see Him in His majesty and power; to know that He is our King and Judge; to experience His love, yes, but to tremble in the presence of His holiness as well. Services of worship that are purely informal, filled with chat and good humor and built upon contemporary praise choruses alone cannot accomplish this end. Our worship needs to be dignified, complete, orderly, and profound, and it should draw on the entire heritage of Christian worship, all the rich prayers and hymns and other elements and forms that previous generations found so useful in expressing their praise and adoration to God.

This is not to say that there is no place for contemporary music in worship, or that preachers should be merely severe and didactic in their sermons. It is simply to help us see that, when postmodern men and women wander into our services of worship, they have come for a very specific reason. *They are looking for something more to their lives, something greater than themselves!* And when all we have to show them is that which is familiar to them, what they are already comfortable and at home with, we do not lift their thoughts to consider heavenly matters or challenge them to go beyond themselves and to reach out in faith to God. Rather, we merely confirm their basic self-centeredness and send them the message that religion can be one more good thing to help keep your life together. A more liturgical approach to worship, coupled with a more devotional, missional, relational, ministerial, and communal approach to Christian life, in addition to being more faithful to the purposes of worship, will be far more effective than what we are currently pursuing in drawing our postmodern neighbors to Christ.

(7) Finally, in order to be effective in reaching contemporary postmodernists, the church, and we as members thereof, must *become more eschatological* in our approach to life. I shall wait to unpack the implications of this until the following chapter. Suffice to say at this time, we need to cultivate and foster a radically different outlook on our lives, one grounded in the conviction that God's kingdom is un-

folding to fill the earth, and that we shall be called to give an account of the stewardship we have exercised and the service we have rendered in that grand undertaking.

The postmodern age offers the church of Christ tremendous opportunities to make its message and distinctives clear to the watching world. Let us not make the mistake, either of failing to understand our postmodern contemporaries, or of showing ourselves to be merely like them. Rather, let us work hard, in the love of Christ, to get to know the people around us and to serve them out of the unique context of our covenant relationship to God. Blessed with His goodness and imbued with His power, let us begin more earnestly and aggressively to reach out to those around us, so that the blessings of God may reach and His grace spread to more and more people (Gen. 12:1–3; 2 Cor. 4:15).

QUESTIONS FOR STUDY OR DISCUSSION

1. In what ways have you observed the characteristics of postmodernism this chapter described?

2. Do you find that the interests and concerns of postmodern thinking tend to filter into the church? In what ways? How should we guard against this?

3. What specific activities is your church currently involved in to reach postmodern people? What makes those activities uniquely capable of doing that?

4. In which of the areas of preparation to reach our postmodern generation does your church need to grow? How about you personally?

5. Do you think most Christians see their everyday lives as a "personal mission field"? Why or why not? What difference would it make if they did? If you did?

THE CONSUMMATION
OF THE COVENANT

Since all these things will be dissolved, what manner of persons ought you to be in holy conduct and godliness, looking for and hastening the coming of the day of God, because of which the heavens will be dissolved, being on fire, and the elements will melt with fervent heat? Nevertheless we, according to His promise, look for new heavens and a new earth in which righteousness dwells.—2 Peter 3:11–12

But we must be ignorant of the secret events of things, as touching the time to come; for there is nothing which may make us more slack in doing our duties, than too careful an inquisition herein, for we will always take counsel according to the future event of things; but the Lord, by hiding the same from us, doth prescribe unto us what we ought to do.—John Calvin[1]

I arranged to have lunch with Mark, the owner of the bistro I habitually haunted. Over the months of my enjoying his excellent service and cuisine, we had become casual friends, exchanging pleasantries and sharing conversation over many things whenever I stopped in for lunch. I felt like we were getting to know one another somewhat, but I wanted to spend some time talking with him about deeper, more significant matters than the mere chit-chat that had passed between us.

In the course of our lunch together we talked about many things, including Mark's spiritual life. Raised in a mainline denomination, he had left the church as a college student and never found his way back. Yet he admitted to a belief in God and expressed sincere interest in spiritual things, although he had made little effort to hammer out anything like a personal faith. At one point I asked him to share with me his views about death and whatever might lie beyond. He confessed that he didn't know, and that he didn't really like to think about it. "Why?" I asked. "It's too frightening, I guess. I mean, what if the grave really is the end? Or worse, what if there is something beyond the grave that I'm not prepared for?" It was clear from our conversation that, while Mark did not like to think about such matters, the question of death and what might follow was never very far from his mind.

In our day we are witnessing a renewal of speculative eschatological thinking. Not only among Christians—which we can see in the runaway popularity of "end-times" novels—but on the part of others as well. Secular thinkers such as Francis Fukuyama have gone on record with their views about the end of history and the final state of man. Spiritualists of various New Age stripes proffer personal and cosmic eschatological schemes, some with disastrous consequences, in order to help their followers cope with the difficulties and disappointments of the present. Marxists and other materialist thinkers continue to press their various visions of a secular utopia. And proponents of Islam and Eastern religions are seeing growing interest in their own views of the afterlife.

Postmodern people are inveterately eschatological, whether they will admit it or not. They live in the present, to be sure, but with one eye on the future. Most of them, like my friend Mark, are mindful of the ever-present specter of death, as the writer of Hebrews reminds us (Heb. 2:15). Yet, in the light of that great certainty, their various eschatological schemes amount to little more than wishful thinking concerning how they will contend with the grim reaper.

For, unless they are members of the covenant community, postmodern men and women have no firm ground on which to take their stand against the course of history and to prepare for the end of all things.

Only to those who have come to know Him has God been pleased to reveal anything about the course of history and the afterlife. Among those who enjoy the benefits of God's covenant, their eschatology, grounded in specious notions of a premature rapture of the church, too often promotes a kind of indifference to the world, even an unspoken scorn for those who do not understand the details or heed the warnings of the various end-time scenarios many believers claim to see in the Scriptures.

But, as Calvin points out, God has not been pleased to reveal the explicit details of Christ's return. In the face of our curious and often far-fetched speculations, the Savior advises us, "It is not for you to know." This does not mean, however, that we may have no idea whatsoever of where history is going, or what its denouement shall be, or that we ought not be preparing ourselves in the present against as much of the outworking of God's cosmic plan as we can discover. Indeed, because, as Calvin noted, "we will always take counsel according to the future event of things," we in the covenant community must be diligent to learn as much as we can about the end of history, the outworking of God's kingdom, and the consummation of His covenant.

In this chapter I want to outline a biblical view of the course of history and the consummation of God's covenant. Readers may note a particular bent to this summary of eschatology; however, my purpose is not to promote a specific millennial perspective but to provide a framework for covenant living that will enable us to see our calling as God's people in the context of history and against the backdrop of Christ's imminent return. To that end we will look first at the pattern of history, then at the end of history, and, finally, at the implications of this for living in God's covenant today.

THE PATTERN OF HISTORY

Regardless of one's view of the book of Revelation, the events portrayed in Revelation 12 can be agreed upon by almost all. Here, in the very middle of this great apocalyptic book, is revealed the pattern of history, the framework for all the events occurring in time. A great spiritual struggle is depicted, and it is in the midst of this struggle, and in view of its direction and end, that we in the covenant community must prepare to live faithfully to our God in our own moment of history.

Three critical elements of the drama of history are depicted in Revelation 12, which, together with a fourth suggested in Revelation 20, can help us to think about what our priorities must be in these post-modern times.

(1) The first element is *the setting for history*. We can see this in Revelation 12:7–9, and verses 3 and 4. In verses 7–9 warfare breaks out in heaven. The dragon and his angels wage war against the ruling power of heaven, probably in a fit of jealousy and lust for the divine throne (cf. Ezek. 28). This dragon is identified as the serpent of the garden of Eden, the devil himself. He is defeated and cast out of heaven to the earth, taking a third of the heavenly host with him in his downfall. On earth he will devote himself to deceiving the nations, so that they may not worship and serve the one true God. In order to expedite his cause, he positions himself before the woman who gives birth to a Son destined to rule all the nations from His throne at the side of God (Rev. 12:5; cf. Ps. 2), that he might devour her Child. Yet the Child is born and taken to rule with God in heaven. Frustrated in his attempt to gain the heavenly throne by direct assault, or to prevent the birth and enthronement of God's appointed King, the devil turns his wrath against the woman, who gave birth to Him, and all her offspring, namely, those "who keep the commandments of God and hold to the testimony of Jesus" (Rev. 12:17 NASB).

The woman, who is adorned with the creation (v. 1; cf. Ps. 8) and wears a crown of twelve stars, probably represents Israel—from whose womb Jesus came—and then the church, the new Israel, who "gives birth" to those who testify to Him and keep His commandments (cf. Heb. 12:22ff.). That is, she represents the covenant people of God, those who in all times are to be identified as His people because of their being the object of His love. She is hated by the devil, and he desires nothing so much as to overwhelm and ruin her. He sets a course to persecute her in hopes of defeating God's plan, and, by association, the Almighty Himself (Rev. 12:13–17).

Thus is the stage of history set for the great drama of the unfolding of God's covenant. What do we know from just this much? First, we know that God's rule and His holy will cannot be thwarted. What He has determined will consistently and ultimately prevail, whether in heaven or on the earth. Second, we who have entered into covenant relationship with God through the blood of His Son know that we can expect opposition in our efforts to live for Him during the course of history. "In the world you have tribulation," Jesus told us (John 16:33); "but be of good cheer, I have overcome the world."

We must not expect life in God's covenant to be without trials, suffering, pain, disappointment, and even occasional despair. In this world, for as long as the course of history runs, God's covenant people can expect to have tribulation. We will be mocked and scorned, abused and mistreated, cheated and slandered, rejected and hated by men. Let us not make the mistake of thinking that people should always like us, will always be nice to our children, always appreciate our efforts at getting to know and to serve them, always listen attentively and courteously to our message of Good News. We are engaged in an ongoing warfare that is animated and sustained by powerful forces of evil (Eph. 6:10ff.). We had better prepare ourselves for the struggle, keeping in mind at all times that our King is on His throne, that He will carry us through every confrontation, and that the end, as we shall see, has already been decided to our advantage.

(2) Revelation 12 reveals what we may describe as *the crisis of history*. We see this in verses 1, 2, and 5. The crisis of history, its turning point, pivot, or centerpiece, occurs when God intervenes in history in the Person of His Son, who comes to establish the rule of God over all the nations. We have already examined this crisis in our discussion of the kingdom of God. The coming of God's kingdom, and the enthronement of His King, accelerates the process of history toward its final outcome.

What can we know from this? Simply that God's kingdom is at work in our midst and that we who have entered into His covenant are the

185

people around whom the powerful unfolding of this kingdom has its outworking. We should expect, therefore, to be at once the locus and beneficiaries of God's power and the focus of the devil's energies as we carry out our covenant calling in the course of history.

As a corollary to this crisis of history we must observe an important event related in Revelation 20:1–5. It is clear from Revelation 12 that Satan's attempts to defeat God's plan will not prevail. All the sovereign might of God—symbolized by the earth swallowing Satan's flood (v. 16)—will be brought to the defense of His people as they pursue their calling of bringing the nations under the authority of God's gracious rule. However, Satan had been cast to the earth that he might deceive the nations, the very thing that the existence of the church proves him ineffective in doing. How shall we reconcile his deceiving work with the existence of the church?

We can assume that the deceiving work of Satan went along quite well up to the time of Christ's coming and the beginning of God's kingdom. Before the time of Christ, only a very few—perhaps a mere handful, compared to the world's population—faithful people could be found clinging to the covenant promises of God. After the ascension of Christ and the day of Pentecost, the ingathering of the nations began rapidly to accelerate and has continued to this day. Given the deceiving work of Satan, how shall we account for this?

In Revelation 20:1–5 we see a "messenger" (the literal meaning of the Greek word, *angelos*) descending from heaven having the key of the abyss and a great chain in his hand. This messenger is identified as Jesus Christ Himself in Revelation 1:18. As part of His incarnation He comes to bind Satan so that he may no longer deceive the nations, and so that the kingdom of God may go forward and His covenant blessings reach to more and more people. Jesus Himself was conscious of this important work. He declared that He had already bound the devil by the time of His confrontation with the Pharisees in Matthew 12:22–29, and that plundering of his house was already underway, as we have seen. This binding of Satan probably occurred at the time of Christ's temptation, when Satan could not prevail against the Word of God, even though Christ was physically at His weakest and most vulnerable.

Thus, the crisis of history includes the binding of Satan. He is "on a chain," as it were. While he still deceives the nations, his effectiveness is bridled. Here is how Augustine described this situation:

> We should not be so fond as to think that these unclean spirits are either to be feared for any hurt or honored for any profit they can bring upon man's fortunes. For they are in power, but even as wicked men on earth are, so that they cannot do what they please, but are mere ministers to His ordinance, whose judgments no man can either comprehend fully or reprehend justly.[2]

The devil cannot prevail against the Spirit of God, who calls God's chosen people to Himself, opening their eyes to the gospel and giving them a new heart and new life. And, while it is not a good idea to stray too close to the devil—as the lost invariably do, becoming captive to his wiles and seductive charms—yet we may know that the power he does enjoy during this period of history is strictly controlled by Him who holds the chain. In short, if we resist the devil and are on constant alert against his attacks (James 4:7; 1 Peter 5:8–9), we may hope to prevail against his wiles, overcome in the midst of temptation (1 Cor. 10:13), and carry on our kingdom work with success.

(3) We come to the last element of the drama of history depicted in Revelation 12, *the flow of history*. What should we expect the course of history to look like? Three features in particular stand out. The first is the coming of God's salvation, power, and kingdom—the end and operative agents of His covenant (v. 10). During the flow of history the kingdom of God will grow like the stone of Daniel's vision (Dan. 2:44–45), spreading out by the grace and power of God to bring the saving blessings of His covenant to the nations of the world through the church (2 Cor. 4:15; Eph. 3:10). This is the work to which we in the covenant community are called. Blessed of God with all the riches of His glory in Christ Jesus, we are called to be a blessing to the nations in turn. This must be our focus, our mission during our moment in history.

Second, as we have seen, the course of history features the opposition of the devil (Rev. 12:13–17), concerning which we have perhaps said enough already. Although the progress of the kingdom and the growth of the church are certain, they will not be unopposed. Satan can assume the form of even our closest friends—as Peter learned—in seeking to frustrate the plan of God. Therefore, we must be ever vigilant against him.

The final feature of the flow of history is the certainty of God's victory (v. 11). God will prevail. His kingdom and His promises cannot fail (Dan. 7:12–27). His church will continue to grow and His grace will reach to increasing throngs of people. But this will not come without some cost. As God's covenant people go forth to make His Word known, living according to His commandments and calling men and women to repentance from sin and faith in Christ, they will be subjected to persecution. Many will be mocked and maligned; others will be driven from their homes; some will be put to death. But they must not love their lives more than their testimony (Rev. 12:11). Kingdom progress and rejoicing come from persevering in the midst of trial, looking to God for His overcoming grace to sustain us in the midst of every difficulty (Rom. 5:3–5).

Thus the pattern of history—its framework, crisis, and flow—is clearly discerned. We know what to expect. We understand what our priorities must be. The details are still fuzzy, but the general outline of things can be clearly seen. God's covenant people will take up their calling to be a blessing to the nations. They will prepare for the opposition to come so that they may stand firm against it. They eagerly look forward to the day of the full outworking of God's covenant and the full realization of His rule, and they trust in His sovereign, protecting grace as they pursue His kingdom agenda here and now. They know and are assured that a great and glorious end of history is about to unfold, to an examination of which we now turn.

THE END OF HISTORY

Again, regardless of our particular millennial view, the final chapters of the book of Revelation are quite clear as to what we should expect as history comes to its end. We see the return of Christ, followed by the final judgment. And we know that eternal life in a realm of glory awaits us beyond the end of history.

The *return of Christ* is shown in Revelation 19:11–21. Jesus Christ will come again, leaving, for a moment, His throne of glory and leading His loyal hosts in a final, climactic battle against all who oppose Him. The trumpet of the Lord will sound, and the dead in Christ will rise first. Then we who are alive and remain will join them, clothed in the righteousness of the saints and joining them, as one with them, in His train (1 Thess. 4:13–17; Rev. 19:4). The rest of the dead shall be raised at that time and will arm themselves for the final struggle against the returning Lord (John 5:28–29; Rev. 19:19). Christ will descend upon them with power and glory, brandishing the Sword of the Spirit and overcoming his foes, casting them away from His presence forever.

We do not know when Christ will return; nor should we enter into vain speculations concerning the times or events that the Father has reserved to His own authority (Acts 1:7). He will come when the world least expects Him, like a thief in the night. We in the covenant community are not blind to the signs that portend His coming (1 Thess. 5:4): we see the gospel advancing daily (Matt. 24:14); we observe the rise of the man of lawlessness on every hand (2 Thess. 2:1–4); we are not ignorant of the growing indications that suggest the last times are upon us and the end of history may be at hand (Matt. 24:37–44; 2 Tim. 3:1–10). We hope, even long for the day of Christ's return, for we know that only in that day will our faith be vindicated and every obstacle to full realization of our covenant fellowship with the Lord be removed.

The *final judgment* occurs immediately upon Christ's return (Rev. 20:11–15). At this time the righteous will be purged of every remaining weight of sin and transformed into glorious new bodies (1 Cor. 3:12–15), and all this in a moment, in the twinkling of an eye (1 Cor. 15:51–55). At the same time, the wicked shall be cast away from the presence of God to a place of everlasting torment and woe. Then the heavens and the earth will be dissolved with a fervent heat (2 Peter

3:10) in preparation for the final, glorious work of God's majestic covenant plan.

This is the *creation of the new heavens and the new earth*—the realm of everlasting glory. God will create a new heavens and a new earth, a wondrous fusion of all creation into one new glorious reality, where He will dwell together with His covenant people forever (Rev. 21:1–3). The full and unobstructed blessings of God's covenant will flow like a river of life to His people for eternity. The church, like a mighty, splendid fortress, will be adorned in perfect beauty, holiness, and humanity, glorious in her consummation and completion (Rev. 21:9–27), and busy about her appointed tasks as she continues developing the new heavens and new earth to ever greater stages of beauty and glory. She will feast with her Husband and King eternally on the abundant and unlimited blessings that His presence among them affords (Rev. 19:7–9). And the members of the covenant community, while engaged in all their works and activities, without fear or sorrow, will worship the Lord in the beauty of His holiness and praise His Name in unending, glorious song (Rev. 4; 5).

God has shown us the end from the beginning, the pattern of history and its course or flow as well as the final outworking of His covenant plan. We know what is to come. We know the end from the beginning, not in exhaustive detail, but in a roughed-out sketch clear enough to give us hope and guide us as we consider how we must live in God's covenant during our own moment of history.

LIVING IN GOD'S COVENANT IN THE LIGHT OF THE END

The apostle Peter is abundantly clear concerning how we in the covenant community must occupy ourselves during this time while we await the outworking of all that God has planned (2 Peter 3:10–14, 17–18). Rather than fritter away our minutes and hours in vain speculations about hidden details of the end times or petty entanglements in worldly affairs, we are to be busy at work for the progress of the kingdom, trusting in the promises of God's covenant as we labor to grow in grace, build God's church, and watch His power unfold in our midst.

This requires (1) that we *keep the end of history in sight,* that we never forget that this time in which we live is given to us as preparation for an eternal life of glory with the Lord (vv. 10–13). This weary world with all its distractions, diversions, misery, corruption, and despair is passing away. Nothing that men now hold so dear will survive the consuming fires of God's judgment. A new heaven and a new earth are coming, in which righteousness will dwell. We will carry nothing of this world into that one. Thus, we must keep looking forward to what lies ahead, not wallowing in what is passing away.

We may nurture this focus on the age to come in our prayers and worship, as well as through mutual encouragement (cf. Pss. 23, 96, etc.; 1 Thess. 4:18). However, we must also study to keep our focus on heavenly realities and the life for which we are ultimately bound even in the midst of our mundane routines and responsibilities (Col. 3:1–3). We must keep seeking the things of the age to come, longing for them earnestly, expressing our desire for them in prayer, clinging to them in our hearts and souls as we encourage one another with the promises of the new heavens and the new earth.

Further, we must remember that Christ is coming, judgment will ensue, and the sheep will be separated from the goats. Let the knowledge of these certainties guide and motivate us in our daily conduct, our relationships, and the priorities we choose. The second coming of Jesus Christ is not merely the stuff of speculative Christian fiction; it is the end of history and will usher in the final age of all men, whether to eternal glory or to eternal misery. There will be no "second chances" once Christ has come. Therefore, since He is coming, let us keep this constantly in mind, longing and praying for it, and letting its certainty inform our conduct and manner of relating to others in the here and now.

(2) Given the above, that this world is passing away and the judgment of Christ is coming, *we must be careful not to allow ourselves to become ensnared by temporal things* (2 Peter 3:11). "Since all these things will be dissolved, what manner of persons ought you to be in holy con-

duct and godliness . . . ?" As a *holy* people we have been set apart for God, to be different, distinct, as we have seen. We have different priorities. Our outlook and approach to life are different. We are a people with a mission to make God's blessings and kingdom known. We do not hold too tightly to the things of this world, lest they should get in the way of our mission, distracting us to lesser things. Certainly we appreciate the good things of this world and use them to benefit ourselves and others, and to bring glory to God as part of our mission of being a blessing.

But we must not dissipate our energies and resources, nor waste our precious time, on things that are perishing. We are called to use all our talents to prepare a return on investment for the Lord who bestowed them on us in the first place (Matt. 25:14–30). Thus, if we do not engage in all the same kinds of activities as our unsaved friends and neighbors, indulge all the same pursuits and interests as they, give our children over to the same diversions and recreations, or occupy ourselves with the same cultural or leisure pursuits, they may think us strange, and may even malign us as religious fanatics (1 Peter 4:3–5). Yet we are prepared for this, given what we know about the course of history; and we know that both we and they shall have to give an accounting to the Lord. Thus, we prefer to give our time and efforts, as well as all our responsibilities and activities, to preparing to meet Him, rather than in the frivolous and vaporous undertakings of a passing age. We are resolved, in all we do, to seek first the kingdom of God and His righteousness, knowing that He will take care of all our needs according to the promises of His unfailing covenant (Matt. 6:33).

(3) Peter calls us to *grow in the grace and knowledge of the Lord* (2 Peter 3:18). What an exciting prospect! That we might be able to experience more of the grace of God and to know Him better and better every day! This does not come naturally to us, or even easily. We must labor to grow, devoting ourselves to the disciplines of grace and to faithfulness in our walk with the Lord.

But what does such growth in grace look like? How can we tell when it is occurring? To what ends should we set our sights as we enter into the disciplines of grace?

Paul, echoing Jesus, tells us that the goal of our instruction is love, love for God, which is the first commandment, and love for our neighbors as ourselves (1 Tim. 1:5; Matt. 22:36–40). Growth in grace is growth in love, in the *experience* of love, as God meets with us in His Word, in prayer and fasting, in worship, in the other disciplines of grace, and in the filling of His Spirit; and in the *expression* of love, first to God, then to our neighbors. As we grow to love God more, we will take more delight in Him, seek Him more fervently, and worship and serve Him more completely. Thoughts of Him will more and more occupy our minds. We will seek His presence in all we do and at all times. As we grow in love for our neighbors, we will invest more time in them, looking for ways to serve them and to show and tell them the Good News of God's covenant love in Jesus Christ. We will take seriously the challenge of our personal mission field and seek to sow the seed of truth and to irrigate it with the love of Christ in all we do. We will know that we are growing in grace when such love for God and for our neighbors begins to be more evident in our lives.

But to grow in grace we must earnestly apply ourselves to the disciplines of grace, giving sufficient time, attention, and reflection to these disciplines, and faithfully seeking to live out what God shows us in them. Without sound discipline we cannot expect to be ready to show the love of God in our personal mission field to the people around us. Discipline trains us heart, mind, and life to be ready to live for Christ and to speak for Him as the Lord opens doors of opportunity. Those who wish to grow in grace will, therefore, make certain that their practice of the disciplines of grace is as full and complete as can be. They will resist the tendency to allow the spiritual disciplines to become mere routines, and will constantly seek ways of expanding the practice of spiritual disciplines into the whole of their lives. They will devote themselves to worship and to seeking the Lord's face at all times. They will labor in the disciplines of grace until they encounter the glory of God and are transformed by it (2 Cor. 3:12–18). And, thus transformed, they will go forth loving God more and seeking ways to show His love to their neighbors.

(4) Peter calls on the members of the covenant community to *devote themselves to the preservation and advancement of God's truth* (2 Peter 3:17). They will drink deeply from the Word of God, seeking His light to guide them at all times (Ps. 36:7–9). They will attend carefully to the teaching and preaching of the Word, searching the Scriptures to know the truth of what they have been taught (Acts 17:11). They will guard against false teaching—in themselves, their families, and their churches—and will work to see that the covenant community of which they are a part is built up strictly on the foundation of the apostles and prophets, with Jesus Christ Himself as the Cornerstone (Eph. 2:19–22). They will not lend their ears to the siren sounds of strange spirits, but will test all they hear to determine whether or not it is faithful to their calling as the followers of Christ (1 John 4:1–3). And they will diligently seek to bring all their thoughts, plans, hopes, and dreams, as well as every notion or speculation they encounter each day, captive to the obedience of Christ (2 Cor. 10:3–5).

The Word of God holds out the promises of His covenant, shows us the way to walk, exalts Jesus as the hope of glory, and charts the only course through the rough and dangerous waters of a hostile world. Those in the covenant community will thus, like the first believers, who turned their world upside down for Christ, be increasingly devoted to the Word of God (Acts 2:42ff.).

(5) Finally, Peter tells us, in the light of where history is going, that we must *be constantly diligent to prepare for the coming of the Lord* (2 Peter 3:14–15). We must study to promote peace within the body of Christ, working hard to maintain the unity we have in the Spirit by strengthening the bonds of love that unite us. We must cultivate the practice of godliness, laying aside the old, sinful person and being clothed each day with the mind and life of Christ (Eph. 4:17–24). And we must not become impatient with the slowness of the Lord's return. His tarrying is so that we might know more of His salvation, and so that we might be more active and effective in making that salvation known to others (v. 15).

We are truly preparing to meet the Lord when peace and unity, holiness, and the progress of salvation are the driving forces in all we do.

Here there is no place for mere selfishness, no room for sluggardliness in doing good, no quarter for sin, no mantel for the idols of this world, no time for anything other than seeking the good pleasure of the Lord. "But who is sufficient for these things?" we might well ask. None of us, to be sure.

But, with God, all things are possible, indeed, things exceedingly abundant above all that we might ask or think, greater works even than Jesus Himself did, for in Him God will supply all our needs, and we shall be able to do all that He sets before us each day (Matt. 19:26; Eph. 3:20; John 14:12; Phil. 4:13, 19).

There is only one thing that can keep us from realizing the ever-increasing glory of God's covenant during our moment of history as we prepare for the age to come.

THE SIN OF UNBELIEF

Our great stumbling block will be, as it ever has been, the sin of unbelief. Because we do not believe God's promises, do not believe in the power of His kingdom, and do not believe that history is working out according to His revealed plan, we will allow our lives to become distracted by worldly issues and concerns, filled with worldly notions and ideas, drunk on worldly hopes and dreams. We will not believe in God and the promises of His Word; rather, we will believe only what our eyes or selfish lusts tell us. Thus captive to unbelief, or misguided belief, we will fail to know the full blessings of God, will walk a compromised path, and will betray our true allegiance to those around us. We will say one thing with our mouths and allow the naturalism of the age to be our guiding light. We will tell ourselves concerning the covenant lifestyle, "Yes, this looks good on paper, but I live in the *real* world." We will take our cues from those around us rather than from Christ seated on His throne and returning in glory. We will want to be like our materialist neighbors and friends, to have what they have rather than what God promises, to indulge in all those things that will soon pass away, and be consumed with ourselves rather than investing in the mission of the covenant community.

And we will end up, like the prodigal son, eating the slop of pigs rather than enjoying the pleasures of our heavenly Father.

The sin of unbelief is the bottom line of all other sin. We choose to believe the allure of the world rather than the promises of God. We believe it is more profitable for us to indulge self than to mortify the members of our bodies for Christ. We believe the lies of getting and spending rather than the promise of self-denial and sacrifice. We believe we are an exception and that one little dalliance will not affect our walk with the Lord. We believe we are of no value to the work of the kingdom and so sit on the sidelines while the members of our church go to battle against the foes of Christ. We believe that others should do for us rather than that we must devote ourselves in service to them. We believe that being saved is enough without the necessity of working out our salvation in fear and trembling. We believe it is nobler to criticize and condemn than to serve in love. We believe the gospel is powerless, or that we are not able to wield it, rather than the straightforward promises of Christ and Paul that we are to be His witnesses to the power of God for all who will believe (Acts 1:8; Rom. 1:16). We believe that merely reading about God's covenant and its calling on our lives is involvement enough, without any necessity of searching our lives to see how we must begin to apply this blessing more fully to ourselves. We believe we can stare the clear and unobstructed commands and promises of God right in the face, and walk away to live as we please, without fear of harm or loss.

Thus believing, we are fools, who profess one thing but live as though the exact opposite were true.

Let us beware of the sin of unbelief and all the many and subtle ways it makes inroads into our lives. Let us confront it at every turn, clinging to the promises of God's covenant and remembering that a day is coming when we shall stare into the loving eyes of Him who died for us and give an account of our faithfulness. And let us seek above all else, in that precious, final moment of history, to hear from His sweet and gracious lips, "Well done, good and faithful servant. Enter into the kingdom prepared for you from before the foundation of the world."

QUESTIONS FOR STUDY OR DISCUSSION

1. Review the goals you set for this study of God's covenant. Have you made any progress? In what ways?

2. This chapter looked at the overall pattern of history as Scripture presents it. What advantages can you see from keeping this pattern in mind? How should knowing this pattern affect our daily lives as members of God's covenant community?

3. Peter exhorts us to prepare for the coming of the new heavens and the new earth. What will that require of you in the areas of priorities, time usage, and the disciplines of grace?

4. How do you expect the devil to try to thwart your efforts at living for the consummation of God's covenant? How will you prepare to resist him?

5. How does the fact that Satan is bound and we are now called to plunder his former domain encourage you to take more seriously your own personal mission? Who are some of the people who should begin to experience the blessings of God's covenant through your ministry? In what ways?

12

RENEWING IN GOD'S COVENANT

Then they entered into a covenant to seek the LORD *God of their fathers with all their heart and with all their soul.*—2 Chronicles 15:12

[Edwards] believed that the church's public rituals should not be a marketplace for people to come and choose what they needed or wanted, but a communal expression of a single commonly understood ideal.—Christopher Grasso[1]

For many years my father-in-law, Dr. Lane Adams, observed what I considered to be a wonderful practice whenever he presided at a wedding ceremony. At the time of leading the couple in their vows, he would ask the married couples in the congregation to join hands and look at one another. Then he would invite them silently to say the wedding vows after him and with the couple to be wed as a way of renewing their own vows before the Lord and to one another. I was present on at least one of those occasions, and I can recall several of the people in the congregation saying to me afterward how moving it was to rehearse again, if only silently, their marriage vows to their spouse.

I picked up on that practice during the course of my own ministry, but with something of a twist. During a study of how to love their wives as Christ loves the church, I encouraged the men in our church to follow a similar practice as part of their anniversary celebration each year. I suggested they write out their marriage vows in their own words, take their wives out to a nice place for dinner, and, just before the meal is served, read their vows over again to their wives, then offer some brief statement of recommitment together with an appropriate gift. Many men reported back to me that this reviewing and restating of their marriage vows had a profound effect, not only upon their wives, but upon them as well. As they rewrote their vows, they were struck again with what it meant to love their wives as Christ loves the church, and they tried to make their restatement relevant to their present situation, at the same time preserving the essence of the vows. Many told me how they were led to think carefully about what they had promised the Lord and their wives, and to make sure that, when they said it this time, they meant it more than ever. Others admitted to being led to confess their failures to their wives and to pledge, with God's help, to do better. There was not a man who actually took this practice to heart who did not report some benefit in terms of a sense of renewal coming into his marriage and his love for his wife.

There is apparently something to be said for restating such fundamental commitments from time to time, especially in keeping us focused on the larger purpose of marriage rather than our own selfish interests and needs.

Over the past generation the church has increasingly become a kind of spiritual mall, offering services and opportunities to people according to their interests and needs, and using these as a means of attracting new people. The inevitable effect of this is that many churches, especially larger congregations, comprise people with varying interests and needs who seem to have little in common except that they do their spiritual shopping at the same place. They hardly know one another except to greet in passing. Except for Sunday morning worship they almost never engage in any common spiritual activity, and, when the church has more than one morning service, even that may not be true. They all have their own groups and programs, their own projects and activities, which they have entered into because of some personal need or concern, without much in the way of common regard for the overarching mission of the church as a congregation or its place in the covenant community as a whole. The church, like a successful mall, bristles with activity: lots of people coming and going, parking lots full, every shop or kiosk with customers, and everybody happy. People are having their needs met. What more could we want?

This kind of "consumer Christianity" may be what people are flocking to in our day, but it is not what we see in the New Testament, not the faith of God's covenant, and not the kind of faith that will turn the world upside down for Christ. Whenever we promote a vision of the church based primarily on felt needs and self-interest, we cannot help but undermine the larger purposes of God, who has called us as a distinct people to declare His excellencies to the world. As Robert E. Webber has observed,

> Our major emphasis, however, must not be to make Christianity attractive, as attractive as it is, nor to make it a panacea for all ills, as much as it does give life and meaning and purpose. Instead, we need to emphasize the cost of discipleship, that absolute claim of God over our entire life, the necessity of faith that issues forth in obedience, and our belonging to an alternative culture shaped by the kingdom of Jesus.[2]

Already, in the early eighteenth century, Jonathan Edwards could see this tendency toward mere self-interest developing in his own congregation. People came to church when they had a need. When they did not, they stayed away.

But Edwards knew that such an approach to the life of faith was inconsistent with the Christian's calling to deny self in the service of God. Further, it did not provide a foundation for "improving" one's baptism and growing in the grace of the Lord. His solution was to lead the people of Northampton, on various occasions, to a public act of covenant renewal. At such times Edwards, following biblical precedent, led the people to declare their faith and restate their commitment before the Lord, so that they might stand united in purpose, outlook, and conviction as they lived for Christ each day. It is not incidental, I believe, that the Northampton church experienced two powerful seasons of revival during Edwards's twenty-three years of ministry there.

In this concluding chapter I want to examine the biblical basis for such an exercise in renewing God's covenant, to suggest some advantages that might come from this practice, and to recommend a format for proceeding as a congregation in renewing covenant with God.

THE BIBLICAL BASIS FOR COVENANT RENEWING

At several times in the Old Testament we see the people of God being brought together under a leader to reaffirm their commitment to God's covenant in a corporate, public expression of devotion to the Lord. Moses is seen to be doing as much in the book of Deuteronomy. Joshua followed suit at the end of his life, calling the people to put aside their selfish interests and to get on with the work of securing the promised land (Josh. 23–24). During the reigns of Solomon, Asa, Hezekiah, and Josiah, and under the leadership of Ezra and Nehemiah, the people of Israel were assembled to renew their vows to the Lord (2 Chron. 6–7; 15:8ff.; 29:5ff.; 34; Ezra 10; Neh. 9; 10). In each case the Lord seems to have honored their recommitment, if only for that generation, granting His blessings to His people once again.

Essentially, these exercises consisted of a public gathering of all the people of God to rehearse His faithfulness, confess their sins, and renew themselves and their commitment to Him by reaffirming their place in His covenant. While each of the periods of covenant renewing indicated above is unique, they all partake of some common elements.

(1) *There was a convening of the leadership* to assess the situation and make preparations for leading the people into covenant renewal. At times the priests and Levites, at other times the elders of the people, and at still other times the princes and leading citizens of the nation came together to assess the situation and consider the need for renewal. During this time key spokesmen—whether the king, governor, or priests—guided the leadership in a review of God's covenant and of His faithfulness to that covenant, and considered the ways and the extent to which the people had drifted from His plan for them. General agree-

ment was reached that an act of corporate covenant renewal was in order, and plans were drawn up for the exercise.

(2) *The people were convened as one assembly.* The importance of all the people being together at the same time is stressed, at times with threat of serious punishment for any delinquents. This was to be a public activity in which all the people were expected to participate or, by their lack of participation, to confess that they had drifted from God's covenant and were, therefore, under His wrath.

During the assembly of the people various things occurred. Among these was *the reciting of God's covenant faithfulness.* We see this especially in Deuteronomy 1–5 and Nehemiah 9 and 10. Beginning at the beginning, the worship leaders summarized the goodness of God to His people throughout the generations. Familiar details were rehearsed, familiar stories were alluded to, and familiar confessional formulas were employed to accomplish this part of the exercise. At times this reciting took the form of prayer; at other times it was through song or another form of joint declaration or confession. The important point of this part of the exercise seems to have been to remind the people of God of His unfailing faithfulness to all that He had promised them, and to set those promises before them once again.

Second, there is *confession of sin and a call to repentance or renewal.* Usually the leaders acted on the people's behalf in this part of the exercise, as we see Solomon doing in 2 Chronicles 6 and 7, although we can imagine faithful and attentive people praying along with them and affirming by their nods and "Amens" the iniquities that were being reviewed.

Yet another part of this service of renewal involved *the consecration of leaders.* Those who would be responsible to help lead the people in fulfilling their vows to the Lord were put forward and consecrated—by anointing or prayer or both—for their service to the Lord. This would have had the advantage of showing the people that the leaders stood behind the action being taken and should be submitted to for the blessings of God that they anticipated.

Fourth, this exercise in covenant renewing also involved some means of *declaring the people's intent to be renewed in God's covenant.* The Passover was used, as well as sacrifices, public confessions and rituals, and written and signed documents, to signal and to seal the nation's common resolve before the Lord. It was important that every member of the community be committed to and involved in the renewing activity.

(3) Finally, a *general season of celebration* seems to have followed many of these exercises in covenant renewal, with the people sharing their homes and goods with one another, participating in smaller celebrations in homes and local communities, and generally seeking out friends and family to rejoice together in the hope of God's blessing.

These then are the elements that the people of Israel employed during various periods of covenant renewing in the Old Testament:

- Gathering of leaders for assessment and planning
- Calling of an assembly of all the people
- Public rehearsal of God's covenant faithfulness
- Confession of sin and call to repentance/renewal
- Consecration of leaders
- Act of covenant renewing
- Congregational celebrations

We may have some doubts about whether such an Old Testament practice might be appropriate in our day. Jonathan Edwards did not. God was pleased to honor this practice as part of his ministry, during which, as noted above, Northampton experienced two seasons of extraordinary revival, each closely associated with Edwards's leading the congregation in an exercise of covenant renewing.

In a much more general way this practice has been observed at other times throughout church history. For example, upon Calvin's return to Geneva in 1541 he first convened the leadership of the churches and led them in the preparation of the *Ecclesiastical Ordinances of 1541*, the basic document of Genevan church order (a kind of covenant), after which the people were convened and led to submit to this new "covenant order." This was followed by twenty years of growth and mission on the part of the churches in Geneva. The Cambridge Platform of 1648, prepared by the Congregational churches of New England, can also be seen as an attempt to call the people under their leadership to covenant renewal in the face of incipient heresies.

Various seasons of large-scale revival have been preceded by times of prayer and rededication to the Lord, as the late J. Edwin Orr has shown in his many books. Even the Lausanne Covenant of 1974 was presented in something of this manner. Participants at the Lausanne Congress on World Evangelization were invited to examine their own hearts, carefully to consider the challenges set forth in the Lausanne Covenant, and then to come forward and sign as an expression of their renewed commitment to the Lord's work.

Various congregations have used some form of covenant to call the people back to renewed diligence in their callings before the Lord. Recently I preached at a service of covenant renewal in a local church that was changing denominations and wanted to declare its purposes and intentions publicly and to all members. During the service the congregational covenant was read and each member came forward to sign the covenant. The members thereby bound themselves to one another and the Lord in this action.

So there is biblical and historical precedent for such exercises in covenant renewing. What might be some of the advantages of this?

ADVANTAGES OF COVENANT RENEWING

Several advantages or benefits might accrue to a congregation of God's people from some kind of periodic renewing of covenant with Him. (1) Foremost among these is the opportunity for *congregation-wide focusing on the excellence and greatness of God.*

How easy it is for our approach to the life of faith to degenerate into mere self-seeking, exercising concern in every way and above all else to have our personal or family needs met by our involvement in the local church. As we have seen, our present "mall mentality" toward church helps to foster such an approach to Christian faith. An exercise in covenant renewing can afford a congregation a wonderful, and perhaps much-needed opportunity for refocusing on the proper object of faith, namely, God Himself. Through various means and in a variety of ways leaders may bring the congregation to reflect on and rehearse the greatness, majesty, sovereign power and might, compassion, goodness, faithfulness, and covenant love of the God who has called them out of darkness into His glorious light (recall our study of Psalm 50). While such should be the focus of the entire life of faith, and all the activities of the congregation, sadly this is not always the case. A time of covenant renewing can thus be most helpful in reorienting the faith of a church toward a more perfect vision and greater devotion to God in His glorious greatness and majestic holiness.

This "beatific vision" should ideally be the desire of every Christian. To see God more clearly is to love Him more completely, and to love Him is to serve Him, denying self and seeking to care for others with the same comfort and love that God has shown to us. Refocusing and improving this beatific vision should be a central aspect of any exercise in covenant renewing, as it allows the people of God to concentrate with greater intensity on the One who affords them such marvelous blessings and exceedingly great and precious promises through His everlasting covenant of glory.

(2) Related to this, an exercise in covenant renewing provides an opportunity for *rehearsing the broad sweep of the promises of God before His people*. Beginning with the promises made to Abraham and enlarging and applying the promises of life and land made through Moses, of kingdom through David, of inward grace and renewal in the Spirit and the New Covenant, and of the new heavens and earth to come, this can be a wonderful time of helping the people of God to refocus their lives and priorities in the light of what God has declared He will do for them. We can only wonder at how God's people might be encouraged and strengthened in their souls, motivated to greater selflessness and service, and drawn into deeper love for God by such a cataloging of His exceedingly great and precious promises on a regular basis.

We must remember that God leads His people by promise, offering freely of His grace to bless them if only they will obey and follow Him. Too often in our preaching and other church activities we want to chart another course to the blessings of God: follow this routine, learn this program, embrace these doctrines, try out these steps to self-improvement. All these may well have their place in the life of a congregation, but not apart from the promises of God. And it is all too easy in preaching and teaching, church programs and activities, to fail to develop those promises as fully as we ought, so that God's people will be drawn into obedience out of gratitude and love, rather than duty or mere self-seeking.

An exercise in covenant renewing can thus be a source of great blessing for leaders and people alike, reminding the former of the need to keep the promises of God before His people at all times, and the latter of the richness of His love for them and the blessings that come from obedience.

(3) An exercise in covenant renewing can help to *situate the people of God in the grand stream of God's covenant faithfulness through the ages*. How careful the biblical leaders of those seasons of renewal were to remind the people of how God had been faithful to His Word throughout the generations! They showed the people that God was as good as His Word. What He had done for past generations He would continue to do for those who followed faithfully where He led.

The degree of ignorance of the history of God's people on the part of contemporary Christians is appalling. Congregations have at best a poor understanding of the unfolding of redemptive history in Scripture, and are almost completely ignorant of what God has done throughout the history of the church to show His faithfulness. When we come together to renew covenant with the Lord we should take the time, if only briefly, to rehearse and review God's faithfulness throughout all the ages up to our own.

Further, we should comment on His faithfulness in other parts of the church today, where He is furthering church growth through revival, sustaining those who are being persecuted, and sending out evangelists and missionaries into new fields day by day. Most Christians in this country have almost no sense of what God is doing in and through His people in other lands, or even in their own communities. This would be an excellent opportunity for their vision of the church to be enlarged and their appreciation of the faithfulness of God to be greatly expanded.

Moreover, this would be an excellent time for members of the congregation to share with one another the various ways that God has shown Himself faithful to them and to their families in the recent past. What an opportunity for the people of God to rejoice together in His faithfulness as they hear testimony after testimony of how He has fulfilled His promises in their very midst!

(4) An exercise in covenant renewing can also be useful to *consecrate church leaders for service*. How easy it is to take for granted the men and women who serve in the various leadership roles in our churches, as pastors, elders, deacons, teachers, project directors, program leaders, and so forth. Most of these serve quietly in the background. Their contribution may be great or small, but each of them is important to the ongoing work of the church. During an exercise in covenant renewal it would be appropriate to have these various leaders identified, recognized, and set apart unto the Lord for their service. Paul tells us to hold selfless servants in high esteem, even to render them public honor for their service (Phil. 2:25–30). There is also clear precedent for consecrating church leaders to their ministries by a season of prayer and fasting (Acts 13:1–3). Thus we are on good ground if, from time to time, we acknowledge and dedicate to the Lord those men and women who give so much of their time, talent, and strength in the service of the Lord as leaders in our congregations. A time of renewing covenant with the Lord provides an excellent occasion for this.

(5) An exercise in covenant renewing gives the local congregation an opportunity to *update its mission and reaffirm its convictions* before the Lord. Our postmodern world is placing new and strange demands on the churches, as we have seen. Most churches are not rising to the challenge of postmodernism, simply because they have not taken the time to reflect on the phenomenon, and have not been able either to identify the various expressions of postmodernism in their own communities or to consider how best to respond. The church's mission statement, if it has one, has remained unchanged for years. Its theological

convictions, summarized in a statement of faith or one of the classic creeds of the church, shows no awareness of the particular claims and challenges of the postmodern world.

It would be easy in such a situation for church members to get the idea that going to church is one thing, and living in the world is something else altogether. The two seem to have little in common, since each appears to ignore the other. Unless the local congregation actually takes note of the threats and changes going on around it, and adjusts its mission and addresses its statement of faith to speak to these challenges, how are the people to understand or believe that life in the covenant community seeks *engagement* with the world for the sake of reconciling it to the Lord? In an exercise of covenant renewing it might be possible to set forth the church's confession in the form of affirmations and denials specifically directed to the current intellectual and spiritual environment. For example, using an outline of the Apostles' Creed, the people might affirm, "I believe in God the Father Almighty," at the same time declaring, "We deny that the universe is eternal and uncreated, or that chance and matter are the only ultimate things." And so forth (see the Postmodern Creed at the beginning of the previous chapter).

Further, it would be possible at such a time to set forth specific church ministry plans designed to speak to the challenges of the day—programs and projects, preaching schedules, course offerings, and so forth. Thus the people could anticipate that they would be led and equipped more effectively to take their place in the covenant community within a particular time and according to the challenges and opportunities of the historical moment.

(6) Another advantage of an exercise in renewing covenant with the Lord is that *it gives an opportunity for the congregation to renew its own commitments to the Lord and to His church*. By providing a variety of elements—affirmations and denials, hymns, prayers, and declarations of faith—an exercise in renewing covenant with the Lord can make it possible for the members of the church to be reminded of their callings in God's covenant and to renew their resolve to serve the Lord with their whole lives.

In congregations of the Reformed tradition it is the custom to re-quire church members to take vows upon entering the membership of the church. Typically, those vows are used in the church only when a new membership class is being received. At that time, while the mem-bers may be encouraged to listen and reflect on the meaning of the vows for themselves, only the new members are expected to affirm them. I have, from time to time, asked church members in various re-formed churches if they remembered their vows. I have never had a sin-gle person answer that question in an unhesitating affirmation. Ap-parently our understanding of church vows and our use of them are not as important as we might think.

During an exercise of covenant renewal churches would have an op-portunity for a thoughtful, relevant, and highly personal declaration of commitment to the Lord and the work of His church, which each member could make with a clear mind and a good conscience. Like the marriage vows that the men in my study group rewrote each year, church members might find this exercise illuminating, challenging, and highly reaffirming as they, like Jacob returning to Bethel, recall the vows they made to God and prepare themselves for the struggles that lie ahead.

(7) During an exercise of renewing covenant a church might expect to *enhance the unity of the church and its visible oneness in the community*. Not only will the various elements of the exercise lead the members of the church to a common appreciation of their heritage and inheri-tance in the covenant community, and to a singularity of focus for their lives together, but it can actually bring them together before the Lord in a way that may not be possible at other times in the church's life. If the exercise is accomplished in a service of worship that includes the Lord's Supper there is an opportunity to strengthen the bonds of love and fellowship between church members in an exciting and deeply spir-itual way. And, if such an exercise can include other congregations in the community, perhaps at a neutral site (like a public building), the visible oneness of the body of Christ in that community will be greatly augmented, and the actual unity of the church much strengthened.

(8) An exercise of covenant renewing can also help to *remind people of the overarching mission of the church and to call them to renewal in that mission*. It is far too easy for the Lord's people to fall into the consumer mind-set when it comes to the life of faith. Unless we regularly hold before them the true nature of our calling in God's covenant, and lead them to reflect on the meaning of that calling for their lives, we run the risk of allowing church members to be satisfied merely with meeting their own needs through their involvement in church, and we may unconsciously perpetuate the "mall" mentality as the true nature of the life of faith and the meaning of church membership.

While, ideally, churches should always be mindful of this tendency and teaching and preaching to countermand it, an exercise in covenant renewing, when all the people of the church are together at once, can serve to give a common focus to their endeavors and activities.

(9) Finally, an exercise in renewing covenant provides a unique opportunity for the church to *push the life of the congregation and the celebration of God's goodness out into the neighborhoods of the community*. If the exercise of renewing covenant is followed by open houses or dinner parties in the homes of church leaders, to which neighbors and friends as well as church members may be invited, there will be a great opportunity to show the reality of the body of Christ and to discuss the nature of our mission with the people around us.

Thus it should be clear that many advantages can be gained from a church periodically sponsoring an exercise in renewing covenant with the Lord. How often should churches do this? There is a danger, of course, that a too frequent use of this exercise could render it meaningless. This does not need to be the case, especially if the exercise is carefully planned and executed; but we need to be mindful that mere routine observance certainly can be an unhappy result. Each church ultimately will decide when and how often it is appropriate for renewing covenant with the Lord. Personally, I do not think that once a year is too often, although that may not suit every congregation. The important thing is that church leaders stay mindful of what is going on in the church—any tendencies toward "consumer Christianity" or other aberrations of the faith—or any changes in the environment beyond the church or directions in church ministry, and that they gather the people to renew themselves to the Lord according to the changes, needs, and challenges of the moment.

A FORMAT FOR RENEWING COVENANT

How might a church proceed in an exercise of renewing covenant with the Lord? The following are simply suggestions or recommendations in response to this question, as no cut-and-dried formula for renewing covenant is presented in Scripture, and various approaches have been used throughout the history of the church. However, the guidelines that follow are based in general on the biblical pattern and historical precedents that we have examined in this chapter.

(1) *Church leaders should gather for a season of assessment, planning, and renewal.* Depending on the size of the church this can be done over a weekend or in a series of meetings spread out over the period of, say, a month. The purpose of this gathering is to bring the leaders together in order to achieve oneness of mind and heart as they prepare to lead the congregation in an exercise of renewing covenant with the Lord.

During this time a great deal of prayer, reflection, discussion, and evaluation should be given to considering the state of the church and changes in the environment in which it is called to pursue its mission; to strengthen the bonds of unity among church leaders; and to prepare for the exercise in renewing covenant (everything else that follows). Using a combination of research and reports, ministry evaluation tools, small group interaction, teaching and exhortation, worship and prayer, and plenary discussion, leaders should be able to arrive at the following:

1. An understanding of the overall state of the health of the church, in the light of such passages as Ephesians 4:11–16, Acts 2:42–47, and so forth. Church leaders should try to reach consensus concerning the strengths, weaknesses, needs, and opportunities facing the church at this time.

2. A review of the church's mission statement and statement of faith, in order to determine ways in which one or both should

be revised or updated to speak more pointedly to the needs of the church and the challenges of the environment.

3. Agreement on changes to the church's ministry plan to address needs and opportunities brought to light in items 1 and 2.
4. Renewed commitment to the Lord, the mission of the church, and one another.
5. Agreement on a format and basic content for the exercise of renewing covenant to follow.

I have found it helpful during such gatherings to schedule at least one or two meals together, as well as time for devotional instruction, prayer in small groups and as a whole gathering, and worship. Coordinators of this leadership gathering should seek to provide formats that will encourage maximum participation on the part of all the leaders in achieving the ends of this part of the exercise in renewing covenant. Unless church leaders are able to arrive at singleness of mind and heart, and have an affirming and encouraging relationship with one another, it is not likely that any real renewal will spread to the congregation as a whole.

(2) The second step in renewing covenant is to *call the people of the congregation together as a community for the purpose of renewing covenant with the Lord*. This should be both as public and as personal a call as possible. Announcements can be made from the pulpit for several weeks in advance. A letter should go out to the congregation, stating the time and place as well as the purpose and importance of the gathering to which they are being called. In addition, church leaders should take the responsibility of personally inviting and challenging the people in their spheres of ministry to come out. It may even be desirable to make sure that each member of the congregation is personally called by telephone and urged to attend. The church roll could be divided up among the leaders of the congregation to facilitate this task. Churches may wish to consider a press release in the local paper stating the details of this meeting and the activities to follow. This would have the benefit of helping to increase the visibility of the congregation and

heightening the sense of seriousness about its calling, and of encouraging other churches to follow suit.

(3) The actual exercise of renewing covenant should be planned as *a special time of gathering and worship before the Lord*. While this could be held during a normal Sunday morning service, a separate time may be more desirable, as the purpose is to emphasize the special nature of the exercise and to focus specifically on the activity of renewing covenant with the Lord. An order of service for this time might look like this:

Call to Worship
Hymn of Praise
Invocation
Call to Confession
Confession of Sins
Assurance of Pardon
Hymn of Thanksgiving
Rehearsal of God's Faithfulness
    Covenant promises
    Historic faithfulness of God
    Blessings to the congregation (ministry and personal)
Declaration of Faith (affirmations and denials)
Hymn of Dedication
Special Offerings (missions, the poor, etc.)
Prayers of Thanksgiving and Intercession
The Reading of the Word
The Preaching of the Word (focus on challenges and
        changes and the sufficiency of God and His
        Covenant)
Hymn of Response
Congregational Declarations of Commitment
    Ministry plans
    Congregational commitment
Preparation for the Lord's Supper
Words of Institution
Sacrament
Hymn of Response
Benediction

Following the worship service opportunity should be provided for church members to fortify their commitment by some additional action designed to get them off on the right foot in their renewal. These might include signing a covenant, ministry tables and sign-up sheets, small group discussions with church leaders, a book and resource table, question and answer sessions, and private counseling (to confess sin, seek guidance in growth or ministry, etc.).

(4) The final step in the exercise of renewing covenant is the *sharing of fellowship and mutual encouragement in the homes and neighborhoods of church leaders*. In the week following the renewal service leaders should open their homes to the congregation for times of fellowship, refreshment, reflection, mutual encouragement, clarification, challenge, and prayer. This can be done by ministries (Sunday school classes, home Bible studies, outreach team, etc.), neighborhoods, or some combination of these. Much of this time can be informal and casual, with leaders circulating about, greeting church members and their guests and making sure that everyone feels right at home. Part of the time should be carefully structured, however. During this structured time leaders will want to review salient aspects of the church's mission and statement of faith, especially as these may have been changed or updated; remind the people of upcoming ministry plans and activities; invite comment and response to the exercise of renewing covenant; answer questions; and challenge the people to faithfulness in seeking the Lord and living in His covenant. The meeting should close with a season of prayer.

Such an activity of renewing covenant with the Lord can be a very special and important time in the life of a church. It is all too easy, in these busy postmodern times, for church members to have their priorities shaken, their vision blurred, and their callings in the Lord sidetracked or indefinitely postponed. While eagerly desiring to live for the Lord within the framework of His covenant, they may find that the pressures and demands of getting by in a postmodern world can cause them to lose sight of their true goal and calling. An exercise in renewing covenant, carefully planned and executed, can help a congregation to know more of the blessings and power of living in God's covenant, and enable them to be a greater source of blessing to the surrounding community and the world.

QUESTIONS FOR STUDY OR DISCUSSION

1. Why do you suppose those biblical leaders—Moses, Joshua, Solomon, et al.—thought it was important to lead the people of Israel in renewing covenant with the Lord? What led them to take such initiatives? What did they hope would result from doing this?

2. What kinds of things might keep a church like yours from renewing covenant with the Lord? How valid are these?

3. How would you personally expect to benefit from being involved in regular seasons of covenant renewing with the other members of your church?

4. Which of the goals that you set for this study of God's covenant have you managed to attain? In which of these do you still hope to make some progress?

5. What has been the most important lesson for you from this study of God's covenant? How do you hope this will strengthen your ability to live in God's covenant?

NOTES

INTRODUCTION

1. Dispensationalism promotes a way of understanding the Bible that sees the Scriptures divided up into various epochs of revelation, demarcated by covenants. In each of these "dispensations" God relates to His people according to certain specific criteria, the inefficacy of which is demonstrated throughout the period covered by the covenant, necessitating a different covenant by the end of the period. Reformed and other scholars have decried what they see as the effects of such an approach to Scripture. Among these are antinomianism, a moralizing approach to the Old Testament, a capricious and inconstant portrayal of God, and a sacrificing of Old Testament revelation on the altar of the New Testament.

2. See, for example, many of the books cited in the chapters that follow.

CHAPTER 1: GOD'S COVENANT

1. O. Palmer Robertson, *The Christ of the Covenants* (Phillipsburg, N.J.: Presbyterian and Reformed, 1980), 15.

2. Meredith G. Kline has provided a detailed description of this process in his book, *The Structure of Biblical Authority* (Grand Rapids: Eerdmans, 1978). See especially pp. 27–44.

3. Ibid. Note that Robertson uses the plural, "covenants," whereas I have been talking exclusively about the singular covenant of God. We shall address the relationship between the several different covenants and the one divine covenant in chapter 6.

4. We ought to acknowledge our debt to dispensational scholars who have carefully identified the various covenants in Scripture and helpfully noted the differences between them. At the same time, we affirm that all these different covenant-making epochs are manifestations of God's covenant as it unfolds to completion in redemptive history.

5. See Herman Hanko's helpful introductory discussion of the gracious character of God's covenant in *God's Everlasting Covenant of Grace* (Grandville, Mich.: Reformed Free Publishing Association, 1988), 13–20.

6. Thomas Edward McComiskey, *The Covenants of Promise: A Theology of the Old Testament Covenants* (Grand Rapids: Baker, 1985), 144, emphasis added.

217

7. On the historical extent of God's covenant, see Kline, *The Structure of Biblical Authority,* 17–25.

8. See the discussion in Russell Maatman, *The Unity in Creation* (Sioux Center, Iowa: Dordt College Press, 1978).

9. It is for this reason that I take exception to the wording of the Westminster Confession of Faith in its chapter on the covenant. The Confession speaks of a covenant of works and a covenant of grace, the former made with Adam and intended to prove his obedience, the latter made with Adam and his seed after the fall, in which the promise of life is realized through Jesus Christ. These two covenants, rather than being separate arrangements between God and men, are aspects of the one covenant, God's covenant, which is, as I argue, all of grace.

CHAPTER 2: THE COVENANT OF PROMISE

1. Thomas Edward McComiskey, *The Covenants of Promise: A Theology of the Old Testament Covenants* (Grand Rapids: Baker, 1985), 58.

2. Geerhardus Vos identifies only three promises (*Biblical Theology: Old and New Testaments* [Grand Rapids: Eerdmans, 1988]). I could agree with this if we group the six I will present under the broader headings of blessing, greatness, and divine provision. Further, Vos, as well as McComiskey and others, want to include the land as one of the promises made to Abraham. However, I prefer to see the land as a temporal provision only, meant for a particular time and place as something of an initial staging ground for the covenantal activity between God and His people. See chapter 6.

3. The translations in this section are my own.

4. I find it curious that such writers as Robertson and McComiskey do not even deal with this passage, although the latter's book would seem to take its name from here.

CHAPTER 3: EXCURSUS: THE COVENANT OF PROMISE IN THE NEW TESTAMENT

1. Readers will, I trust, pardon the somewhat more academic tone of this chapter. My purpose is to demonstrate in a more strictly exegetical mode the conclusions reached in the previous chapter. Given the widespread influence of dispensational thinking in the evangelical church, this excursus holds a particularly important place in the overall argument of this book.

2. Willem Van Gemeren, *The Progress of Redemption* (Grand Rapids: Zondervan, 1988), 127.

3. Cf. William Hendriksen, *Exposition of the Gospel According to Luke* (Grand Rapids: Eerdmans, 1978), 109. Hendriksen comments here on the Magnificat, but see his remarks in the same reference on the song of Zacharias.

4. Fred H. Klooster, "The Biblical Method of Salvation: A Case for Continuity" in John S. Feinberg, ed., *Continuity and Discontinuity* (Westchester, Ill.: Crossway, 1988), 158.

5. Herman Ridderbos, *The Epistle of Paul to the Churches of Galatia* (Grand Rapids: Eerdmans, 1953, 1981), 120.

6. Ibid., 132.

7. Richard Longenecker, *Biblical Exegesis in the Apostolic Period* (Grand Rapids: Eerdmans, 1975), 123–24, emphasis added.

CHAPTER 4: THE COVENANT OF GLORY

1. Jonathan Edwards, "Dissertation Concerning the End for Which God Created the World," in Edward Hickman, ed., *The Works of Jonathan Edwards*, 2 vols. (Edinburgh: Banner of Truth Trust, 1974), 1:109.

2. For a detailed discussion of the means of grace see my *Disciplines of Grace* (Downers Grove, Ill.: InterVarsity, 2001).

CHAPTER 5: THE EVERLASTING COVENANT

1. Willem Van Gemeren, *The Progress of Redemption* (Grand Rapids: Zondervan, 1988), 404–5.

2. As Robertson and Vos point out, God also entered into covenant with Adam; however, the distinctive language of covenant making is not so evident during this period.

3. We can assume that this included Noah. Although Peter describes him as "a preacher of righteousness" (2 Peter 2:5), this can only have been after he had "found grace in the eyes of the LORD" (Gen. 6:8) and had entered into covenant with God.

CHAPTER 6: THE PEOPLE OF THE COVENANT

1. John Calvin, *Institutes of the Christian Religion*, ed. John T. McNeill, trans. Ford Lewis Battles (Philadelphia: Westminster, 1960), 1012 (4.1.1).

2. Francis A. Schaeffer, *True Spirituality* (Wheaton, Ill.: Tyndale House, 1973), 60.

3. See, for example, his sermon, "The Preciousness of Time" in Edward Hickman, ed., *The Works of Jonathan Edwards*, 2 vols. (Edinburgh: Banner of Truth Trust, 1974), 2:233ff.

4. Abraham Kuyper, "Sphere Sovereignty," in James D. Bratt, ed., *Abraham Kuyper: A Centennial Reader* (Grand Rapids: Eerdmans, 1998), 488.

CHAPTER 7: THE COVENANT AND THE KINGDOM

1. Edmund Clowney, *The Church* (Downers Grove, Ill.: InterVarsity, 1995), 189.

2. Herman Ridderbos, *The Coming of the Kingdom* (Phillipsburg, N.J.: Presbyterian and Reformed, 1962), 23.

3. Robert E. Webber, *Ancient-Future Faith* (Grand Rapids: Baker, 1999), 145.

CHAPTER 8: THE CHURCH, THE COVENANT COMMUNITY

1. Robert E. Webber, *Ancient-Future Faith* (Grand Rapids: Baker, 1999), 71.

2. Douglas John Hall, *The End of Christendom and the Future of Christianity* (Harrisburg: Trinity Press International, 1995), 54.

3. See my book, *Disciplines of Grace* (Downers Grove, Ill.: InterVarsity, 2001).

4. James F. White, *Documents of Christian Worship* (Louisville: Westminster/John Knox, 1992), 75–91.

5. See my article, "A Famine of Hearing" in *Spirit of Revival*, December 1999, 27ff.

6. Webber, *Ancient-Future Faith*, 145.

7. See, e.g., the works of Francis Schaeffer, David Wells, and Stephen L. Carter, among others.

8. Cyprian, "On the Unity of the Church," in Alexander Roberts and James Donaldson, eds., *Ante-Nicene Fathers*, 10 vols. (Peabody, Mass.: Hendrickson, 1995), 5:421. Cyprian was

writing against the Novatians, who refused to extend grace to those who had lapsed during persecution and were now petitioning the church for restoration to the flock of Christ. Calvin cited this passage in arguing the unity of the church in book 4 of the *Institutes*.

9. John Calvin, *Institutes of the Christian Religion*, ed. John T. McNeill, trans. Ford Lewis Battles (Philadelphia: Westminster, 1960), 1026 (4.1.12).

10. Paul Tournier, *The Whole Person in a Broken World* (New York: Harper and Row, 1964), 34.

CHAPTER 9: WORSHIP IN GOD'S COVENANT

1. Eddie Gibbs, *Church Next* (Downers Grove: InterVarsity, 2000), 156.

2. I would encourage the reader to consult, among others, John M. Frame, *Worship in Spirit and Truth* (Phillipsburg, N..J: P&R Publishing, 1996); Donald P. Hustad, *True Worship* (Wheaton: Harold Shaw, 1998); Robert G. Rayburn, *O Come, Let Us Worship* (Grand Rapids: Baker, 1987); and Robert E. Webber, *Worship Old and New* (Grand Rapids: Zondervan, 1982).

3. Robert E. Webber, *Ancient-Future Faith* (Grand Rapids: Baker, 1999), 124.

4. Unhappily, most English translations of this verse give the impression that Zion is the perfection of beauty. While this is a possible translation, it is not required by the text. In fact, given God's excoriating remarks that follow, it is difficult to image that He considers His people to be "the perfection of beauty." It is much more likely that this phrase refers to God, who rises up and shines His perfection and beauty into the sin and self-centeredness of His chosen people.

5. Another way of translating this verse might be, "I *have not come* to reprove you."

CHAPTER 10: COVENANT LIVING IN A POSTMODERN WORLD

1. For an excellent overview of postmodernism see J. Richard Middleton and Brian J. Walsh, *Truth Is Stranger than It Used to Be* (Downers Grove: InterVarsity, 1995).

2. Paulo Freire, *Education for Critical Consciousness* (New York: Seabury, 1973), 34.

3. Eddie Gibbs, *Church Next* (Downers Grove: InterVarsity, 2000), 29.

CHAPTER 11: THE CONSUMMATION OF THE COVENANT

1. John Calvin, *Acts of the Apostles* (Grand Rapids: Eerdmans, 1949), 45, comment on Acts 1:7.

2. Augustine, *City of God*, vol. 1, bk. 2, trans. John Healey, ed. R. V. Tasker (London: Everyman's Library, 1967), 67.

CHAPTER 12: RENEWING IN GOD'S COVENANT

1. Christopher Grasso, "Misrepresentations Corrected: Jonathan Edwards and the Regulation of Religious Discourse," in Stephen J. Stein, ed., *Jonathan Edwards's Writings: Text, Context, Interpretation* (Bloomington: Indiana University Press, 1996), 21.

2. Robert E. Webber, *Ancient-Future Faith* (Grand Rapids: Baker, 1999), 145.

INDEX OF SCRIPTURE

221

T. M. Moore is pastor of teaching ministries at Cedar Springs Church in Knoxville, Tennessee. He is a graduate of the University of Missouri (B.A.) and Reformed Theological Seminary (M.Div., M.C.E.), and has pursued additional studies at the University of Pretoria, the University of Miami, and the University of Wales.

He is a fellow of the Wilberforce Forum and editor of their online journal, *Findings*. His column, Ars Musica et Poetica, appears on the *BreakPoint* Webpage, along with his daily devotionals. He is North American editor for Scripture Union Publications, a ministry associate with Reformation and Revival Ministries and the Jonathan Edwards Institute, and associate editor of *Reformation and Revival Journal*.

Moore is also the author of eight books and has contributed chapters to numerous others. His book *Ecclesiastes* (IVP) received a 2002 Award of Merit from *Christianity Today*. His essays, reviews, articles, and poetry have appeared in numerous journals and periodicals. He is a frequent speaker in churches, conferences, and seminars.

He and his wife, Susie, have four children and ten grandchildren, and make their home in Concord, Tennessee. When he is not working, T. M. wiles away the time listening to Celtic music, reading poetry, playing the mountain dulcimer, and enjoying the glory of God in creation.